1500
#

The Surrealist Look

THE SURREALIST LOOK

AN EROTICS OF ENCOUNTER

MARY ANN CAWS

THE MIT PRESS
CAMBRIDGE, MASSACHUSETTS
LONDON, ENGLAND

This book was set in Bembo by Graphic Composition, Inc. and was printed and bound in the
United States of America.

Library of Congress Cataloging-in-Publication Data

Caws, Mary Ann.
   The surrealist look : an erotics of encounter / Mary Ann Caws.
     p. cm.
   Includes bibliographical references and index.
   ISBN 0-262-03244-9 (hardcover : alk. paper)
   1. Surrealism.   2. Arts, Modern—20th century.   3. Arts, Baroque.   4. Comparative
arts.   I. Title.
NX456.5.S8C28   1997
700′.41163—dc21   96-44541
                                                     CIP

Contents

Looking is such a marvelous thing, of which we know but little; through it, we are turned absolutely towards the Outside, but when we are most of all so, things happen in us that have waited longingly to be observed, and while they reach completion in us, intact and curiously anonymous, *without our aid*,—their significance grows up in the object outside.

—*Rainer Maria Rilke,* Selected Letters, 1902–1926

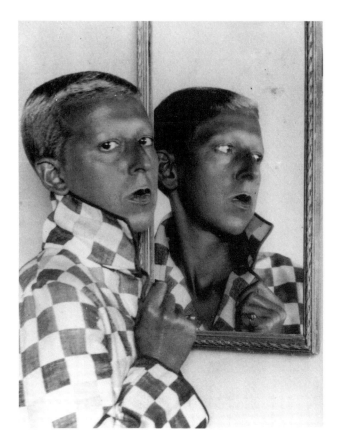

Claude Cahun, *Untitled* (self-portrait), 1928. Gelatin silver print, 24 × 19 cm. Courtesy of Virginia Zabriskie, the Zabriskie Gallery, New York.

PREFACE: LE LOOK

There they are, looking. I want to see how they find themselves and each other, these men and women in observance. How we look at them looking, how they all look.

Now what we are used to knowing of the male representation of surrealism is men's way of working over the female body; we believe, in fact we know, that there is an absolute relation between what you represent and what you believe of the other or the self you represent. Look at René Magritte's *Representation* (1937) (figure 1). The male surrealist look at the female, dressed or undressed, presents a body quite often in parts. To be sure, the Renaissance celebrated, iconicized even, the individual body parts as emblems—as in the *New York Times* advertisement of the Bandolino shoe (figure 2), with a lovely leg as the object of adoration—but in surrealism, these are ribald reductions (the woman as self-pleasuring, licking her nipple in the shower, as in Magritte's *Pebble*, figure 3). We are used to these partialities, these particulars, but here they seem often opposite in their effect from celebration Renaissance mode. Instead of a hand, we see a glove in bronze on Breton's desk, we see ankles parading over the streets as Robert Desnos pictures surrealist woman. The Czech artist Jindřich Štyrský places a firecracker in a suggestive loop above a woman's ankle, *slipped* from its high-heel shoe, just timed to go off and to set off (figure 4). In every case, the woman is in slippage. Worse, she is an amalgam: take Magritte's *Invention Collective* as woman and fish, with woman legs and fish head is a mermaid's horrendous opposite, gasping its way to its end, unlovely,

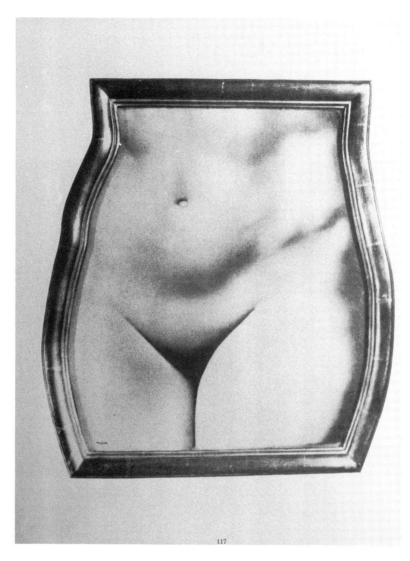

Figure 1 René Magritte, *Representation,* 1937. Oil on canvas on wood, 19⅛ × 17⅜ (irregular). Penrose Collection, London. © 1997 C. Herscovici, Brussels/ARS, New York.

Figure 2 Ad in *New York Times,* 1988, for Bandolino.

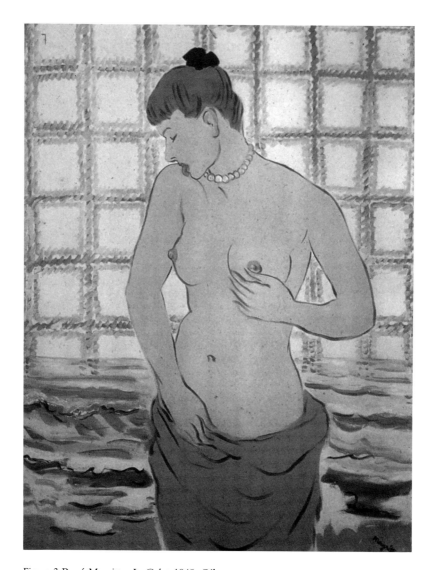

Figure 3 René Magritte, *Le Galet,* 1948. Oil on paper.

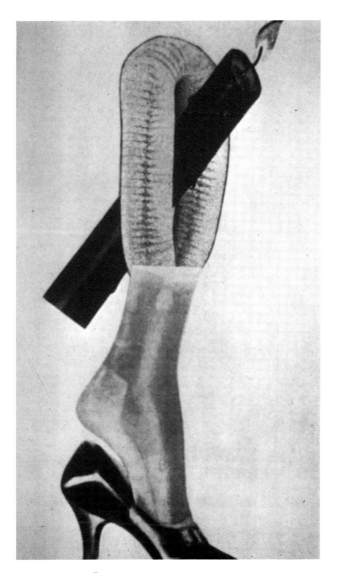

Figure 4 Jindřich Štyrský, *Collage,* 1934.

Figure 5 Hans Bellmer, *Doll,* 1936 (from *Jointure de boules,* 1936, *Minotaure* no. 8, illustrating E. Tériade, "La Peinture surréaliste"). © 1997 ARS, New York/ADAGP, Paris.

Figure 6 Hans Bellmer, *Doll,* 1936 (from *La Poupée*). © 1997 ARS, New York/ADAGP, Paris.

unloved, and forlorn on a beach. Clearly, Hans Bellmer's famously terrible and terrifying images, all reduced to the "middle essential," leave nothing but the macabre behind them (figures 5 and 6). This kind of *doll,* not even the Stepford Wife variety, is just one step beyond René Magritte's *Le Viol* (figure 7)[1], his *Rape* scenes, and their use by the leader of surrealism, André Breton, on the cover of his book *defining* surrealism in 1934: *What is Surrealism?* and then this image (figure 8). Little wonder that in the following year, the *Bulletin international du surréalisme* (*International Bulletin of Surrealism*) in Brussels puts a female body with a skull on it: where do we go from here? (figure 9)

We have been angry at these images; we still are.[2]

So I want to unbeach that woman, and look at the parallel look, from other eyes, for we are just getting used to looking at female looking. Magritte

Figure 7 René Magritte, *Le Viol,* 1934. Gouache on paper,
28½ × 21 in. Collection George Melly, London. © 1997
C. Herscovici, Brussels/ARS, New York.

Figure 8 Cover of André Breton, *Qu'est-ce que le surréalisme,*
Brussels: René Henriquez, 1934.

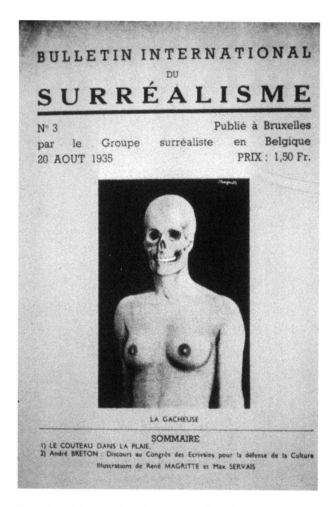

Figure 9 *Bulletin international du surréalisme,* Brussels, no. 3,
August 1935.

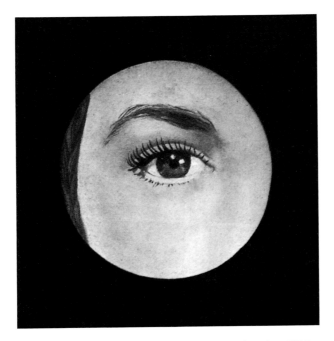

Figure 10 René Magritte, *L'Oeil: Objet peint,* second version, 1936 or 1937, 6 in. Private Collection, New York. Copy of antique eye. © 1997 C. Herscovici, Brussels/ARS, New York.

even appropriates the woman's eye in his painted object called just *Eye (L'Oeil: Objet peint* (figure 10)—copied from an eye on an ancient Egyptian box, and given to his wife. Negatively read, he is taking over even the looking; positively, he is giving her *le look.* This surrealist gift, like the surrealist *look,* is very different indeed from Redon's symbolist vision (figure 11). In any case, the women included here: the artist and writer Dorothea Tanning and the writer and photographer and artist Claude Cahun in particular, will have their word to say.

This *look* will cut both ways, and, so far as I can manage it, every which way, starting with the baroque view, a shifty one. But I want also to look at what might be, as a 1996 exhibition of female artists entitles it, "Inside the Visible," alluding to the experience "folded into visibility."[3] This too is part of the look, as I see it.

Figure 11 Odilon Redon, *The Vision,* no 8 of *Dans le Rêve,* 1879. Lithograph. 274 × 198 cm. Bibliothèque nationale, Paris.

Acknowledgments

For permission to reprint (or adapt) material from articles previously appearing, I am grateful to the editors and publishers of the following: *Surrealism and Women,* ed. Mary Ann Caws, Rudolf Kuenzli, and Gwen Raaberg (Cambridge: MIT Press, 1991), first published as an issue of *Dada and Surrealism* (Iowa City: University of Iowa, 1990); "Regard et représentation: problématique du corps féminin: tel qu'en lui-même," in Jacqueline Chénieux-Gendron, *Du Surréalisme et du plaisir* (Paris: José Corti, 1987), 169–78; "L'Oeil fixe, les yeux croisés," in Jacqueline Chénieux-Gendron, *Lire le regard: André Breton et la peinture,* Collection Pleine Marge, no. 2 (Paris: Lachenal & Ritter, 1993), 231–49; "Joseph Cornell et Robert Motherwell: Choisir et Construire," in *Regard d'écrivain Parole de peintre,* ed. Monique Chefdor et Dalton Krauss (Nantes: Joca seria, 1994).

My thanks to so many friends, students, and colleagues who have helped me look, through their writings and conversations and receptiveness. In particular to Carol Armstrong, Timothy Baum, Yves Bonnefoy, Michèle Cone, Tom Conley, John Hollander, Etienne-Alain Hubert, Rosalind Krauss, Gerhard Joseph, Charles Landesman, Christie McDonald, Nancy Miller, Linda Nochlin, Martha Otis, Martica Sawin, Ellen Handler Spitz, Richard Stamelman, Susan Suleiman, and many others in the fields of surrealism and art history. For their gracious help with reproductions, thanks to Richard Adar, Geraldine Aramanda, Jacklyn Burns, Mikki Carpenter, Marie-Claude Char, Marie-Claire Dumas, Joanne Greenbaum, Christina Houstian, Steve Infantino, Alison Jasonides, Serge Malaussena, Luisa Orto, Peter Namuth, Hubert Neumann, Yuki Puar, Margit Rowell, Dorothea Tanning, Virginia Zabriskie. To Roger Conover, Julie Grimaldi, Katherine Arnoldi, and the designer of The MIT Press: I am really grateful for your patience and more. Thank you all.

I

Looking and Listening

1

LOOK: LARGE AND BAROQUE

Everything on earth is baroque. The boat is no more made for the
sea than the sky.

—*Robert Desnos,* Nouvelles Hébrides [1]

LOOKING

Surrealism brought about a new way of looking. Like much else in that movement and manner of thinking, the word has two senses: what it looks like and
how it looks at the world outside it and then inward, to an "interior model." I
will look at both kinds of looking, theirs and ours, that is, at what and how
those whom we call surrealists saw, as if we could look through their eyes, and
also what we see when looking at them and their gaze. Such a double intention
seems already to split, consciously, into a willed presence (looking with them)
and a certain distance (looking at them). They had "le look" in advance, and a
lot more. Borrowing a properly surrealist optimism, I will interweave these
looks and lookings.[2]

Surrealism still looks large from here. Whether we concentrate on its
images of communicating vessels and glass houses or on its linguistic and famously visible gestures, they all seem to contain within them a kind of spaciousness, radiating the same spirit. Surrealist discourse expresses and incites to excess. Surrealism causes problems. It disturbs, as it wants to, even now.[3] It calls
upon whatever energies we have to reread it.[4]

It is not, any more than Dada, a movement that wants to put itself or the observer at ease. I differ from those who construe Dada as totally negative and surrealism as positive. Dada is always Dada, or it is not; in its major moments, it writes itself with a capital letter. Surrealism absorbed much dadaist energy, which its own contradictory tendencies were able to sustain.

LOOKING BAROQUE

In surrealism nothing stays where it should or used to. Things keep pouring into each other—as in the image of those *Communicating Vessels* (1991)[5] by which André Breton characterized the surrealist mingling of night and day, death and life, and all other contraries, or in René Magritte's *The False Mirror* (1928) where clouds cross the sight (figure 1.1). Things and people and ideas refuse to stay in their own domains, the way we remember them, the way they are often presented. They are—*just look at them!*—spilling all over the place, no longer willing to be read only "one in the other," as in the crucial surrealist game of curious title, *l'un dans l'autre.* Instead they insist, across centuries and countries, that they can best be seen not just in but *through* the other, as in Benjamin Péret's poem "Rosa": "Today I look out through your hair. . . . And I think through your exploding breasts." I see surrealism's look through the way it looks, thinking this gesture of interpenetration part of the great baroque tradition I associate with the gestures of surrealism.

The ways the baroque approach teaches us to think about reversals, upside-downness, and in-outness I would summarize briefly as fascination with what is complex, multiple, clouded, and changeable. As for traditional or "classic" definitions of the baroque I will cite a few sources: Heinrich Wölfflin's celebrated distinction between Renaissance and baroque, with the well-marked polarities of linear versus painterly, planar and clear versus recessional and unclear construction:

> Every picture has recession, but the recession has a very different effect according to whether the space organizes itself into planes or is experienced as a homogenous recessional movement . . . The great contrast between linear and painterly style corresponds to rad-

Figure 1.1 René Magritte, *The False Mirror (Le Faux Miroir),* 1928. Oil on canvas, 21¼ × 31⅞ in. Collection, The Museum of Modern Art, New York. © 1997 C. Herscovici, Brussels/ARS, New York.

ically different interests in the world. In the former case, it is the solid figure, in the latter, the changing appearance; in the former, the enduring form, measurable, finite; in the latter, the movement, the form in function; in the former, the thing in itself; in the latter, the thing in its relations. . . . The former represents things as they are, the latter as they seem to be.[6]

Jean Rousset arranges his analyses of baroque images and themes around changeability or mutation, including indeterminacy and cloudiness, and disguise. Baroque poetry relies on such images as soap bubbles for their formal change and their fragility, water as it reflects and alters in form, and water's imagined hard form, the mirror. Associated with change or material conversion is psychological conversion: thus the appropriate figure of Mary Magdalen, rendered and rerendered by Georges de La Tour. To the list of baroque figures, Christine Buci-Glücksmann adds Salomé, as the baroque heroine staging her desire. In *La Raison baroque,* Buci-Glücksmann illustrates the aesthetics of otherness, in which the feminine acts as the place and origin of knowledge for baroque male poets.[7] It is clearly preferable to render her mute, as André Masson does his mannequin (1938) (figure 1.2).

No figures better illustrate changeability than Proteus, on one hand, and Don Juan on the other. Rousset sums up the baroque:

> To the intuition of an unstable and moving world, of a multiple and inconstant life, hesitating between being and seeming, fond of disguise and of theatrical representation, there correspond, on the expressive and structural level a rhetoric of metaphor and *trompe l'oeil,* a poetics of surprise and variousness, and a style of metamorphosis, of dynamic spread and dispersion in unity.
>
> In order to produce the desired effect of motion and expansion, of an action constantly beginning over and never completed, of perpetual transmutation central to the work, the baroque creator will have recourse to several stylistic means: open and complex forms, the elimination of articulations, a construction on several levels at once, an unstable equilibrium due to the multiplicity of perspectives, of organizing centers, and of mental and imaginative registers.[8]

Such complex forms as the play within a play, an obvious part of this aesthetic, have definite implications for the *mise-en-abyme,*[9] as for the associated theory of fractals. Whether we view the baroque as a period spanning 1520 to 1680 and include in it mannerism (1520–80) or identify its characteristics as illusion and mutability the baroque sensibility pictures the world in reverse and upside down.[10] The baroque is generally associated with the visual: in *Downcast Eyes,* Martin Jay describes the baroque as "the art of the thing seen" and views theatrical baroque performance as directed at that art, as authoritarian controls over

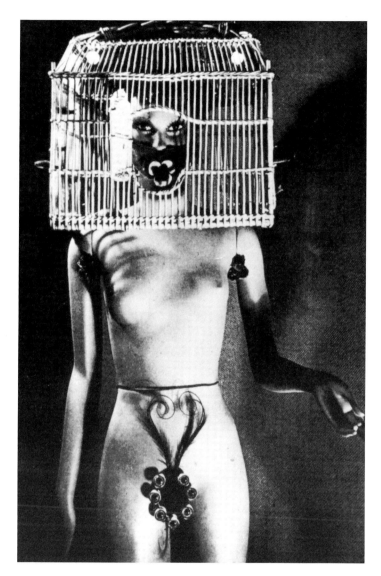

Figure 1.2 André Masson, *Mannequin with Bird Cage* (for the Surrealist Exhibition of 1938), Construction, 1938. © 1997 ARS, New York/ADAGP, Paris.

Figure 1.3 Man Ray, *Rrose Sélavy,* 1920. Gelatin silver print,
8¹¹⁄₁₆ × 6¹⁵⁄₁₆ in. The J. Paul Getty Museum, Los Angeles.
© 1997 ARS, New York/ADAGP/Man Ray Trust, Paris.

the people and their festivities.[11] He refers to Buci-Glücksmann's study of *la folie du voir* (madness of vision), which disparages "lucid clarity and essential form," celebrating instead "the confusing interplay of form and chaos, surface and depth, transparency and obscurity."

The baroque sensibility and techniques have an urgent application in the world of surrealism and its reversal of words, thoughts and concepts and its exuberant ways of thinking and expressing in general. Already in the first number of the luxurious surrealist journal *Minotaure,* Max Raphael presents a telling "Remarque sur le baroque," with Tintoretto, Rubens, and Poussin as illustrations.[12] Just as those great Renaissance wordplayers, the Grands Rhétoriqueurs,

Figure 1.4 El Greco [Domenikos Theotokopoulos, called], *Laocoön*, c. 1610/1614. Oil on canvas, 54⅛ × 67⅞ in. Samuel H. Kress Collection. © 1996 Board of Trustees, National Gallery of Art, Washington.

put a combinatorial verbal spin on their world, so does Robert Desnos speak—grand-rhetorically—as Rrose Sélavy, the alter ego of Marcel Duchamp. Meet Rrose in 1920 (figure 1.3). The affection that Desnos shows for the Spanish mannerist/baroque poet Luis de Góngora and his reversals, twists, and serpentine constructions testifies to the link I hope to reinforce here, in which the contortions of the famous *Laocoön* (figure 1.4) and of Tintoretto's *Leda* (figure 1.5) do a remarkable double twist and turn. Compare the swerves of a Góngora poem, in which Leda is compared with the peacock and Juno with the swan, with the normal associations reversed: "pavon de Venus es, cisne de Juno" (peacock of Venus she is, swan of Juno).[13] Similarly, in the dream poems or *Songes* of the Renaissance poet Joachim Du Bellay, everything is constructed only to be deconstructed and decomposed.

Figure 1.5 Tintoretto, *Leda and the Swan*. Oil on canvas, 63⅜ × 85¾ in. Galleria dell'Uffizi, Florence. Photo: Anderson.

No image better links surrealism and the baroque, I think, than André Breton's phrase of optimism, reversal, and openness: "Les oiseaux n'ont jamais mieux chanté que dans cet aquarium" ("The birds have never sung better than in this aquarium"). Indeed they have not, and it is up to us to learn how to listen. Breton, tone-deaf and totally impenetrable to musical sound in general— think of his categorical demand: "Let the curtain fall on the orchestra!"—knows how to hear, from inside, what matters for the tone of surrealism.[14] "le la." This does.

We have to learn to listen, but also to look. One image seems to me perfectly to introduce the surrealist experiment within the baroque one. In Man Ray's extraordinary *Indestructible Object,* (1958) (figure 1.6) the cover of the metronome box is unhooked and laid aside, although still touching the box, in

Figure 1.6 Man Ray, *Indestructible Object,* 1958 replica of 1923 original.
Metronome with photograph and paper clip, 8¾ × 4¼ × 4¼ in. New York,
Morton G. Neumann Family Collection. Photo: Quiriconi–Tropea.

which a photograph of one eye with its lashes is detached from its face, and flimsily attached with a homely paper clip to the pendulum of a metronome. So, it would seem to say, seeing takes its own time. If the look is inseparable from its timing, it is remarkably and uncomfortably separable from its agent. The eye as emblem or icon, once it is set in motion, will tick right along. Things do not necessarily belong in their human context. The surrealist look exists independent from the looker. All of this is, for the time and space of this one image, true. *Fecit Man Ray,* as so often.

2

MODE: SEEING THROUGH

What one would like to say is "seeing by seeing."

—*Ludwig Wittgenstein,* Zettel[1]

The act of seeing one thing through another, this *mode* of interpenetration, is presided over by the figures of the child-woman and the mermaid Mélusine, these boundary figures whom Breton places at the center of his meditation on flexibility and revolution against the mechanistic way of seeing. Here in *The Surrealist Look* Mélusine as model and heroine opens the way for three chapters on the problems of female creation and self-portraiture as exemplified in the work of Dorothea Tanning and Claude Cahun, as opposed to Man Ray's representation, manipulation, and fashioning of the female body.

I choose to move from personal to impersonal, reading the body of surrealism against a decor of high and often lonely lyricism, as in Robert Desnos's *Deuil pour deuil* (*Mourning for Mourning*), and then its absolute contrast: an excessive and violent surrealist painting by François de Nomé (often confused with Monsu Desiderio or "Monsieur Désir"), read in the light of Antonin Artaud's reflections on repassioning the universe via an explosive sensibility.

Continuing with excess, I then take up the emblematic *game* of surrealist collective excess, *cadavre exquis* (exquisite corpse). The kinds of philosophical games or toys that Joseph Cornell invents are seen as containers of memorable scenes and as architectural structures of containment. More subtly, they are also transgressions against the architecture of things,[2] as is his feminized representation in *Laundry Boy's Charge* (1966) (figure 2.1) of Man Ray's representation of Breton, to be compared with Duchamp's representation of Man Ray's representation of Duchamp as Rrose Sélavy (see figure 1.3). These transgressive figures perform the central play of surrealism as I see it, baroque as they can be and as it can be.

Figure 1.3

My concluding discussion concentrates on the surrealist *look* in its different possible rhythms, exemplified by how René Char reads the painters around him, and then on its sharp focus on a point, as does the Dada subject/object of Marcel Duchamp's pointing finger of *Tu m'* (1918) (figure 2.2), illustrated by Wittgenstein's meditation on the subject. Finally, I look at its own *language* in the baroque light already mentioned, the light of willed and willing change that Mélusine emblematizes in the initial chapter and continues to represent.

Baroque and surrealist views and representations reflect upon each other in an interconnecting perspective, each *through the other.* If Man Ray's picture of Lee Miller's *Neck* in 1929, later portrayed in *Anatomies* 1930 (figure 2.3) looks like a penis, so be it. More power to the neck, as it were, or to both. Fluid interpenetration is a major point of surrealism, too often overlooked in favor of the more easily explained automatism that was the object of the first *Surrealist Manifesto* of 1924. Indeed, Breton's philosophical, alchemical, playfully serious game title "one in the other" was leverage enough to reverse elements into each other, but his emblematic metaphor of communicating vessels went still further.

So *The Surrealist Look* is about accepting the invitation to communication and interpenetration that Desnos implicitly holds out in his invocation of the baroque, taking the sky as a potential container for a boat and the sea for a plane. When Breton demands—for his tone goes far past an asking—that we learn to see afresh, to replace things anew, we may well find that the sort of birds he invites us to hear "have never sung better than in this aquarium." So René Char draws a bird and labels it a snake (figure 2.4). If the relation of the baroque and the surrealist spirit and text is close, it has always been so. It is up to us to hear and see that relation right now.[3]

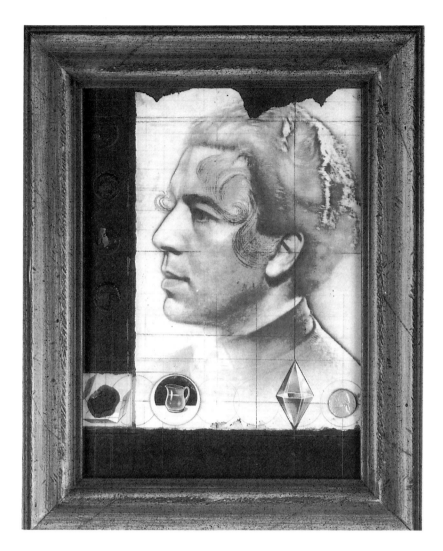

Figure 2.1 Joseph Cornell, *Laundry Boy's Charge,* 1966. (Photograph of André Breton by Man Ray, from 1931). © The Joseph and Robert Cornell Memorial Foundation.

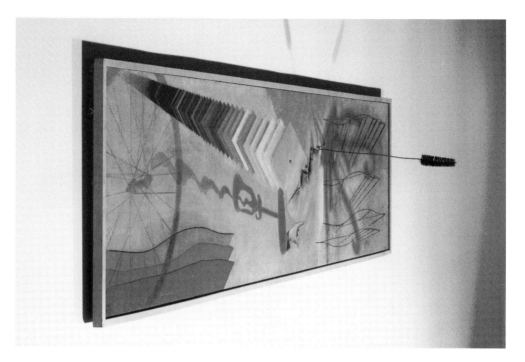

Figure 2.2 Marcel Duchamp, *Tu m'*, 1918. Oil on canvas with bottle brush, three safety pins, and one bolt, 27¼ × 10 ft 3 in. Yale University Art Gallery, New Haven, Conn. © 1997 ARS, New York/ADAGP, Paris.

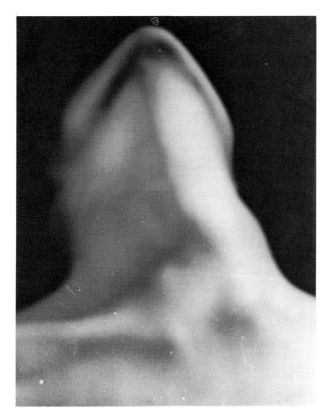

Figure 2.3 Man Ray, from *Anatomies,* c. 1930. Gelatin silver print, 28.9 × 21.6 cm. New York: Museum of Modern Art. © ADAGP/DACS 1989.

Figure 2.4 René Char, *Le Serpent* (*The Snake*) (from René Char, *La Nuit talismanique* [Paris: Skira, 1972]). Courtesy of Marie-Claude Char.

3

PROBLEM: THE PERSONAL SURREALIST

We are very high up, and not at all disposed to come down.

—*André Breton,* Nadja[1]

Surrealism was surely as *personalized* as it was collective. This is as clear as it is
seldom discussed. So a question arises straight off: How does the reader of this
movement reconcile the vastly differing individual surrealist profiles of the
selves making up the movement with the collective revolutionary style that
surrealism promised, believed in, and—at its best moments—delivered? When
and how does the objective spirit dominate the subjective differences? To the
extent that the personal is now political, as we are so relentlessly cautioned,
should we read this consideration back into the heyday of surrealism? How
would it then affect the wonderfully eccentric enthusiasms of the personalities
through whom we latter-day readers have often found our most appealing entry
into the matter?

What sort of self are we expecting ourselves to find, along this path we
choose to call surrealist? Aren't we really discussing a losing of the self, in our
difficult knowledge that we must either renounce any fixity or ignore the fluidity that surrealism cherishes? Surrealism's overall motto, after all, was that of the
freedom to change by the moment, to address the passerby in the street for an
always possible encounter. This is set up, albeit implicitly, as the opposite of
Baudelaire's romantically tragic sense, his already inbred nostalgia about what

was always marked as impossible, never going past the past conditional ("Oh how I would have loved you, Oh how you knew . . ."). To find oneself but to find oneself *other* would be the great project of the whole surrealist enterprise. Altogether other but not always other together with all the others, for that would seem an odd principle of freedom—and yet. And yet.

This is precisely one of the inbred contradictions that fascinate us about the surrealist movement. We know how the surrealist group always met in the same cafés, like the Café Certa, and always drank the same thing, like a *mandarine curaçao,* and celebrated the same *passages,* like Aragon's salute to the Passage de l'Opéra in his *Paris Peasant.* Open to chance, to the large as to the small, the surrealists maintained their belief, as in Breton's *Nadja,* in a world willed as "sudden encounters, petrifying coincidences . . . flashes that could make you see, but really *see,* if they were not still more rapid than the others" (N, 18–19).

Of course, as with so many other instances, this was already the dada perspective. Breton's manifesto of those years, his "Disdainful Confession," reads as a salvo against stasis and settling down: "I used only to leave my dwelling after having said a definitive farewell to everything that had accumulated there in the way of enveloping memories, everything of myself I felt like perpetuating."[2] "You must forgive me for thinking," he continues, that "quite unlike ivy, I'll die if I get attached to something" (PP, 131).

At least two questions arise here, even at the outset. This is plainly, in spirit as in date, a "confession" in the dada and not the surrealist spirit. To be attached to *nothing* speaks more loudly of refusal than of a relatively *ordered* revolution of the sort Breton will later formulate for surrealism. For the members of the surrealist group, originally and later, were supposed to be attached to the movement and its beliefs—to its games and projects as to its leader. But who is to assert that attachment to one movement is any less conformist than to another? A second question arises even within the tenets of surrealism: What does openness to everything leave you with? Of what does the surrealist personality consist, when interesting in itself rather than just a self-discipline along the lines laid down by collective or party credos?

The most reliable model, at least for surrealist feminism, is Mélusine the shape-shifter. She was Breton's favorite figure; she is mine too.

4

Figure: Breton's Mélusine

No hope of synthesis.

—*René Crevel,* Le Clavecin de Diderot[1]

To think surrealism is to rethink the self. Let's assume this project is at once personal and literary: How do we find ourselves, as readers of this surrealism, deliberately revolutionary in style as in content? It was always, in spite of the continuities visible on first reading, a surrealism as individual to our own thinking of it as it was determined by its founders.

Yet we must also assume from the start that this project is without possible closure, inconclusive by nature as by choice, even as it is contemporary, given the struggle between manners of thinking. A common desire for objectivity frequently and easily wins out over our private selves and any personal optimism about highly individualizing possibilities, in the moment we are forced to admit the superior strength of depersonalized structures. Our learned cultural mistrust of anything concerning individual and generally inexplicable emotions can only reinforce our tendency to flee the personal. We flee often to escape toward simpler explicative models, whether semiotic or psychoanalytic or anthropological. In place of the deauthored and deselfed, I would choose, here and now, a personal, even emotional, relation between subject and object, subject and subject. The most collective project can become individualized, if one determines it so.

You have to believe it to see it.

I believe it.

Who Finds One Thing Only, Loses

We cannot, naturally, give up the spontaneous self and all of the possibilities of motion it entails. Like the protean self, the surrealist self has to take its consciousness from drift. Since we know how shape-shifting works, we might wonder in what shape we will continue.

This surrealizing person found as a protean self and reader, who might that be anyway? Who could guarantee that it is us and not someone else, some cypher or token person supposed in this idealizing function? To find ourselves, but to find ourselves *other,* and then still other, this is central to the surrealist enterprise. Any of our *others* is already problematic, to say the least, and already potentially lost to the next, whether an other person or the most loved text or belief. What do we then get to keep, in this recreation of the self in movement?

Breton's "Disdainful Confession" of his Dada years refuses to serve as a limit case of unsettling down. His conception of life remains as open to risk later as at this moment. In *Nadja* he insists on exposure to everything the street might offer: the world in which he chooses to dwell will be "opened to chances, to the most trivial and to the most important," made up of "sudden encounters, petrifying coincidences" and traversed with the flashes of insight these provoke.

The surrealist *état d'attente* (state of expectation) today comes under what British psychologist Adam Phillips stresses in his essays on the uncommitted life, provocatively called *On Flirtation:* whatever is contingent that can teach us most about ourselves. "Coincidences belong to those who can use them," he says.[2] The surrealist knew and still knows how to see and use them and knows how to teach us, in turn, about all that. That is what we get to keep: our redefinition of ourselves. *It has to be good enough.*[3]

Being Good Enough

Now what mental gestures might we best make, in language and the visual world, to declare this credo? How can we declare, for ourselves and others, our openness to the contingent? We have to continue to insist on surrealism's initial credo bound to believe in an objective chance that defines itself as an answer in the outside world to an inner question we didn't realize we had. Such gestures must bear primary witness to our willingness to shift our emotional as well as our mental state.

One of Breton's less well-known essays, "First Hand," prefixes a statement about our necessary trust in and encouragement of the emotions by the formal verbal equivalent of a typographical finger pointing or an arrow aimed at the point, like Duchamp's *Tu m'* (see figure 2.2): "Never shall we be able to insist enough on this: only by the emotional threshold can we gain access to the royal way; otherwise, the paths of knowledge never lead there."[4] Many surrealist texts testify openly to the emotional sway under which surrealism works, in the wake of romanticism ("We are the tail of romanticism," Breton was inclined to say, adding, "but now prehensile!"). So surrealism must want to hold on to something, with its prehensile tail. What it holds on to, just as we do, is its own definition.

Figure 2.2

I am dwelling at such length, initially, upon surrealism's own credos because I want to emphasize how they do not seem to me out of date. To be sure, the techniques of automatic writing and the hypnotic sleep experiments, delightful and revealing as they were, were *of that time*. This is however not true of the basic philosophical tenets of the surrealism as now reread. It lasts.

CHANGING THE SELF

To reinforce these initial statements about how we can make a true change of self, about the growing up one can do through surrealism, I want to call on the surrealists Louis Aragon, René Crevel, Octavio Paz, and Benjamin Péret before calling on that child-woman, that mermaid-maiden Mélusine, whose path they prepare.[5]

For each being, says Aragon in his *Le Paysan de Paris (Paris Peasant)* (1926), there is an image that will change the universe, bringing about a great dizziness that will completely alter what is seen, thought, felt. Such faith in a singular image and its attendant emotional state must hold firm against the discouragement Breton faces in *L'Amour fou (Mad Love)* (1937) when, walking with his newfound beloved along the streets of Les Halles in the very early morning, he hesitates, saying: "There would still be time to turn back."[6] Breton did not, of course, turn back; but his weakening faith here gives weight to his later meditations on what courage can be, even at its lowest point.

From Breton's standpoint, Aragon did turn back when he left the surrealist dizziness for political commitment in stasis, including a stasis of language. Aragon felt that he should simplify his poetic technique and thought, and did so. What he asks in his "Voyage to Holland" (1964)—in part echoing Baudelaire's "Invitation au voyage" and other voyages to Holland and their invitations[7]—is anguished and unanswerable except by the self in its questioning of the emotions: he wonders if some day we will have to reach the limit of our thoughts,

> The end of what we were the end of what we are
>   losing the sense
> Of what we feel we are saying; stopping halfway through
>   the sentence.[8]

In an important essay against conventions entitled "The Mind Against Reason," René Crevel speaks of the links between the emotions and poetry, between poetic revolution and real daily experience. That he so early on committed suicide does not invalidate his claim on poetry or life. "Any intelligence that fears the power, the embrace of life, becomes reciprocally incapable of power, of embrace. . . . Moods of the soul have nothing to do with fixed landscapes. Instead of flotsam, jetsam, and wreckage, the emotional flood brings the lively fruits of desire."[9]

Emotion is tied to invention in this world where language creates the outer and inner landscapes. Spaciousness must be found within the changing self as well as beyond it. Here being and becoming depend on voicing. In "Draft of Shadows," Octavio Paz examines the relations between the self and its phrasing of possibilities, between individual thinking and epic motion:

> I drift away from myself,
> following this meandering phrase,
> the path of rocks and goats.
>
>   . . .

> From my forehead I set out
> Toward a noon the size of time.
> . . .
>
> I am where I was:
> I walk behind the murmur,
> footsteps within me, heard with my eyes,
> the murmur is in the mind, I am my footsteps,
> I hear the voices that I think
> The voices that think me as I think them.
> I am the shadow my words cast.[10]

The world here is full, the song is large enough to absorb not just the murmur of the mind but the footsteps of the one walking. The shadow cast by language makes room for others, as for the self, for things as for living creatures. The sense of place is strong within the universe of this lastingly contemporary poetry, which is not in drift.[11] More than timelessness and boundlessness, it is about the timeful and the spacious, as an intense timefulness and spacefulness develop from the private and pensive forehead. Here the walker-poet can set out "toward a noon the size of time" and know it not to be colorless. Here the positive easily dominates the negative, whether implicit or explicit.

The world created through the phrasing and walking-as-making accommodates the self in the surrealist plenitude so well represented by Benjamin Péret, Breton's right-hand man. Péret's love poetry, which clearly permits seeing through another's self in this open-form universe, permits much else besides:

> where the pointed breasts of women stare out through
>   the eyes of men
> Today I look out through your hair
> Rosa of morning opal
> And I wake up through your eyes
> Rosa of armor
> And I think through your exploding breasts
> Rosa of black forest drenched with blue-green postage stamps.
> Rosa of cigar smoke

Rosa of sea foam made crystal
Rosa.[12]

Like Breton's famous "Free Union," where the beloved's attributes are successively celebrated as in the emblemizations of mannerist poetry, themselves harking back to the *blasons* or the emblems of the Renaissance, Péret's voiced celebrations of the self in the other and the other in the self seem to depend uniquely upon the power of, the fact of, loving. Yet I think they depend just as gravely and finally upon language and its power, the rediscovery of which is the crucial insight of surrealism at its finest moments.

Finding or inventing the fullness of the universe through language is what matters most deeply. Paz speaks of a country "Beyond Love": "Beyond ourselves/on the frontier of being and becoming/a life more alive claims us" (DS, 20–21). And Breton, saluting the work of Jorge-Luis Borges and his "lucid perplexity" about the world, praises the way in which his self is always and already an other: "Courage, exulting even in its moments of weakness, honing itself anew in each courageous death, is the driving force of this poetry where the 'I' is already intensely 'an other' because it assumes all the exigencies, including that of the inanimate, and can only conceive of itself as their global consciousness."[13]

Elsewhere, in an essay gathered in *Perspective cavalière,* the posthumous collection that includes the essay just quoted, Breton insists that we oppose anything threatening the dignity of our lives, made up of "freedom and love: the whole diamond we are carrying in ourselves" (PC, 166). When Robert Desnos salutes, in the title of his brilliant novel *La Liberté ou l'amour!* (Freedom or Love!) (1927) even the conjunction shines in its ambivalent glory: it both separates love from liberty and makes them equivalent. What conjunctive power—this is surrealist ambivalence at its most intense: freedom or love! The question becomes the shout, the choice becomes the affirmation.

MÉLUSINE'S MAKEUP

Melusine, after the cry . . .

—*André Breton,* Arcane 17[14]

Mélusine, the surrealist heroine par excellence, is undeniably the feminist model for surrealism at its best.[15] One of Breton's most convincing passages, in the lyric musing of *Arcane 17* extends a fitting salute to the mermaid, as he reclaims a power to place in woman's hands. It begins:

> Mélusine after the cry . . . I see no one else who can redeem this savage time. She is entirely woman and yet such as she is today, deprived of her human place, a prisoner of her roots however mobile they are and nevertheless, through them, in providential communication with the elemental natural forces. Woman deprived of her human place, as legend has it, through man's impatience and jealousy. This place can be returned to her only after he has meditated at length on his mistake, a length proportionate to the resulting misfortune. For Mélusine, before and after the metamorphosis, is Mélusine.[16]

A first cry will announce her return to the world; a second will announce childbirth with no suffering and other miracles. Breton celebrates her uniquely feminine attributes: her stomach is like an August harvest, her breasts are like

> ermines caught in their own cry, blinding with the burning coal of their raging mouth. And her arms are the soul of streams singing and perfuming. And under the fall of her hair, with its gilt worn off, are found forever all the distinctive traits of the woman-child, this particular variety which has always captivated poets *because time has no power over her. (Arcane 17,* 93–94)

She is both composite and shape-shifter, both fish and woman, woman and child. Around her, she undoes the best-organized systems because, like time itself, they have no sway over her. She is invincible *because she changes,* being the victim of no categorization. The perfect model of surrealism, its ideal representation, she is the woman that Breton would have wanted to be, to which implicit desire Cornell's *Laundry Boy Charge* (see figure 2.1) pays homage.

Figure 2.1

> Her complexion disarms any harshness, beginning with those of time, as I don't need to tell her. Even that which strikes her makes her stronger, suppler, clearer in outline, and finally completes her as would the chisel of an ideal sculptor, docile to the laws of a preestablished harmony and which will never find closure because, without any possible misstep, it is on the road to perfection and this road could not end. And even corporeal death, the physical destruction of the work happens not to be an end. Still the radiance subsists, what am I saying, it's the entire statue, still lovelier and possible, waking to the imperishable without losing anything of her earthly appearance, made up of a sublime meeting of light rays. (A, 97)

A legend, yes, but strong as a model for the legendary ability of the female temperament to overthrow what is already too clear and hardened. The woman-child exemplifies the transformative power of the *possible* for others, the ones who have learned to read surrealism and the ones who learn later, sometimes from those who did before. Upon Mélusine, we can model our openness to contingency and faith in the positive inventions of everyday life. Landscapes, like lives, have to be created before you can hold on to them, even as they change. They are not given, they have to be earned.

And Mélusine is *always* good enough.

5

RHYTHM: CHAR AND HIS OTHERS

Cher vieux frère, jamais assez de colère, jamais assez d'amour, d'amitiés pour te dire combien je t'aime . . .

(Dear old brother, never enough anger, never enough love, friendship, to tell you how I love you)

—*Nicolas de Staël to René Char, September 15, 1952*[1]

One of the most challenging certainties about surrealism is the astonishing contrast between its rhythms of creation and of reception, from the very rapid to the very slow. Already in the "automatic writing" that Breton did with Philippe Soupault, *Le Poisson soluble* (1924), there are notations of the speed of writing. (Rapid transcription of the automatic dictation the surrealist hand felt it was taking down was supposed to release the mind from its ordinary logical constraints, breaking down the resistance to this flood of expression.)

So, for a while, surrealism seemed to me to be about speed. I saw in my mind's eye those figures of the early surrealism, Breton and Soupault, writing *Le Poisson soluble* as rapidly as they could, walking as quickly as possible down the street to defamiliarize themselves with it so as to see it afresh. I thought of the surrealist artists imitating Victorien Sardou's etching hand, moving "nonstop and with an unheard of swiftness from one side of the plate to the other without lifting from it, returning a hundred times to the same point. Thus all parts were begun and continued simultaneously, no one part being completed before another was begun."[2] Neutral observers said that the resultant mess was totally incoherent and incomprehensible before the work was seen as a whole, while certain detractors seemed to find that true even at the end.

Such an obsessive speed, desperate to get things down, verged at times upon hysteria in its wish to close the gap between perception and the subsequent representation.[3] The *delay* between one moment and the next in the work of art—a cousin of Marcel Duchamp's *Delay in Glass*—has its equivalent in such modernist authors as Henry James, for example, especially the late writings of James,[4] where situations and perceptions are held suspended, in deliberate and sustained delay.

Delay is everywhere evident in surrealism, in narration that endlessly leaves us expectant, trying to catch up, almost hysterical ourselves, with this impossible faith in what would be, could be "always for the fist time."[5] That is how it has often felt to me, a rushing after significance—"Les poètes tiennent du seismographe plus que du citoyen," says Aragon in his "Introduction à 1930."[6] He tells this particular poetic tale about and for young men, whose more serious spoofs even were marked by an impatience at once touching and inimitable. The sense of quick breathing comes from their just plain going along too fast, at least much of the time. For them and their feet—but that is the source, often, of our responding excitement.

Wanting to experiment with rhythm for a while now, I have taken to reading these essays in their translations, putting a distance between myself and the original, setting experience itself in delay, as it were. From that vantage point, much of the language, many of the actions, seem marked by the same near-hysterical pace and outlook. In a recent publication for example, *The Surrealists Look at Art*,[7] Paul Eluard addresses Hans Bellmer's revolting doll (see preface, figure 5) in these engaging terms:

Figure 5

> It is a girl—where are her eyes?
> It is a girl—where are her breasts?
> It is a girl—what does she say?
> It is a girl—what is she playing at?
> It is a girl, it is my desire![8]

Enough said.

Figure 5.1 Jean (Hans) Arp, *Bois déchiré (Torn up Woodcut)*, 1920/54. Wood engraving torn and mounted on card backing, 8¾ × 6½ in. Tate Gallery, London, Great Britain. Tate Gallery, London/Art Resource, N.Y. [Originally made as woodcut for Tristan Tzara's *Cinéma du coeur abstrait* in 1920, torn and reassembled in 1954.] © 1997 ARS, New York/VG Bild-Kunst, Bonn.

Many such surrealist acts seem hysterical in themselves, seen from here, or from where I am looking: René Magritte chalking a drawing on a slate so that, precisely, it can be erased; André Derain scraping off the actual newspaper in his painting *Portrait of Chevalier X,* which is then exhibited with a painted newspaper in Leningrad and called, with a slight difference, *Portrait of an Unknown Man with a Newspaper;*[9] Max Ernst's obsession with the technique of *frottage,* entailing not just a pleasant erotics but the whole rather unpleasant notion of irritability; Soupault's taking a piece of asphalt from the street and framing it to hang between an empty frame (*Portrait d'un Inconnu*) and a mirror (*Portrait d'un imbécile*); Jean Arp's tearing up of one of his woodcuts (figure 5.1); Salvador

Dali's placing a piece of bark on a collage to make *Nu féminin*. This is all inventive, funny, and incontrovertibly exhausting. As if one could catch on, but never up.

One summer, as I was contemplating the subjects of exhaustion and never catching up, I revisited the René Char exhibition in the Palais des Papes in Avignon, slowly. I was suddenly stopped dead in my tracks by a picture. The text alongside it was one of Char's aphorisms about a space stretching out to infinity; the painting was done, in the Vaucluse, by Nicolas de Staël and was just a road. It stretched out too, in blue and yellow and in flat but shimmering white light, and held you fixed. I felt my mind taking its time again, at last, as it had in the days when Char was alive, in the Vaucluse where I spend my summers because of him. Over the years he taught me, with a poet's patience, to take the time to wander, as he used to put it, in the great spaces of the self.

That was the phrase he used to me, about what I was learning, from his poems, his landscape, and himself. For his poetry knows how to take its time. The landscape in which he lived is full of that lesson he leaned so well. Char took his time with his friends, like Paul Eluard (figures 5.2 and 5.3), who introduced him to surrealism and the surrealists, and then later, and always, with his landscape, dominated by Mont Ventoux (figure 5.4). I place here, as witness, the picture that he gave me of it, taken by his friend P. A. Benoit (figure 5.5). It could all be conceived in the light of the dialogue that Char envisages having with Georges Braque one summer afternoon in 1950:

> Le Peintre:
>> Quoi de neuf dans votre Midi?
> Le Poète:
>> Les orangers déjà sont en fleurs, le pêcher fait son
>> averse. D'autres arbres vont bientôt suivre. Mais leur
>> maturité est insérée dans une unique saison.[10]

In the light of that *unique saison,* I have wanted to see what a *slow poem* by Char might be: here are three examples.[11] The first, from *Fureur et mystère,* bears the monumental name "Fastes," already indicating the passing of the seasons

Figure 5.2 *Paul Eluard et René Char à Nice,* 1930 (from *Faire du chemin avec . . . ,* Marie-Claude Char, Paris: Gallimard, 1992). Photograph courtesy of Marie-Claude Char.

Figure 5.3 *René Char avec Paul Eluard à L'Isle-sur-Sorgue*, 1930
(from *Faire du chemin avec . . .*). Photograph courtesy of
Marie-Claude Char.

Figure 5.4 *René Char, with Pablo Picasso on the Mont Ventoux,*
protesting the nuclear installations (from Marie-Claude Char,
op. cit.) © ARS.

and the tides, binding together the landscape of the mountain and that of the
sea, in a slow union along the length of the poem's three sections, up to its
central height.[12]

Fastes

    L'été chantait sur son roc préféré quand tu m'es apparue, l'été
chantait à l'écart de nous qui étions silence, sympathie, liberté triste,
mer plus encore que la mer dont la longue pelle bleue s'amusait à
nos pieds.

Figure 5.5 P. A. Benoit, 1960s, photograph of Le Mont Ventoux, in the Vaucluse, given by René Char to the author.

L'été chantait et ton cœur nageait loin de lui. Je baisais ton courage, entendais ton désarroi. Route par l'absolu des vagues vers ces hauts pics d'écume où croisent des vertus meurtrières pour les mains qui portent nos maisons. Nous n'étions pas crédules. Nous étions entourés.

Les ans passèrent. Les orages moururent. Le monde s'en alla. J'avais mal de sentir que ton cœur justement ne m'apercevait plus. Je t'aimais. En mon absence de visage et mon vide de bonheur. Je t'aimais, changeant en tout, fidèle à toi.

(Annals

Summer was singing on its favorite rock when you appeared to me, summer was singing apart as we who were silence, sympathy, sorrowful freedom, were sea still more than the sea whose long blue spade was playing at our feet.

Summer was singing and your heart swam far from it. I embraced your courage, heard your confusion. Road along the absolute of waves toward those high peaks of foam where virtues sail, murderous to hands bearing our houses. We were not credulous. We were surrounded.

The years passed by. The storms died down. The world went its way. I suffered to think it was your heart which no longer perceived me. I loved you. In my absence of visage and my emptiness of joy. I loved you, changing in every way, faithful to you.

[MAC])

The second, from *La Parole en archipel,* is briefer, containing, in its small space, the whole history of a life, a judgment, and a truth that has known how to take its own time. "Traverse," it is called, "Short-Cut," like that of a schoolchild going home:

Traverse

La colline qu'il a bien servie descend en torrent dans son dos. Les langues pauvres le saluent; les mulets au pré lui font fête. La face rose de l'ornière tourne deux fois vers lui l'onde de son miroir. La méchanceté dort. Il est tel qu'il se rêvait.

(Short-Cut

The hill he has served so well descends torrential at his back. Poor tongues salute him; the mules in the meadow welcome him. The gulley's rose-hued face turns toward him twice the waters of its mirror. Meanness sleeps. He is as he dreamt himself to be.[13]

[MAC])

The third poem, "Prière rogue" ("Unbending Prayer") from *Recherche de la base et du sommet,* is at once solemn, sad, and quietly, triumphantly wise:

Prière rogue

Gardez-nous la révolte, l'éclair, l'accord illusoire, un rire pour le trophée glissé des mains, même l'entier et long fardeau qui succède, dont la difficulté nous mène à une révolte nouvelle. Gardez-nous la primevère et le destin.

(Unbending Prayer

Preserve for us rebellion, lightning, the illusory agreement, a laugh for the trophy slipped from our hands, even the whole lengthy burden that follows, whose difficulty leads us to a new rebellion. Preserve for us fate and the primose.[14]

[MAC])

This poem as prayer, while inscribing itself in a future, demands nothing so passive as patience—this is Char's condensed equivalent of a long-term credo: "I believe," and it is the belief that preserves the long-term credit.

From the point of view of rhythm, the speed of surrealism seems to line up with that of futurism, whereas that of such meditative poets as Char and Bonnefoy calls for another kind of reading and commentary, set in a slower mode.

How does the artist choose the poet who seems to be in the closest correspondence? I will briefly glance at three painters—Georges Braque, Vieira da Silva, and Nicolas de Staël—as they opt for certain of Char's texts. I like to think that they chose him for texts such as those just quoted. They found in him, no doubt, the spaciousness and timelessness yet the presence and the specific taking of time that work and friendship require. The passages I invoke date from 1950 to 1953: good years for poetry and for friendship.

Georges Braque, "the master of invisible relationships," is, of the three painters, most frequently associated with Char, whose celebrated text of bridging, "Le Requin et la Mouette" ("The Shark and the Seagull") is dedicated to Braque. He was perhaps the greatest of all of Char's "alliés substantiels"—the name of a collection containing a text called "Avec Braque, on disait. . . ." The two worked together over long periods (figure 5.6), and one of Braque's works

Figure 5.6 *René Char chez Georges Braque,* photograph (from *Faire du chemin avec . . .*). Photograph courtesy of Marie-Claude Char.

occupied the place of honor above Char's fireplace, at the center of his study, where it was the background for our conversations on long afternoons, winter and summer. Along with Miró, Braque illustrated more of Char's works than any other artist, and they remained close. Braque's work, says Char, is about continuity—we need too many things, he says, to be satisfied with one (figure 5.7):

> par conséquent il faut assurer, à tout prix, la continuité de la création, même si nous ne devons jamais en bénéficier. Dans notre monde concret de résurrection et d'angoisse de non-résurrection, Braque assume le perpétuel.[15]

Figure 5.7 Georges Braque, illustration for René Char (from *Le Monde de l'art n'est pas le monde du pardon* [Paris: Maeght, 1974]). Gallery Maeght, Paris. © ARS, New York.

(consequently, we have to guarantee the continuity of creation, even if we never have any benefit from it. In our creation, even if we never benefit from it. In our concrete world of resurrection and the anguish of nonresurrection, Braque takes on what is perpetual.)

Continuity may seem a vague concept, but it covers exactly what is most clearly to be sensed in this bridge builder—a profession that Char always shared.

Vieira da Silva had once heard André Breton say that he had just discovered a giant in the south of France. Having read *Fureur et mystère* and *Les Matinaux,* she was eager to work with Char's texts, which she described as "cette poésie où les mots deviennent incommensurables avec eux-mêmes, projetés comme ils sont sur une étendue qu'ils attirent" ("this poetry in which the words cannot be measured against themselves, so projected are they against a space that they attract"). They met in the fall of 1953, became friends, and had a beneficent mutual influence upon each other. Her gouaches for his poems were

Figure 5.8 Vieira da Silva, engraving, illustration for René Char, *L'Inclémence lointaine* (from Marie-Claude Char, *Faire du chemin avec . . .*). © ARS.

done in 1954: this poetry in its concision encouraged her stringent limitation on herself, her increasing concision, her minimalism (figure 5.8). Of her dry-point engraving, she said: "Je n'aimais que les traits fins de la pointe sèche, les plus légers). Les noirs ne me plaisaient pas" ("I only liked the lightest, the most delicate tracings of drypoint. The heaviness of black were displeasing to me").

Something of Char's passionate language taught her the technique she subsequently used to construct her art parallel to his—we have only to look at her great portrait of him, quivering as it is with emotion, strange in its intensity. The influence of his poetry upon the actual character of her lines is clear: for example, swerving lines replace her usual vertical ones, others mark diagonals across the canvas, and ellipses abound instead of fully filled in strokes. Above all, she labored slowly—and found the space needed both by her work and his poems.

Of this great artist, Char wrote that she held in her hands something mysterious, "quelque chose qui est à la fois lumière d'un sol et promesse d'une graine." Of this undetermined "something," further inquiry is useless, for one of Char's firmest links with da Silva is the determination not to "strip the heart of the rose" ("ne pas effeuiller le coeur de la rose.") Her sense of the labyrinth won out by conferring magic upon the vertebrae of the mountains: "Nous ne sommes plus, dans cette oeuvre, pliés et passifs, nous sommes aux prises avec notre propre mystère, notre rougeur obscure, notre avidité, produisant pour le lendemain ce que demain attend" ("In this work, we are no longer doubled up and passive, we are delving into our own mystery, our obscure redness, our avidity, producing for the next day what tomorrow is waiting for").[16]

Through Georges Duthuit, Nicolas de Staël met Char, whose poems he had longed to illustrate; their first publication together dates from 1951. Staël was attracted by Char as he was by all elements out of the ordinary in size. "Il y a des moments où je te vois comme un monument très rude," Staël wrote Char.[17] They were two giants together, recognizing in each other this stature they were never to lose. Two tall columns, they seemed. Together they prepared the layout for their joint work, placed it in black cover, placed the blacks and whites of Char's *Poèmes* inside. Velvet and snow (figure 5.9).

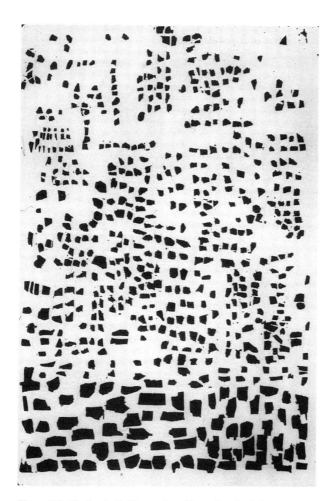

Figure 5.9 Nicolas de Staël, woodcut illustration for *Poèmes de René Char* (from Marie-Claude Char, *Faire du chemin avec . . .*). © 1997 ARS, New York/ADAGP, Paris.

Char's description of the work insists on the heroic:

Ces bois gravés sont un triomphe contre la résistance du matériau
le plus dur, blocs de buis debout. Staël recherche le plus rebelle, ce
qu'il aura jouissance de mater dans la vie comme dans la création
manuelle.[18]

(These engravings are a triumph over the most resistant of materials, blocks of boxwood standing upright. Staël searches for the most
rebellious matter, that he will delight in crushing in life as in man-
ual creation.)

A lyric and lay plainsong, their communal work has been called. Together
they prepared the costumes and text for a ballet about the abominable snow
man, "L'Homme des neiges," consulted Dallapiccola and Stravinsky, and
thought of Messiaen, but it never came to pass.[19] Yet lessons were learned for
good: "Staël et moi," says Char, "nous ne sommes pas, hélas, des Yetis! Mais
nous nous approchons quelquefois plus près qu'il n'est permis de l'inconnu
et de l'empire des étoiles" ("Staël and I are not Yetis, alas. But sometimes we
come nearer to the unknown and to the empire of stars than it is permitted
to do").[20]

Nicolas de Staël hammered out—against the resistance of the wood—
his visual texts with the same massively slow rhythm we sense in Char's writing.
If Char admires his *paresse lumineuse* (luminous laziness), it is because he knows
the value both of light and of time set slow. Their modes corresponded—and
that road so present in Char's exhibition in Le Palais des Papes has its correspondent image of an interior road, which Char mentions in relation to the artist
Pierre Charbonnier. Along that road both painter and poet traveled, and the
painter must have sensed it from the beginning in Char's work, never to forget
it afterward. "Il y a cela de vraiment merveilleux entre nous c'est qu'on peut se
donner tout ce qui est possible et impossible sans limite parce qu'on ne voit pas
la fin de nos possibilités" ("What is truly marvelous between us is that we can
give each other everything possible and impossible without any limit because
we never see the end of our possibilities") Staël wrote Char on November
9, 1953.[21]

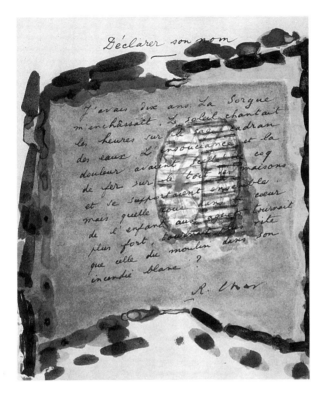

Figure 5.10 René Char, *Déclarer son nom* (from René Char, *La Nuit talismanique,* [Paris: Skira, 1972]). Courtesy of Marie-Claude Char.

This limitless road, outside or in, figures forth the openness that Char finally represents for these artists and for us. This openness takes its time, gives us back our breathing space, like the landscape. As happens often in the best essays, what Char writes of de Staël is true also of himself: his space is one he knows how to share: it is beyond any doubt "Le champ de tous et celui de chacun" ("The field of all and of each"), a name to be declared (figure 5.10).

The lessons of these three painters are clear: from Braque, continuity; from da Silva, an irreducible promise; from Staël, openness and largeness in the light. Theirs is the slowness that nourishes thought, that will not permit us to rush unheedingly into comparisons, writing, or seeing. Of course we will never

Figure 5.11 René Char, "*There is Ouranos the present one, rolling down with the wolves, and there is Orpheus. Both struggling, spitting out the earth of their captivity*" (from René Char, *La Nuit talismanique*). Courtesy of Marie-Claude Char.

catch up: we have to learn to work in just the space of that slippage between perception and representation that was so frequently deplored by Breton and that we might otherwise have found ourselves lamenting. It is, paradoxically and marvelously, exactly the delay that bestows time upon us.

Within Char's work, one great production bears the marks of deliberate slowness, anguish, and illumination. Called *La Nuit talismanique* (*Talismanic Night;* figures 5.10 to 5.14), it represents his work at its most intense and most deep. For from 1955 to 1958, when he was afflicted by insomnia, he created a series of aphorisms and works of art whose texture he never again attempted. These are at once stones and pages engraved, scratched, and lit by candlelight, experiences of thought and vision and craft that perfectly respond to each other. It is as if in them and in their dark light his different modes of being and seeing, his thought and his vision had merged for a moment. The baroque and meta-

Figure 5.12 René Char, "*I am not alone because I am abandoned. I am alone because I am alone, an almond between the walls of its close*" (from René Char, *La Nuit talismanique*). Courtesy Marie-Claude Char.

physical illumination of a dazzling darkness finds its place here, from his autobiographical statements, as he "declares his name" like a child in the Sorgue's waters, by the mill wheel and as he contemplates the planet Uranus. These are meditations on solitude and on the light of a candle, burning in a long delay. These are the works of a poet who knew how to be interior to his being and, taking his time along the road uphill, how to accept uncertainty.

Blindness and insight perhaps. There is a strange and obscure alliance between the outwardly unseeing and the inwardly great. Char's poems of *Aromates chasseurs,* with their theme of the hunter blinded but led on by the scent of the magic herbs, particularly his "Blinded Orion" with its salute to Nicolas Poussin's *Blind Orion Searching for the Rising Son* (1658) in New York's Metropolitan Museum of Art, represent this dark certainty (figure 5.15). On the other side of surrealist looking is poetic seeing, probing into itself. "J'aime

47

Figure 5.13 René Char, "*The flower is in the flame, the flame is in the tempest*" (from René Char, *La Nuit talismanique*). Courtesy of Marie-Claude Char.

Figure 5.14 René Char, "*To hold your book with a sure hand is difficult*" (from René Char, *La Nuit talismanique*). Courtesy of Marie-Claude Char.

Figure 5.15 Nicolas Poussin, *The Blind Orion Searching for the Rising Sun (Landscape with Orion),* 1658. Oil on canvas, 46⅞ × 72 in. The Metropolitan Museum of Art, Fletcher Fund.

l'homme," says Char, "incertain de ses fins comme l'est, en avril, l'arbre fruitier" ("I love the man who is unsure of his ends like the fruit tree in April").[21] "Slowness of the future," he entitles one of his poems, reminding us that we are always making our journey upstream and uphill—*amont*—in continuous pursuit of some undefined point, uncharacterized except by its mystery, a road undefined except by ardor and openness along which we have to learn to take our time.[22]

II

REPRESENTING

6

Body: Seeing the Surrealist Woman

Nous porterons ailleurs le luxe de la peste
Nous un peu de gelée blanche sur les fagots humains
Et c'est tout . . .
Nous le pain sec et l'eau dans les prisons du ciel

(We'll carry the luxury of the plague elsewhere
We a bit of hoarfrost on human firewood
And that's all
We plain bread and water in the prisons of the sky)
—*André Breton,* "Broken Line"[1]

Headless. And also footless. Often armless too; and almost always unarmed, except with poetry and passion (figure 6.1). There they are, the surrealist women so shot and painted,[2] so stressed and dismembered, punctured and severed: Is it any wonder they have (we have) gone to pieces? It is not just the dolls of Hans Bellmer, lying about, it is more. Worse, because more lustily appealing, as in Man Ray's images (figure 6.2).

I am looking at one of the most problematic: to describe her (or the part of her that exists, confronting me) is already to feel nervous. She poses like a challenge, wrapped like a dubious present in shimmering dark water-patterned and tight moiré, glistening just about everywhere she is (no head, no feet, no anything but that body mesmerizing, arms akimbo); this dame Man Ray so

Figure 6.1 René Magritte, *La Lumière des coincidences (The Light of Coincidences),* illustrating E. Tériade, "La Peinture surréaliste," in *Minotaure* no. 8, 1935, n.p. © 1997 C. Herscovici, Brussels/ARS, New York.

severs and swaddles and stresses is none of us, exactly. But maybe she is us all, as we are seen. Sure and strident, ready to do anything we can—except that she can neither speak nor think nor see, nor walk and run, certainly not love and paint and write and be. Surrealist woman, problematic and imprisoned, for the other eyes. She may be lit or framed (preface figure 1), but she is not whole.

GIVE THEM THEIR HEAD: THEY HAD ONE

Figure 1

The women or the woman seen by the surrealist painters and photographers are often made to seem the equivalent of the dame wrapped up and shiny that Man Ray so shot. Yet many of them wrote or painted, saw and thought and

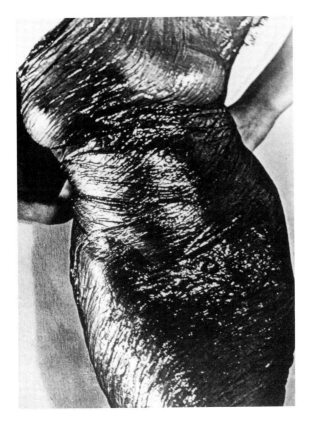

Figure 6.2 Man Ray, *Untitled,* 1929. Bibliothèque nationale,
Paris.

were, not necessarily as the others of men but not as their mothers either. We
feminist viewers of surrealism have wanted to give them their head, their eyes,
and their hands, not just on their hips to provoke, but free to use as they pleased
and did.

GIVE THEM THEIR VOICE: THEY HAD ONE

Sure, they spoke in differing accents, and their voice was not always pleasing.
It was, from time to time, cruel, jesting, acerbic; and, from time to time (harder

to take, for some of us), self-effacing. But we have wanted to give their multiple voices their due, so we could listen. And keep on listening.

LET THEM STAND ON THEIR OWN TWO FEET: THEY HAD TWO

They were not necessarily the runners-around with or the runners-after their male companions, if they had or wanted one. They were capable of going, and of going fast and often first. We have wanted to let them choose and take their stride. Are they, then, strident women? Yes, sometimes, even frequently. And does that bother us? Not in the slightest.

BESIDES, NADJA KNEW HOW TO DRAW

And there she is, drawing away in those pages, with Breton looking on. Only he gets bored.

Let him.

Now, Breton had perhaps some problem with the female gender.

The buildup was fine, and even glorious: In *Mad Love,*[3] he exclaims in horror about love burning itself out: "So Juliet, continuing to live, would no longer be always more Juliet for Romeo!" She should have been, of course, and in the innocence that love creates—and that he would have believed it possible to create—that would have been quite surely so. But Breton himself, continually, is skeptical of the continuity of the sublime in love.

Look what happens to all his heroines: Nadja, fascinating because mad, is then disappointing, because she is not interesting enough; she reads the menu aloud and, says Breton, "I was bored." Later, of course, when she has gone truly (therefore, for him, terrifyingly) mad and been put away—after a pause ("They came to tell me Nadja was insane"), he can confess he was not up to loving her as he should have. But at the moment, boredom. In *The Communicating Vessels,*[4] Breton is enchanted at one moment by a woman who dangles her perfect legs sitting across from him, next to her dreadfully dull companion ("probably a teacher"—!), at another, walking along, by some lovely eyes. He goes back to meet those eyes but panics at the thought that actually, he wouldn't be able to recognize the girl were she not looking, because, well, of course, he had forgotten everything else . . . What matters matters, and if you don't see it, the rest gets lost: "J'avais en effet, tout oublié de sa silhouette, de son maintien et, pour peu que ses yeux fussent baissés, je ne me sentais pas capable de l'identifier à trois pas" ("I had, in fact, forgotten everything about her silhouette and the way she carried herself, and if she were to lower her eyes, I would not have felt capable of identifying her three steps away").[5] Then the thing diminishes, and, although he is terribly grateful she was there that first Sunday, now when he meets her, and is not hoping to, her eyes may be still as lovely as before, but she has lost something, in fact all of her meaning for him. The passage bears reading, with its impersonals: "*il était donc vrai . . . il* m'arrive . . . *il* faut bien reconnaître"—as if, through the impersonal, he as a person were to be let off the hook of caring, feeling, seeing more than the eyes, or of seeing at all. She has lost out, and lost him, whether she cared or not: she did break it off, but then, he somehow wins out in the expression. It is like the case of Nadja, however different. It is the problem of the surrealist woman, in these texts:

> Il était donc vrai qu'elle n'avait à se trouver sur ma route que ce premier dimanche. Je lui sais encore un gré infini de s'y être trouvée. Maintenant que je ne la cherche plus, il m'arrive de la rencontrer quelquefois. Elle a toujours les yeux aussi beaux, mais il faut bien reconnaître qu'elle a perdu pour moi son prestige. (98)

> (It was true then that all she had to do was to be in my path that very first Sunday. I am still grateful to her for having been there. Now that I am no longer looking for her, I happen to run into her sometimes. She still has eyes just as beautiful, but it has to be admitted that she has lost her importance for me.)

And now, he says, she turns her head aside when they pass in the street. It somehow seems all very sad.

AH, THE SEABIRDS

Mad Love, a beach walk where everything goes wrong. All of the presages are against the love, and it had no chance, that day: it was, says Breton, the nature of the site. "I remember, as I passed rather far from them, the singular irritation provoked in me by a bustling flock of seabirds squawking against a last ridge of foam. I even started throwing stones at them" (102). Now they are walking not right by the water, because he hated taking off his shoes, and they are walking more and more distant from each other, this non-shoe-removal decision being the only definite thing about the situation. His mood progressively worsens; even with his shoes on, he longs to turn back—this is a constant in his love-walking, see the passage in Les Halles—and the mental distance between the lovers is suddenly immense: "The rift between us was deeper still, as if by all the height of the rock in which the stream we had crossed had been swallowed up. There was no point even in waiting for each other: impossible to exchange a word, to approach each other without turning aside and taking longer steps" (103). And then it turns out, it is indeed the site's problem, for they are walking near the House of the Hanged Man, painted by Cézanne (who, thinks Breton, painted things that were even more important than his apples). The *aura* around the house is, like the aura around the apples, what matters.

Now the issue is, in a sense, what has an aura and what does not. We know from Walter Benjamin how important the aura is, and we know, from Breton, that the urgent thing is the mystery of it all—they are on the same frequency, the aura and the strangeness of woman, as long as she remains other. Or at least somewhat other.

According to Xavière Gauthier, in *Surréalisme et sexualité,* everything in surrealist art is *piégé* or mined and trapped and undermined because it is all highly ambivalent.[6] She studies several canvases by Magritte, such as *Le Chant d'amour* with its red shoes turning to feet, and discusses the strong urges to violence and torture: in surrealist poetry, she says, women are loved, but in surrealist art they are hated (331). And indeed the images, even the seemingly most loving, have an edge to them. To say nothing of the least loving, by René Magritte.

This is strangely true often, even in the poetry. Take the following examples from four different poems, two prose poems and two in verse: "Rendez-vous," about the sky ringed around by storms, ends with stifling and with the cozy words: "la bague au châton vide que je t'ai donnée et qui te tuera" ("this ring with the empty setting that I gave you and that will kill you" [*Poems,* 21]). That is what happens with gifts.

The dense and lyric "Forest in the Axe," full of oxymorons, ends with the opposite gender-murder but the same feeling: "Il n'y a plus qu'une femme sur l'absence de pensée qui caractérise en noir pur cette époque maudite. Cette femme tient un bouquet d'immortelles de la forme de mon sang" ("No more than one woman out of the absence of thought which characterizes in pure black this damned age. That woman holds a bouquet of everlasting in the shape of my blood" [*Poems*, 58–59]). Something may indeed last, but in a very odd form: the violence of the setting, for that rings of emptiness and for this bouquet of blood, disconcerts and tells what seems to be the truth. Bloody as it is.

One of the most moving verse poems, "Vigilance," ends with the statement of unity so often quoted: "Je ne touche plus que le coeur des choses / Je tiens le fil" ("I touch nothing but the heart of things / I hold the thread" [*Poems*, 78–79]), but it is preceded by a shell-shaped bit of lace from which, as in Botticelli's *Birth of Venus*, the woman emerges, here, just in the shape of one breast ("la forme parfaite d'un sein"). Of course two breasts have twice the same shape as one, usually, but all the same, the impression is less one of wholeness than one of partialness—less, I would say, partiality, in the positive sense—than partialness. It depends upon the way we read, of course, but at a certain angle, as Breton often said of his own vision, this is the way it looks. Even when the surrealized female contemplates herself, something is off as Magritte looks at it (see preface, figure 1).

Figure 1

Finally, in the poem of birth that begins "Il allait être cinq heures du matin" ("It was about to be five in the morning" [*Poems*, 102–3]), the ending, about a magic spell cast upon the narrator, takes effect again in the sort of violence that Gauthier perceived in the art:

> Tu avais gravé les signes infaillibles
> De mon enchantement
> Au moyen d'un poignard dont le manche de
> corail bifurque à l'infini
> Pour que ton sang et le mien
> N'en fassent qu'un
>
> (You had etched the unfailing signs
> Of my enchantment

By means of a dagger whose coral handle
Bifurcates to infinity
So that your blood and mine
Make but one [*Poems,* 103])

Now of course it is deeply erotic to be so joined, but one does wonder what the reader, so enjoined to participate in the sexual and emotional union here, however "free,"[7] is free to do and to read.

It is not so much that I want to begin reading surrealism over as that I see increasingly the problematics of the surrealist woman within that reading. We have wanted, some of us, to *make free* with the reading and to let her creations make free. Let it not be taken as negative for surrealism and its male leaders but as a positive revisioning, rethinking, and call to re-reading—to a *representation* that will be fuller than what Magritte has framed.

7

PERSON: TANNING'S SELF-PORTRAITURE

One thing is certain: no one else could bring it off—your picture. How could they? The very smallest touch, the smudge called up from your own cache of smudges, the bold swath you will dare to trace across a rectangular surface, these are yours.

—*Dorothea Tanning,* Birthday[1]

In a vast network of references and self-references, the diverse forms of Tanning's work, both the visual and the verbal—for she writes with the same dramatic verve as she draws and paints—open into each other like the doors so prevalent in her imagery as early as her *Birthday* of 1942 (figure 7.1). I have chosen to view it in exactly that way. For example, the image of a door serves as an *opening* into something else, frequently, into the color green, as if the constructed door led out to the natural world, culture making way for nature.

Once outside, in the swirls of Tanning green, in the large painting of *On Avalon* (1987), for instance, the observer is caught up in a dynamics of force. A meditation upon that dynamics, in those swirls and in the explicit force lines in certain of Tanning's works, leads me to the diagonal line, an inheritance from the baroque tradition. Tanning, so closely associated with the surrealists for a time, inherits all the same some techniques and concerns of the romantic tradition, but particularly those of the baroque: I take this appellation in its strongest and most positive sense. I see this in her excited rhythms, her complex

Figure 7.1 Dorothea Tanning, *Birthday,* 1942. Oil on canvas, 40¼ × 25½ in. Collection of the artist. Property of the Dorothea Tanning Foundation, Inc. © 1996.

intertwinings, her stressed diagonal and vertical movements. For me, the baroque, a gathering of complex and unresolvable tendencies that choose not to resolve or calm its contradictory impulses, remains of supreme importance for the contemporary spirit. The baroque position called *contrapposto* permits one stress, or a turning in one direction, to pull against the other, turning in the other direction. One detects the tension between opposite directions, as between the different parts of Tanning's heritage, already in her development from her early work in its precise brush strokes and clear profiles that provide an unambiguous *reading* of all the forms and outlines within the frame toward her later work, with its looser brush strokes and whirling and prismatic forms, the flurry and cascading planes enabling multiple interpretations. Thus, the perception of one moment shifts into an opposing perception without any clear markers in time, space, or dimension. The reader of Tanning's forms falls prey to the rhythmic and impulsive forces within the work; the artist is in complete control of the viewer.

An almost ecstatic drama appears here, reaching past what has so often been called eroticism toward something else, something behind and beyond. Something more profound and more troubling, indefinable.

A SURREALIST START

Many of the themes and techniques that I perceive in Tanning's works connect with the surrealist imagination and style. Having been so closely associated with surrealism, Tanning retains both an affection for it and a complex relation to it. From my point of view, a surrealizing vision such as hers does not bypass but adds actively to the ongoing surrealist heritage, as the verb *to surrealize* is more active than the simple observation that a work is surrealist.

Nothing is boringly smooth or unknotted in Tanning's painting, writing, or drawing: that she retains from surrealism. Let me say immediately what does *not* seem to me crucial about Tanning's connections with surrealism, and they are first, the more easily visible, such as those remarked upon at the time of her last London exhibition. I quote: "Tanning's most famous and familiar works date from the late Forties, and are the most instantly classifiable as surrealist. They have the hard, precise finish of a typical surrealist picture, and something

approaching typical surrealist subject matter; little girls in Victorian dress, end-
less cosmic vistas of sky, disquietingly large dogs and plants, ambiguous as to
whether they are friend or foe."[2] These are indeed *kinds* of surrealist subject
matter, images, and the kind of finish is indeed like that of the surrealist painters,
but what I see in Tanning of surrealism is of a different nature, one that develops past this early simple play of imagery. Important, it seems to me, is the
fact that after Tanning's early paintings there are no horizons, nothing to give
the viewing a particular known basis; rather, they maintain a deliberately vertig-
inous quality, never clear.

The automatic scribble or starting point that Robert Desnos sketched out
in his drawings for *The Night of Loveless Nights* (figure 7.2) in 1927 was taken
up by Matta and others, particularly Robert Motherwell, in the world of surrealist poets and artists.[3] It is paralleled by Tanning's applying a wash of color to
the canvas at the very beginning, as an inspiration for continuing. This consti-
tutes a latter-day equivalent of the canvas preparation undertaken by surrealist
writers and artists. I am thinking also of the haunting and sometimes paralyzing
white formlessness so strongly presented by the French poet Stéphane Mallarmé: the terror of the blank page. When Tanning lays down a wash of color
("Sometimes, I just want to make a mauve painting," she says), she can start:
"That gets me going and I start to see things."

The other principal lesson that Tanning derives from surrealism concerns
the art of "intertwining," the way in which one element mingles with, joins
with another in a back-and-forth swerve. Three of her works illustrate this
move she continually makes in her painting, from early to late.

The Rose and the Dog (1952) makes a wonderful exchange of the natural
and mineral worlds. The rose is steel yet like a tree, with its metal peeling off
to reveal the flesh of the same copper color, permitting the mysteries of a metallic rose and a strange dog with hairs on its feet to merge under an overcast of
shadow. The setup is as complicated as in Baudelaire's celebrated correspondences, where the synesthesia of the various senses mingles in a profundity
unavailable from one source alone.

In *Reality* (1973–83), the ultimate strangeness of this particular and peculiar reality is of the same kind felt in the many other paintings of dog and
woman intertwined. At times the dog, Kachina, is upright in a dance with the

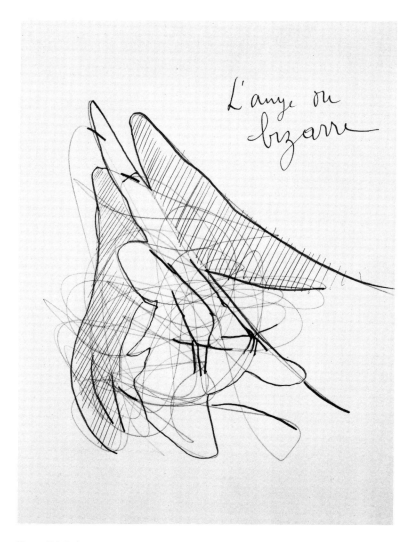

Figure 7.2 Robert Desnos: Original illustration, 1925, *L'Ange du bizarre* ("The Strange Angel"). Illustration found by the author in the manuscript of *The night of loveless nights,* by Robert Desnos, in the Paul Eluard-Camille Dausse Collection, Museum of Modern Art, New York. (Anvers, published privately, 1930.) Pencil and ink on paper, sheet: 8⁵⁄₁₆ × 11⅛ in. The Museum of Modern Art Library, New York. © 1997 ARS, New York/ADAGP, Paris. Photograph © 1996 The Museum of Modern Art, New York.

artist, at other times seated or lying down, but in each case, the viewer's eye is caught by the remarkably intimate connection between dog and woman, animal and human in an omnipresent and ambiguous relation. At the end of her novel *Abyss,* a panther tears at the face of one female figure before padding along companionably with another: intimacy and terror join here, as often in Tanning—see the painting *Guardian Angels* (1946), for example (figure 7.3).

A few of these implicit dances, of these singular embraces, stand out for specific reasons. Here, the immense and immensely protruding eyes of the dog, not unseeing but—as the artist puts it—"seeing in a different way" guide our own to perceive what we might not have seen otherwise. The surrealists, Breton and Aragon in particular, placed an enormous weight upon the idea of the *état d'attente,* that general feeling of expectation and readiness. It is not a matter of what we might be waiting for but of what we might be willing to expect in the limits of such a highly charged, erotic yet familiar encounter as this ironically entitled *Reality.* It is not any reality we as observers generally recognize, yet its possibilities may awaken our own latent imagining. Seeing in a different way is already a start toward the openness that is part of Tanning's aim.

Still on the theme of the dance, *Paper Aunt II* (1992) intertwines three figures: two outer ones in blue and white leaning toward each other and surrounding a central figure, wrapped as in a mummy cloth, red at the top. Two blue arms overhead, either joined to the figure at the left or independent, twist together in a fan shape, penetrated at the bottom by the left arm of the figure to the right. These figures interpenetrating, with only one head between them, are at once disturbing and provocative. On either side, a ghostly white leg, sharply outlined, dangles above the dance, and to the lower right, another unidentified, unattached member rises.

This is a witty dance, if dance it be, in any case a humorous intertwining, with those two arms beckoning. The very fact that there is no way of knowing how many participants could be involved in whatever dance this might be lends its own humor to this pencil and crayon undertaking. Her art of intertwining is baroque, as well as surrealist and symbolist, particularly in such whirling works as her *Insomnies* (1957) and the dramatic *Notes for an Apocalypse* (1977) twenty years later. These are works of high drama, dramatic as the baroque generally is.

Figure 7.3 Dorothea Tanning, *Guardian Angels,* 1946. Oil on canvas, 48⅓ × 35 in. The New Orleans Museum of Art. Property of the Dorothea Tanning Foundation, Inc. © 1996.

HIGH DRAMA AND THE BAROQUE

One of Tanning's most baroque canvases, *Notes for an Apocalypse* combines stability and tension in a way quite unlike any of her other works. From the left, a great thrusting table/altar/tomb, covered with a gray cloth, pushes in a middle horizontal band against a naked yellow-pink body, bending back in a striking diagonal from a smaller figure crouching on the floor beside its left leg toward another leg of a different body entirely, one of those typical Tanning legs—found, for instance, all the way from *Plein-Air Philosophy* (1969) to *Murmurs* (1976), *Hail, Delirium!* (1979), and *Door 84* (1984). The sight coninues upward to a head with closed eyes, a replacement for the head of the graceful first figure bending backward, hidden by the sheet. Upon the stomach of this first figure falls the white-gold light, and also upon this ankle and foot, while above and to the right, the hand reaching back spreads itself over a globe of pinkish light.

This is, finally, the focal point of the entire horizontal picture, all of which pushes from left to right, the energy conveyed by the folds of the tablecloth/winding sheet, the upper portion of which, like pair of wings (again like the *Guardian Angels*), gives an upward motion to the otherwise stable horizontal mass and perfectly balances that illuminated leg, itself foregrounded against a backdrop of assorted greyish-lavender limbs. When I call this a baroque sensibility, I am remembering that celebrated *Double Portrait of Gabrielle d'Estrées and Her Sister* (figure 7.4) of the Fontainebleau school, where some of these elements are found, in different combinations. There too the body parts are severed from any wholeness, the illumination of a fire is the source of energy, and the trousseau chest, like this table/tomb, gives mystery and depth to the whole. This important piece shows Tanning at her dramatic best.

Baroque in its very being, even in its colors—red-orange, black, gray, and white—this major painting refers to death and life, as they are mutually each other's challenge. The very human, very aliveness of the pink stomach pushing against the folds of the sheet marks at once the double possibility of reading: this is at once a table and a tomb. The sheet is at once a tablecloth and a winding sheet, with the meaning stretched between them.

As a further baroque element, the unusual gap between the big toe and the other toes on the foot stretching toward the upper right calls attention to

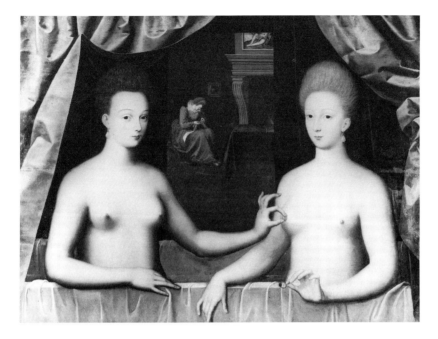

Figure 7.4 Ecole de Fontainebleau, *Gabrielle d'Estrées et sa soeur* (also called *Gabrielle d'Estrées and The Duchess of Balagny*), 17th century. Oil on canvas. Paris: the Louvre. Documentation photographique, Réunion des musées nationaux.

itself, signaling a stress and stretch, an intense effort seemingly in contrast with the pinkness of the stomach. Above that gap, like a hidden source of energy, light streams through the fingers held aloft, as in a canvas by Georges de La Tour, an *Education of the Virgin* or a *Nativity,* or one of the repentant *Magdalens* (figure 7.5). How do you light an Apocalypse? How do you point to both its imminent terror and its eventual illumination? Like this.

To produce her intense effects, Tanning calls upon a whole constellation of techniques, including pounding rhythmic stress and a frequent use of both diagonal and vertical lines. The diagonal line can be a force of integration, as in the impressive drawing *Emotion II* (1988), where the bright orangish line slanting up from lower left to middle right balances the enormous upside-down gray *V,* giving the whole dynamism and intensity. It can, on the other hand, realize

Figure 7.5 Georges de La Tour, *(La Madeleine) The Magdalen,* c. 1625–28, 1 m. 28 × 94 cm. Documentation photographique de la Réunion des musées nationaux.

some sort of human and material chaos, particularly in the late Tanning works with their upsets and their accidents; I am thinking of *Pounding Strong* (1981), with the roller skates, and the interrelated works of 1989 and 1990 about messages and bicycle accidents, like some Greek tragedy made contemporary in the spinning wheels of disaster: *Further Chaos* (1988), *Traffic* (1988), *Between Lives* (1989), and *Swarm* (1990). All of these provoke pain, upset, and dizziness. Everything spins about, touches everything, pulses. A pocketbook swings from a shoulder bent backward, caressed by a snail shape with its spiral echoing the wheels. A television set in the middle of the canvas simply reflects the cloudy forms passing across it, the rhythm pulses all about, and in the background, the turbulence never ceases. Like the later bicycle pictures, the forms—here the skate wheel, there the bicycle wheel—do more than reinvent the wheel. The observer is swept up in their mad spin, the human and the mechanical intertwining like some offshoot of futurism. In the nightmarish precision of fatal accidents and their attendant revelations, these depictions in lethal terms of the hurtling through space of a capsized vehicle, one or more bodies falling and pierced by another, deal with pain and its dreadful energy.

When the body falls in a Tanning work, as if to the side, there is all around it a great space, an openness spreading all about the diagonal forms that seem to stretch their meaning out into the universe beyond the simple accident. The suggestion is, then, not only of the human body as it is menaced by human invention—and the oldest of all, the wheel—but of life itself as it is so precariously poised on the edge of death. The spattered blood, the crisis: all of this seems, also, to give a kind of birth. As in Greek literature, the terror is cathartic: no, some of these messages will not arrive because the messenger himself has to be sacrificed. The whole drama takes place high up, by vertical extension, and not just in the street. By the time a gorilla's face is inserted beneath or between the handlebars, the vehicle has already taken on the mythic force of culture that meets the animal force of nature. The gorilla replaces the dog as the animal respondent to the human, intertwined with it.

These elements of fate make a contemporary form of the classic presentation of forces beyond the human, of sacrifice, terror, alarm, and fatal reversal. Nothing, it would seem to me, in Tanning's earlier works prepares us for this. In *Dream Bikes* (1989), for instance, the dotted lines of the overturning and collision sketch out either a prediction or a trace, yet not, not ever a presence. On the other hand, both *Hell Bent* (1988) with its twisted black wheels above the strokes of yellow, blue, and orange, and *Between Lives* (1989) with its crumpled tire wrenched from its rim and its handlebars lying upside down, on a lavender background offsetting the pallor of the white forms, are matters of high drama in the present, like a tragedy we *should be able to do something about.* And cannot. This is our complicity in the tragic, that we know this, cannot change this, and know this to be high art.

The gorillas mark the age of the primitive in tension with the modern movement; such a juncture of the animal and the technical can be positive, even vivifying, the diametrical opposite of the death-dealing accidents. These messages are sent—to whom?—by the artist to herself, to us, to the inhabitants of the quiet realms within the drawing. Surely somewhere, Tanning's messages, these and others, will be delivered. Perhaps not always with the same dramatic and negative results. But what sticks in the observer's mind is how control is foregone and the gods, or fates, take over. These are the least rational of Tanning's works and in no way the least powerful. As the wheel spins out fatally from control, so it puts a spin on our own thoughts, chaotic, uncontrollable, tragic. This is the end of desire, this death. This *is* the message. Such an ecstatic eroticism deals a not necessarily unpleasant violence. For within these works, violence is a matter as much for exultation as for terror. They go together in the complex world of drama.

As for verticality, one of the strongest constructions of all, *To Climb a Ladder* (1987), divides in three, with the clearly marked vertical climb in the center of a series of pink figures who rise up elongated, naked, wispy, and disquieting. At the top of the ladder, a constellated glow spatters across the night. On either side, the painting is dark, with a glowing patch of light on the left and a series of rungs set in a blue space on the right. The play of the pink central figure against the stable rungs and lines gives tension to the picture, done in green, lavender, pink, and black. Toward what is the figure climbing? Is this a fair question, is it even justified by the painting? In any case, there is a reach toward something beyond that dark, by that figure, a classic Tanning pink, winding her way upward, to be compared with the pinkish figure in the window frame of *Still in the Studio* (1979), another scene of climbing and mystery.

There is something peculiar indeed about both works, something unavailable to the grasp, as if the observer were climbing *beyond* our sight or even our imaginative capacities.

Another significantly vertical work, *Zealots* (1989), with its three vertically joined figures, a standing male, a seated female, and, clinging to her feet, a childish form, calls upon both the diagonal and the vertical force with their potential energies. The forces pull against each other, the strong upright line on the far right of the drawing including the back and rear legs of the chair and the male figure branching to the left twice. Along the horizontal table form upon which the middle figure's arm stretches, marking the link from right to left against the normal reading direction, one's glance travels toward the child nestling against the female figure. The three figures are joined, as in a family, yet in some terrible way, we know something terrible is happening. Zealotry, if you like. Some drama is taking place, some signing away of human autonomy. Something having to do with the gods and with fate. The classic lines of this drawing, with some rapid overhatching strokes, give the feeling of an instant masterpiece. Sober, restrained, yet with high drama, as the title indicates. The passion of zealotry is the opposite of anything mediocre: so is this drawing.

But above all the whirling and prismatic forms of the later Tanning works, after 1965, mark her work as baroque. Of all of the whirling pictures, perhaps *Insomnias* (1957), a key picture in Tanning's oeuvre, is the height of a certain way of painting, a particular way of looking. The work is full of reach, both literally, as arms bend and pull and stretch, and figuratively, of figures reaching behind themselves, of creatures emerging and disappearing back into the prisms of the variously lit parts: orange, pink, purple, like spreading stains. In all of the recessive and protruding planes in this picture, the dimensions are intentionally confused, the directions deliberately hard to read. There no horizon, so that nothing has a known base. The forms intermingle without a definite starting or stopping place. Limitless and mystifying, on the left, the grey shapes emit gleams and then diffuse their light.

Is there a center to this kaleidoscopic swirl? Various heads, creatures, permit themselves to be seen and then fade out. Toward the bottom are the reversed form of an animal on the left and its correspondent dog/fox figure to the right; directly above the fox head is the soft form of a human body with a child's head, its eyes lowered, its face pillowed against some soft and prismatic forms to its right. This is the center, possibly, and retains our gaze, reinforced by the orange-yellowish glow above.

Insomnias, indeed. The work is between sleep and waking, clear and unclear. It spins beyond any limited signification that we might have wanted to place upon it. I am thinking here of André Breton's definition of the "sublime point" at which all contraries meet in a surrealist union, a "free union" of up and down, life and death, day and night, the rational and the irrational, the pragmatic and the dream. These are so many *Communicating Vessels*,[4] joining one thing to another, as in the scientific experiment by the same name, in which gases circulate from one tube to another. Tanning's work, from the creations based on the dance to those based on the architectural examination of inside as it joins outside, is often about mingling circulation, based on intertwining elements.

Another prismatic work, *Dogs of Cythera* (1963), is filled with receding and advancing planes, its intertwined shapes caught between storm and sun, between the protrusions and intrusions that are one of Tanning's signature forms. The complexities are infinite. Bodies bend over backward, parts thrust through other parts, and underlying the whole are a child's head and body at the center, as with *Insomnias*. Directly below the head and to the right, a dog's face looks straight up, its eyes closed, the animal counterpart to the sleeping child. Strange glows and gleams abound, with their reddish-orange set against the purple, white, and gray of the rest.

In these epic pictures, and through the whirl of shapes, is a sense of plenitude and wholeness. It is not that the observer actively has to question what the work is about but rather that the multiple signs indicate many things. The open brush strokes here convey a sensuality missing in the early surrealist works, stressed all the more by the glowing reds and yellows, incandescent sources for the entire canvas. Somewhere, hair is whirling in a golden haze. Elsewhere, things go on, not imperceptible but unperceived. Arms reach out, back, through other arms and legs and forms. We may focus on a clearly identifiable object or a central fullness (take the round, dark purple child's head bowed in *Dogs of Cythera* or, at the other pole of color, the central, white moonlike object, identified ironically as "Faith," in *Faith Surrounded by Hope, Charity, and Other*

Monsters [1976], where the white stands out from the other colors), or it may be a gap: between the fingers, between the paws, between the grip and what is seized. We spin in our consciousness, losing our grip. Ancient wounds are healed here, old ecstasies are summoned into the place of complicated light and purplish shadows.

MENACES

The surrealist spirit depends on shaking up the world; it is anything but reassuring. It is, in fact, generally associated with menace. This mood is prevalent in Tanning's paintings, certainly the earlier ones.

In the celebrated *Birthday* (1942) (see figure 7.1) as doors open one upon another, with at least seven pairs of doorknobs in echo, they correspond alarmingly with the round eyes of the dread winged beast with the donkey ears and the breasts of the standing artist, all reaching back in infinite regress.[5] These doors, in presence and regression, recur endlessly: in *Children's Games* (1942)(figure 7.6), where the menace is clear and as unplayful as possible; in the equally menacing *Eine kleine Nachtmusik* (A Little Night Music, 1943) (figure 7.7) in *Fatala* (1947) (figure 7.8), where the human figure outside, a maiden with flowing hair, reaches through the keyhole into the pages of a book with a game inside. Here, the four inset figures, each different, variously refer back to her hair and figure: round at the top and columnar below, they are lit at the edges or sheathed or draped, and one has flowing hair exactly recalling the figure outside. To the right of the book-game is a thinner, shorter, off-white book facing the other way, fanning its pages toward a building with closed arched windows. The pair of standing books, one dark, one light, form between them a triangle on the ground, echoing the upper and lower triangles of the books fanning out into the imagination. These are all doors opening just that way. In the architecturally complex *On Time, Off Time* (1948) (figure 7.9), the door frame stands alone and leads outside, so that you are clearly looking out and in, like a further play on Magritte's doors and windows leading out and in. Later, this will be made explicit, as in the 1951 title: *And if You're Outside Looking In*. In *Lumière du foyer* (1952) (figure 7.10) the beast with a human face poises painfully outside, clinging to the door hinge against closure, as light streams out

Figure 7.1

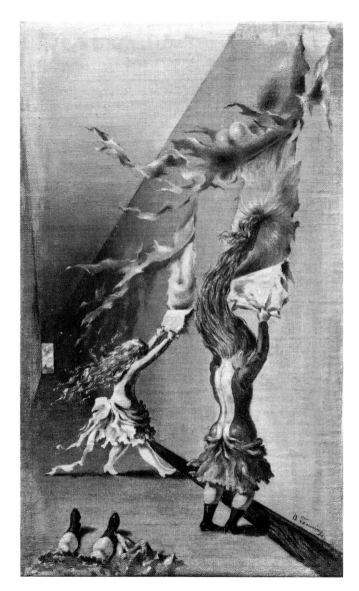

Figure 7.6 Dorothea Tanning, *Children's Games,* 1942. Oil on canvas, 11 × 7¹⁄₁₆ in. Collection Grimberg, Dallas. Property of the Dorothea Tanning Foundation, Inc. © 1996.

Figure 7.7 Dorothea Tanning, *Eine Kleine Nachtmusik,* 1943. Oil on canvas, 16⅛ × 24 in. Collection Penrose, London. Property of the Dorothea Tanning Foundation, Inc. © 1996.

under the large triangular door shape. This door itself has a surreal look. It opens upon itself, repeated in a Magritte-like impossibility, and confronts us with an enigma, like Marcel Duchamp's ambivalent studio door at 13 rue Larrey, with its anomalous ability to be both open and closed—a deliberate contradiction of Alfred Musset's play based on the cliché *"A door must be opened or closed."* This door divides, joins, is perfectly and impossibly situated. One of Tanning's strongest statements about balance and tension, pull and possibility, this work demonstrates the power of suggestion that she has so thoroughly mastered.

Doors are about division: of space, of sight, of imagination. in a sense, all of these doors recall Duchamp's exterior door of *Etant donnés* (1944–66) (figure 7.11): they both block visual access and invite seeing through. In his door are tiny holes through which you must look, with the added complication that, in its installation in the Philadelphia Museum of Art, there may be impatient

77

Figure 7.8 Dorothea Tanning, *Fatala,* 1947. Oil on canvas, 9 × 6 in. Private Collection. Property of the Dorothea Tanning Foundation, Inc. © 1996

Figure 7.9 Dorothea Tanning, *On Time Off Time,* 1948. Oil on canvas, 14⅛ × 20½ in. Private collection. Property of the Dorothea Tanning Foundation, Inc. © 1996.

and/or amused and knowledgeable Duchamp viewers behind you, looking at you looking. All of Tanning's doors question, use, and endlessly repeat the idea of door itself. Years later than the doors just looked at, Tanning's post-surrealist work continues to combine the thematic with the formal examination of the door. *Door 84* with its pair of figures pushing against a door on either side, shows the baroque tensions on both sides of the central dividing structure. In Tanning's work, the door as image develops from the literal (that which opens out or in upon something, either mundane or mysterious) to the psychological (that which excludes the outsider) to the formal and metaphoric combined in this diptych (the side of the door as division and the idea of division as the source of energy).

In this divided picture, each figure reaches toward the center with one leg and stretches out in a mutual push and pull against the violence of a yellow background, with the colors scumbled and tormented. We the observers look at the edge of the door, remembering the series of doors opening one into and

Figure 7.10 Dorothea Tanning, *Lumière du foyer (Home Light),* 1952. Oil on canvas, 19¾ × 6¾ in. Collection Schwarz, Milan. Property of the Dorothea Tanning Foundation, Inc. © 1996.

Figure 7.11 Marcel Duchamp, *The Door,* 1946–66 (from *Etant donnés*). Mixed-medium, assemblage, 95.1.2 × 70 in. Philadelphia Museum of Art. © 1997 ARS, New York/ADAGP, Paris.

beyond the other in the early *Birthday:* but how much closer to us this is. Our own vision here is divided, as we feel the reach of the diagonal figure on our left and the calmer pose of the girl on the right, seated upon a phantom lap with two ghostly legs surrounding hers. The outline of this larger body behind her cradles her form, supports it, and gives it birth. With the half of the face we can see, she stares into the distance where we are, her expression defiant, regretful, or uncertain: we cannot know. Nor can we know beyond that half of her face, the other hidden in shadow. Whereas the other figure, the violent one on our left, is hidden by her own arm, by her will perhaps.

INTERLUDE: THROUGH THE DOOR

As I stated at the beginning, I'd like to look through the door of the imagination at an imagined world: first at a brightly colored one, Tanning's world, all in lavender-gray, blue, yellow, reds and oranges, and, above all, green, the color of hope, wonderfully captured in *Philosophie en Plein Air* (1969) and *On Avalon* (1987). Both works, as I read them, deal with the relation of the color green to the thought of nature and the nature of thought.

Philosophie en Plein Air, a testament to and advocacy of philosophy in the open air, exhibits a clear freshness of color supplied by barite green. Seeing the outstretched leg to the right, some viewers will think back to other celebrated open-air works, such as Manet's *Déjeuner sur l'herbe* (1863), where the male figure to the right, the one telling the story, extends his leg toward the two seated figures to the left. We might remember the poet Stéphane Mallarmé writing his famous piece on Manet and the impressionists, as they worked in the open; that the original is lost and that it has had to be translated from English back into French, different with each translator, only adds to its prestige. The implicit reference to Manet and other such references, conscious or unconscious, explicit or not, whether they arise in the mind of the artist or only that of the commentator, deepen the visual and emotional/intellectual experience of the work and thus are to be treasured in almost all cases.

In this work appear two of Tanning's signature forms, horseshoe and the open mouth frequently found afloat upon the voluptuous and voluptuously painted flesh of a female figure. Even in the tranquility of such a setting, on such a green afternoon, one senses menace. The luck of the horseshoe might offset it, or not. *On Avalon* ironically plays bare legs against the bursts of circular light among the green, the human posed against nature.

I think about green. I ask Dorothea Tanning:
—Do you sometimes begin with color, and sometimes with an idea of form?
—Yes, she replies, sometimes, I want just to make a mauve painting . . .

Here, and in a companion picture called *To the Rescue* (1965), the painting and the feeling are green. ("Verde, yo to quiero verde" ["Green, I want you green"] wrote the great Spanish poet Garcia Lorca in one of his gypsy ballads.)

BACK TO THE DOOR

Given Tanning's strong architectural sense and intense interest in the relations between interior and exterior, the image of the door is a natural-cultural given. One of the more remarkable uses of the door as architectural element, with its openness and complications exposed and exposing, is the triptych *On Time, Off Time* (1948) (see figure 7.9). I would compare its atmosphere to De Chirico's early metaphysical/architectural constructions; its construction to some of the Japanese paintings of such importance to French art; and its conceptualization to Magritte's celebrated picture of the human eye with clouds passing over it,

Figure 7.9

False Mirror (1928), for its realization of the complex interrelations of seeing and seen, of inside and outside. *On Time, Off Time* is uniquely constructed, a triptych with clouds on the left, sky and half-door on the right, and a great moving swerve-curve in the center veering to the right, under the sunflower as timepiece. Sunflower and mirror combine in the intense vision of *The Mirror* (1951) (figure 7.12), round like a mandala, like an eye. At this point, the sunflower (as in *Eine Kleine Nachtmusik* also) serves as a surrealist signature, but its upending here *in the place of time* stands it in relation to the clouds on the left, the sky on the right, beyond which the recognizable female figure watches us looking.

Among other things at which we are looking is the portrait, precisely, of the female. This persists through myriad other paintings, whether set in the

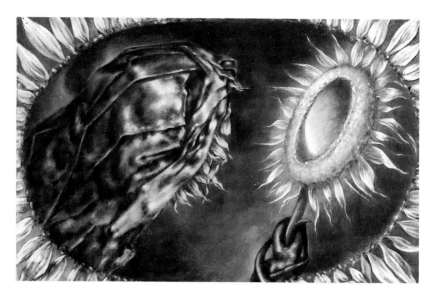

Figure 7.12 Dorothea Tanning, *The Mirror,* 1951. Oil on canvas, 12 × 18¼ in. Collection Schefler, Aspen. Property of the Dorothea Tanning Foundation, Inc. © 1996.

Figure 7.6

world of a grownup artist's studio or in that of children's games. In the dread-provoking canvas *Children's Games* (1947) (see figure 7.6) hair streams down the backs of the terrible little girls like flames or stands up on their heads; their smallish beings are convulsed and sexualized, lined up against the wall in rapidly receding perspective. When they pull aside the wallpaper, they reveal what we might have known all along: it was really the skin of a body. Outside, in a tiny space with a door in the far wall, other things happen—a woman gives birth, a landscape is born. But here inside, the scene is violent, and creation is associated with utter cruelty.

Beyond these visible elements speaks the voice of an awful desire, awful even, awe-inspiring. The voice of the unseen, conjuring something we do not want to, or *cannot,* face. Where in the work of the other surrealist painters do we see such *extreme* terror, such a paroxysm of frenzy? I would rather compare Tanning's work to some of the strongest and scariest writing of Antonin Artaud: for example, his essay on blood and passion and ritual in the Indian tribe of the

Tarahumara—*there* is the intensity, the cruelty, and the vitalizing pain felt at its height. Artaud associates, as in his *Theater of Cruelty,* intense passion with intense precision: the precise is cruel, ritualistic, as it is in Tanning.

Indeed ritual lies at the core of much of Tanning's painting and drawing, gathering into itself the repetitions of theme and form, the conjuring and execration of this erotic extension of the self into some other, unknown world not to be resumed in words. Her images—tearing, pulling, execrating, banishing—only hint at the terror behind that wall.

Eine kleine Nachtmusik (see figure 7.7) features trademarks of Tanning's early work. The ends of the tree branch are as ragged as the flames springing forth from the sunflower, from the edges of the girls' skirts, from their long hair, drifting down or rising skyward. Flames, energy, and mystery mingle terribly. By comparison, Breton's sunflower poem, simply called "Tournesol" ("Sunflower") has no such sense of menace. Everything here is too large: the flower, the leaves. Tanning's early work displays a deliberate excess of everything, paradoxically present in spite of the tight and precise strokes.

Figure 7.7

As in *Birthday* (see figure 7.1), here a door opens onto a blaze of light—but the girls are not looking, whereas we who *are* looking have no idea where the door might lead. Tanning, in her catalogue for a 1974 exhibition, speaks of the "grave replies" her pictures give to the question ceaselessly posed by those coming to see her work, and wondering about its meaning. They give the replies the painter does not have to give; still we have to be ready to understand them, even if we have asked no questions.

Figure 7.1

Each of us might ask different questions. Mine would go something like this: Why are two petals missing from the gigantic sunflower at the top of the steps? (What if there were three missing, or one? Would it make any difference, symbolically or aesthetically?) What is a sunflower doing at the top of the steps anyway? How and why did it get in? What does it represent? Why is it so very large? Why does the hair of the girl nearer to the observer rise upward whereas that of the other girl falls downward? Is this purposeful? How does its likeness to flame serve this picture?

Striking a new note, where the menace is counterweighted by joy, the painting *Max in a Blue Boat* (1947) holds manifold enigmas. The bird Loplop, guardian mascot of Ernst's dada works and the initial surrealist group, laughs from a partially folded form to the left, like a sail or a bedsheet, of the same color as the rising moon and as Ernst's white hair and vest. The sail protrudes out over the boat, cutting like a benevolent phantom across the blue boat and its chess board, while the woman's brown hair dangles over the game. This, presumably, is Dorothea the artist, her presence in the stern balancing that of Max in the prow, holding a flame whose color echoes in a rust-colored wall. To the rear is an unidentified shape, like an iceberg or an island, conferring mystery. Something caught up in the folds of that sheet makes its profound and perhaps dangerous nest in this painting, before it sails out. The sheet/wing form reappears in the ironically titled *Guardian Angels* (1946) (see figure 7.3), where the wings hanging over the beds seem more menacing than protective: few things are simple or clear in Tanning's work.

Figure 7.3

SELF-PORTRAITURE FROM EARLY TO LATE

In a *Self-Portrait* (1944) (figure 7.13), a woman stands on a cliff overlooking a vast landscape of mountains, her fragile figure with its long hair and slender legs making an attractive center. In this painting, Tanning has constructed a self-portrait with the scope and reach of the eighteenth-century German romantic painter Caspar David Friedrich; as his figures stand looking out on immense land- or seascapes; the observer contemplates through their eyes the whole scene. In the Tanning painting, the viewer is at once enabled to see far into the distance through the eyes of the portrayed artist and to contemplate her fragile form as it stands, scantily dressed and unprotected, vulnerable against the rocky expanse.

The visual and psychological impact of self posed against horizon, of human figure upon the cliff, and of the vision so doubly posed is great. Given that so many of Tanning's works are undeclared self-portraits, this particular identification is all the more singular and important. Contrast this figure with the later *Nude Standing Nude* (1984–87) (figure 7.14) and *Woman Artist, Nude, Standing* (1985–87), where the form is seen from the front instead of the rear and where it is all-important against its abstract and background of scumbled paint. Here the figure is no more important than the natural forms that surround it, envelop it—indeed, that might threaten to engulf it, were not the figure so strong.

Figure 7.13 Dorothea Tanning, *Self-Portrait,* 1944. Oil on canvas, 24 × 30 in. Collection Johnson, Sedona, Arizona. Property of the Dorothea Tanning Foundation, Inc. © 1996.

This painting bears meditation. Tanning has always been crucially aware of her own position as an artist and of her own awareness as essential to the project both of art and of self-creation. I take this as a credo and as a starting place, finding it more credible even than *Birthday,* with which so much writing about the artist begins. Outside in nature, no doors open upon each other, no face appears with inquiring gaze; the observer sees *with* the artist, instead of seeing her alone. This work, profound and magisterial, opens out, not just in.

Harking back to Goya's *Maja* clothed and naked (*vestida* and *desnuda*), this strong and voluptuous female with a hat that looks very much like an

Figure 7.14 Dorothea Tanning, *Nude Standing Nude,* 1984–87. Oil on canvas, 64 × 51 in. Collection of the artist. Property of the Dorothea Tanning Foundation, Inc. © 1996.

overturned wastebasket, with a red flower on the right, places her hand on her hip in jaunty assurance while all about her wavy lines emphasize the *spin* she puts on the idea of nakedness. The wonderfully dense texture of what she stands *against* reinforces as nothing else could what she stands *for:* a kind of gaiety, her left hip swinging to one side, her tiny chin and delicate mouth just visible under the hat, with a rose splash on her right cheek just below the actual flower. That this artist so self-depicted cannot see beyond the hat may only intensify her inner vision: this self-portrait in intaglio, in its effrontery, its blatant *being-thereness,* has the conviction of its own singularity—no dog to waltz with, dream with, sleep with. Just the self, presented and self-sufficient, creating its own selfhood.

Tanning, in her self-portraits, from the early *Self-Portrait* (see figure 7.13) seen from the rear to this series of standing nudes, avoids the clichés of self-consciousness and preciosity. When, at the beginning of her novel *Abyss,* a young woman stares at herself in the mirror, a topos that could have been a stereotype, Tanning saves it by describing a strange collection of knotted and gnarled juniper woods, scattered all over the room, which "bears a curious and disagreeable air of arrested agony, mutely twisted in a motionless spasm."[7] The spasm is dynamism taken to its utmost.

Figure 7.13

Corresponding to the *Woman Artist, Nude, Standing* (1985–87) (see figure 7.14), *Standing Nude* (1983) and *Nude Standing Nude* (1984–87) both wear flowers on the right ears and swing short skirts. In *Standing Nude* a mailbox at the left has a seductive vertical shape, with a tiny flag waving from its top. These paintings are full of humor, joy, and fun. The two sides of the body, with a wavy line joining them in the center, are voluptuously full of protrusions and gleams—instead of the noticeable elbows of the figures in *Pounding Strong,* for example, the body is soft, touchable. In *Nude Standing Nude* the figure holds a fan at her left side, inspired by Velasquez's Spanish women, Picasso's hieratic woman with a fan held out, and Tanning's own previous rendering of the artist nude. Compare these with Man Ray's vulnerable *Kiki, Nude, Standing* (1925) (figure 7.15) in her simple direct pose, unadorned.

Figure 7.14

We cannot fail to notice how the figure is always standing in Tanning's self-portraits. In these dynamic renderings no reclining is possible. These self-assertions are about action, even as they are about creation. One of the most

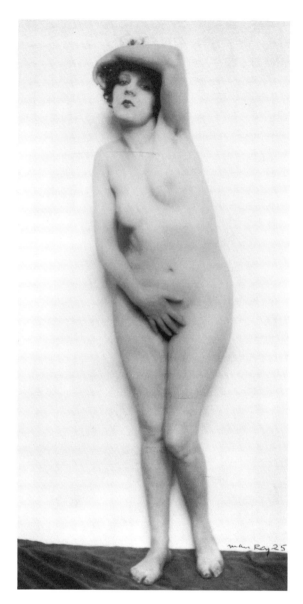

Figure 7.15 Man Ray, *Kiki, Nude, Standing,* 1925. Gelatin
silver print, 11¹⁄₁₆ × 5⅝ in. The J. Paul Getty Museum,
Los Angeles. © 1997 ARS, New York/ADAGP/Man Ray
Trust, Paris.

remarkable self-portraits is *Still in the Studio* (1979); the play on words explains the fascination of this canvas. Tanning is still, at the time of this painting, in her studio on the rue de Lille, which she will have to leave, leaving Paris. It is, then, a farewell. Yet it is also a statement of presence and not only of anticipated absence—this "still" is also a still life, a presentation of materiality in full consciousness of the complexity of stillness in both senses.

This is a major achievement in the autobiographical vein—face-on—presenting the artist's body with a box of paints set into the torso and another set out on the drawing table, in close proximity to a set of pencils and brushes. Overhead an architect's lamp bends down, its sharp line angling into the soft pink body, echoed by the upright lines of the chair back and reinforced by the ledge of the drawing table, running parallel to the bottom frame. Reminiscent of the trompe l'oeil still lifes of the great masters, this display of art and artist and artist's tools is a complete statement.

Yet a tragedy of unwilling. Something will be left behind, and not only in Paris. The force of this study picture—a *peinture d'atelier*—places it among the great *ateliers* of Matisse and Picasso and the written studio pieces of, say, Francis Ponge, Georges Braque, and Alberto Giacometti. This is the sacred place where creation is born. Never mind that it must be left behind. The testimonial to its fullest presence is that inset box of paints, that desk like an altar. Something will take place here, and we are permitted, for a time, to be witnesses.

Later, in her lyric and often witty book *Birthday*, Tanning describes, from her youth, the joy of spreading out these tools of this trade, in eager expectation:

> Alone. Self-consciously, uncompromisingly alone. No to sisters. No to friends. No to boys. No, no. Instead, the clear ritual of laying out paper, pencils, crayons, watercolors, the usual stuff, on the (ah, the simple word!) table. Something would happen, had to happen. It filled me up and down, back to front, and my head said that it would spill out.[8]

Still in the same book, toward the end, we read of that same eagerness: "The beginning is uneasy. Only witness: the studio where an event is about to take place. Not proud, not humble, not at all certain of anything nor yet uncertain, you play with the light, although there is no need, so filled is your inner vision with promise, the kind that shifts behind your eyes in and out of focus."[9] This painting is a farewell to the artist's studio, so strong as to stun the viewer, forced to contemplate both the paints replacing the body and the blur of the head, turned away. A melancholy painting, says the artist, in which decay is taking over. Indeed, even to the left of the window frame—through which we see Parisian roofs in their grays and browns—another gaseous form awaits, a vaguely female shape, pink and foggy, drifting down to the bottom of the window as a blob of indeterminate matter. The shock of contrast between soft lines and hard, pink and gray, the forethrust *chest of paints* like an intricate surrealist word/image game, the window—with its recalling of Juan Gris' paintings of Paris windows enriching both the melancholy and the meaning—make of this particularly strong work an important hinge to future paintings, after Paris.

Finally, in the whole gamut of effects related to self-conscious artistry, is the remarkable emphasis that Tanning places on the indexical trace of the creator's hand, whether literal or transposed onto canvas or paper through the hand of another. To put alongside the art of the self-portrait, nothing is more fitting than the hand—the artist's own or that of another—in a collage or a painting, leaving one's own mark on one's own creation. Tanning has made particular use of the hand—from its mysterious appearance, inserted in an implicit narrative in *Mrs. Radcliffe Called Again, Left No Message* (a recall of the earlier drawing, *A Mrs. Radcliffe Called Today* [1944], to its more formal use as the image of the instrument performing the operation of art. Like her use of the door or the crescent moon as image, symbol, and form, depending on the epoch in which it is used, the hand too is all those things: the image of the very idea of creation, the symbol of the artist herself as artist, and a formal object, with fingers, palm, and shape.

The imprint left by the hand, the indexical representation of writing and painting, marks her awareness, her self-conscious thought about art and making it. The use of the hand in a work of art made by the hand reveals high wit. In *Hotel* (1988), the handprint to the left and the torn shapes all about signal the making of collage and the acceptance of the fragmentary, the imperfect. Underpinning this work, the long, pink unattached form can be an arm or leg. Above it yet another unattached leg protrudes from the window of a fortress—in ironic play with the idea of "hotel." The *handling* of these unattached elements, obliquely referred to in such works, is funny, surrealist, light hearted yet potentially terrible. The separation of parts from whole cannot be treated simply as an amusing technique: it means something, and what it means all of Tanning's work says.

The hand, as presented in these works of 1988, is *never* attached to an arm or anything else. These are studies of detachment, of isolation—if you like, of the creative act as it knows itself to be detached, even as it is most significant. Tanning never falls into the romantic trap of painting herself isolated; it is enough to paint, to paste, to draw a hand in isolation from the rest of the body and the rest of life.

Exactly as it is detached, it is significant. Tanning and the hand. Tanning and the door. These images, whether the center of certain works or detached from the works and considered by themselves as marks designating the construction of the art works signal Tanning's modern consciousness. They reach out to the viewer and to the creating self at once:

> Now all the doors are open, the air is mother-of-pearl, and you know the way to tame a tiger. It will not elude you today for you have grabbed a brush, you have dipped it almost at random, so high is our rage, into the amalgam of color, formless on a docile palette.
>
> . . .
>
> It was, after all, your hand, your will, your turmoil that has produced it all, this brand new event in a very old world.[10]

8

Doubling: Claude Cahun's Split Self

Confondu parmi l'invisible, vous tous—les incrédules—vous me
passerez à travers la poitrine, sans vous blesser, sans le savoir.
(Mingled with the invisible, all of you—unbelievers—you will
walk right through my chest, without hurting yourself or even
knowing it.)

—*Claude Cahun,* "L'Insensé"[1]

No one had more *ways of looking* than Claude Cahun. She fascinates. She horri-
fies. She is monstrous. There is no better way of putting it.

In the most familiar self-portrait, heavy-lidded eyes look to the side under
a shaved skull. The left ear protrudes. You are tempted to look away.[2]

What we know about Lucy Schwob's life, intriguing as it is, isn't enough.
She is born in 1894, in Nantes, the daughter of Maurice Schwob, the brother
of the literary personality Marcel Schwob, one of the founders of the *Mercure
de France*. In 1909 she meets her great love, Suzanne Malherbe (descended from
the poet François Malherbe), who calls herself Marcel Moore, or Moore, as
Schwob calls herself Claude Cahun, both names deliberately androgynous.[3] In
the early 1920s they settle at 70 bis, Notre-Dame des Champs. In 1923 Cahun
joins the Union of the Friends of the Esoteric Arts, where she meets Béatrice
Wanger, the American dancer whose stage name Nadja, is adopted by Léonie-
Camille D., the heroine of André Breton's 1928 book of the same name. In
1929 Cahun plays men's and women's roles at Pierre-Albert Birot's Théâtre du

Plateau. In 1930 she meets Robert Desnos, and in 1932, André Breton; she joins the Association des Ecrivains et Artistes Révolutionaires (Association of Revolutionary Writers and Artists), known as the AEAR. In 1934 she writes her best-known work, *Les Paris sont ouverts,* (Place your Bets) visits the Clinique de Sainte-Anne with Breton and Henri Michaux, and participates in *Contre-Attaque* with Breton, Georges Bataille, and Roger Caillois. In 1937 she moves with Moore to "La Rocquaise" on the Bay of Saint Brelade on the island of Jersey, a place in which, she says, she is finally able to feel her full value.[4] In 1939 she joins the Fédération Internationale de l'Art Révolutionnaire Indépendant (International Federation of Independent Revolutionary Art); the painter Jacqueline Lamba Breton and her daughter Aube come to visit Cahun, and she gives them a Mexican sugar-candy skull. From 1940 on Cahun actively participates in subversive activities against the German occupiers of the island. She is arrested in 1944 and condemned to death. The Island is liberated in 1945. In 1953 Cahun returns to Paris, thinking of residing there; instead she returns to the island, where she dies in 1954.

That is what we know.

Here is what we see.

1911: She is beautiful, not monstrous. Heavy black hair and heavily costumed, staring at you with pouting lips. A real star. But she is polymorphous, this monstrous self seeing, always, itself, as man, as woman, as androgynous being. She thinks of herself as undefined.

1919: She is represented in profile (figure 8.1), her beaked nose above her tight lips and fully rounded chin, one hand clutching her ribbed sweater, against a black background. She poses so as to show her profile, closely resembling that of her father, who poses in the same attitude in 1920. But now she looks away from us. I am glad.

1920: Dressed in flat black slippers with diamond-patterned white socks beneath knee-length corduroy pants and a high-collared white sweater, she looks out just above our eyes and to the right while her sailor hat covers everything above *her* eyes. Arms akimbo, she poses against a black scrim against a white wall. What are we supposed to be thinking?

1921: Still in front of scrim, she is dressed in a man's black costume, same corduroy trousers, a black jacket, her right hand on her hip, her left hand loosely

Figure 8.1 Claude Cahun, *Self-Portrait as a Young Man,* 1919,
Silver print, 9⁵⁄₁₆ × 7 in. Courtesy of Virginia Zabriskie, the
Zabriskie Gallery, New York.

clenched in a fist. The white handkerchief in her left pocket has its own charm, like the white scarf wrapped around her neck. Her shaved head looks quizzically out at us, in a post almost hieratic, against a square black scrim.

1923: In the lotus position, Claude Cahun meditates, her eyes to our right, her silken robes folded over her knees, five strings of pearls draped around her neck. She is a triangular monument to unbudgingness, to luxury restyled as majestic meditativeness. Everything feels opulent.

1925: Her head looks out from something like a fencing helmet, like a box by Joseph Cornell, like a fishbowl on a ledge. Her head tilts to the side, and she cannot breathe in the glass bowl. I think decapitation, I think experiments with the wooden box and the saw; I think, in short, the drama to be a bit overwhelming.

1927: With bright red spots on her cheeks and on her breasts, she plays Harlequinades. She plays for a long time. In the play *Barbebleue* (Blue Beard) in Pierre-Albert Birot's theater, and in her own being. In costume and feminine-convincing; and in the same year, as a man at a café table in the play *Banlieue,* (Suburb) with crew cut and tie, her lids heavy.

1929: In fact, her face as a man is always more gripping: in 1929 also she dresses as a magic prince, her helmet and robe studded with jewels, her upslanting eyebrows above her hostile eyes and stern mouth are riveting.

1931: Her self-portraits never let up: now she stands in a bed of lava, her arms outstretched.

1932: She curls up in a cupboard, imitating one of Hans Bellmer's dolls.

1937: She poses by a milliner's model, all proper in her smoothed hair.

1938: She poses behind a cobweb, behind the leaded panes of a high window, as if prefiguring the prison she will inhabit during the German occupation of Jersey.

1939: She makes a self-portrait, stretched out among flowers like Kiki de Montparnasse amid the seashells, and photographs a decorated sugar skull in exactly the same position, beneath the same flowers. Unafraid, she is uncompromising, she is not a social being.

She is as unlike herself as she is unlike others, in all of her self-portraits, throughout the years. She masks herself in 1928 and after, in a smooth-faced covering, surrounding herself with more masks, the ones on her cape repeating her own masked face. *Cahun is masquerade itself,* extreme in the extreme (figure 8.2). She is camp as camp can be. Masks and half-masks. In 1948, in a half-mask, she walks her cat through the cemetery, in *Le Chemin des chats*. It is a blindman's cat, for the all-too-seeing Claude Cahun. "J'avais passé mes heures solitaires à déguiser mon âme. Les masques en étaient si parfaits que lorsqu'il leur arrivait de se croiser sur la grand'place de ma conscience, ils ne se reconnaissaient plus" ("I had spent my hours alone disguising my soul. The masks were so perfect that when they met on the central plaza of my conscience, they no longer recognized each other").[5]

Of all the self-portraits, those of 1929, with her head and eyebrows shaved, her mouth heavily rouged and pulled down at the edges, pictured alone or with her partner Moore—see, for instance, the double portrait on the cover of *Frontières humaines*—make the most impact. In one, her head stretches up egg-shaped above protruding ears while her eyes stare roundly and sadly to her right; her black dress drapes far down her shoulders.

None of these is real. All of these are real. Behind each the real disappears, making itself as small and undetectable as possible:

> Il y a trop de tout. Je me tais. Je retiens mon haleine. Je me couche en rond, j'abandonne mes bords, je me replie vers un centre imaginaire . . . Je me fais raser les cheveux, arracher les dents les seins— tout ce qui gêne ou impatiente mon regard—l'estomac, les ovaires, le cerveau conscient et enkysté. Quand je n'aurai plus qu'un battement de coeur à noter, mais à la perfection, bien sûr je gagnerai la partie.
>
> (There is too much of everything. I keep silent. I hold my breath. I curl up in a ball, I give up my boundaries, I retreat towards an imaginary center . . . I have my head shaved, my teeth pulled and my breasts cut off—everything that bothers my gaze or slows it down—the stomach, the ovaries, the conscious and cysted brain. When I have nothing more than a heartbeat to note, to perfection, I will have won.)[6]

Figure 8.2 Claude Cahun, *Untitled* (self-portrait), 1928. Gelatin silver print, 9⁵⁄₁₆ × 7 in. Courtesy of Virginia Zabriskie, the Zabriskie Gallery, New York.

To be sure, this is an effort toward nothingness, toward minimalism. But it is also a major salute to the powers of language toward the self, an oath of lessness as sleekness, made in a perfect stripping down of language all the more empowered, like the look whose trajectory nothing impedes or halts.

To disguise, mask, and look at yourself single and double as Claude Cahun does, in so many ways, is not only a polymorphic, brave, and exhausting act. With her hair, lashes, and nails pink or green or gilded, with metallic streaks, she was the least natural imaginable ("Que d'artifice en moi, si peu de primitif'") Instead of spontaneity, the cultivated masking and mask; instead of the natural and the "abomination of the everyday," the thought-out, spied on. Her applied colors and artificial appearance would have delighted Baudelaire, for whom makeup was the only weapon against the natural and the "abomination of the everyday," the thought-out, and the already given, bringing the person close to a statue, both divine and superior. Everything was to excess, as it is supposed to be in the surrealist world. Yet Cahun was too much for Breton, who was indeed—as he suspected and said—not up to loving Nadja the mad-woman or Cahun the polymorphous.

A significant and conscious contemporary dandy, everything enabled her to be also the witness to and transcriber of herself as artist, as auto-interpreter, and as object extreme among extremes: "Je ne voudrais coudre, piquer, tuer qu'avec l'extrême pointe. . . . Ne voyager qu'à la proue de moi-même" ("I wouldn't like to sew, stick, kill with anything but the extreme point. . . . Only travel at the very tip of myself").

I see four of her portraits as closely linked in self-construction and con-struction of the other. Each is about mirroring. Each plays against a curtain, implicit or explicit, like Breton's "Rideau rideau" ("Curtain curtain").

In the most mysterious of these mirroring self-portraits (figure 8.3), dat-ing from 1927, Claude Cahun, seated, stares at us, a scalloped fringe of dark hair framing her forehead, her white face unsmiling, with pouting lips and sul-len eyes, ears protruding against the dark background. Her arms make a rectan-gular frame around a globe-shaped form, in which is reflected an image at once unclear and clearly composed of inside and outside, a dark form against a lit pair of arches. The self-artist is cradling a world to which, as it were, she has

Figure 8.3 Claude Cahun, *Untitled* (self-portrait), 1927. Gelatin silver print, 11.7 × 8.9 cm. Courtesy of Virginia Zabriskie, the Zabriskie Gallery, New York.

Figure 8.4 Claude Cahun, *Untitled* (self-portrait), 1928. Gelatin silver print, 24 × 19 cm. Courtesy of Virginia Zabriskie, the Zabriskie Gallery, New York.

given birth. She stares soberly at us as we try to figure out what she is holding. The image seems to concern what it is to hold an enigma up close, to cradle its depths and force us to see.

In a haunting image of 1928 (figure 8.4), her serious, anxious gaze comes at us sideways, as she stands close against a mirror. There her the image is deflected away. The eyes are both knowing and sad. Whatever her concerns, she cannot tell them and we cannot share them. The double image is not about

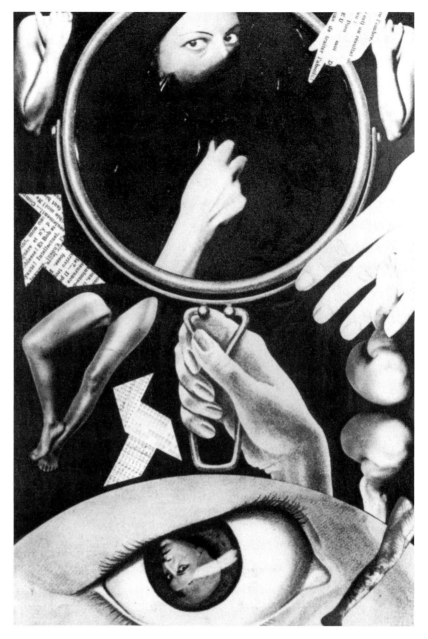

Figure 8.5 Claude Cahun and Moore, *Untitled,* 1928. Gelatin silver print. Courtesy of Virginia Zabriskie, the Zabriskie Gallery, New York.

self-reflection only but more urgently about how we cannot really reflect on either our own deeper self nor on someone else's. The image refuses any but its own interior reflection—outside no look is exchanged between subject and mirror.

A remarkable photomontage made by Cahun and Moore, between 1929 and 1930 (figure 8.5), makes a multiple display of discrete and separated hands, eyes, legs, and fingers. This enormously erotic *discretion* lays out the acts of folding, of self-mirroring, of pointing. The close-up examination is signaled by a handheld mirror, where Cahun's disquieting look, her hand turned slightly sideways, and right arm are pointed to by a gloved left hand jutting inward into the mirror, on which words are written—in the age-old tradition in which the virgin receives a message straight from God. It says: "l'ombre . . . un résultat . . . Dieu . . . moi . . . de traiter l'absolu" ("the shadow . . . a result . . . God . . . me . . . from treating the absolute"). Such an absolute is best treated, perhaps, best handled through the fragment. This is, of course, to discuss the workings of that absolute against a ground of difference, made of a series of "discrete, ungeneralizable situations," as Linda Nochlin puts it in her reflection on the fragment in *The Body in Pieces: The Fragment as a Metaphor of Modernity.*[7] The basis must be difference instead of any "unified field of discourse," and the present photomontage is truly a composite field of fragments, scattered like our perception of ourselves.

To this hand from on high responds a thumbless right hand, jutting into the picture from below, touching the rim of the mirror, held by another ungloved right hand with shapely fingernails. Directly below it, the eye contains another face upside down, in a tight cap, presumably that of Moore (Suzanne Malherbe), with a beam of light extending to the forehead. This is thinking, this is seeing, straight and reversed, with these surrealist women lovers. Masking, masquerade, and fragmentation are parts of Cahun and Moore's self-portraiture.[8]

Their doubling is also doubled by other pairings. In the upper corners, a pair of arms folds themselves up against a shoulder, like a doubling of something doubled up already, right arm in left corner, left arm in right corner, holding up the picture. Like a child's paper airplane, a pair of folded paper arrows point at a pair of elegantly highlighted legs, and at the mirror, already pointed to by the uppermost finger. Everything is doubled or grotesquely echoed, as is the shapely pair of legs by a gangrened single leg crossing the eye on the lower right corner. A pair of organic and squishy mushroom shapes, like some sort of testicle separated from its context, extrudes a foot between the bare fingers of the left and thumbless hand, and a bony form into the eye that stretches along the lower frame. It is enough to make you want to walk out of the picture right along with that leg heavily scored and leaving in the lower right corner, walking away from the eye staring at us, staring like the two eyes mirrored. Velasquez's celebrated *La Meniñas* is no more complex than this.

This play on hands is also a play on Magritte's play on seeing, called the *False Mirror* (see figure 1.1)—this is a true mirror, truly more complex. All three images are about the enigma of reflection and what it is to reflect on it, about a true and a false invitation to enter this construction of the other by the other, who stares out at us.

Figure 1.1

Claude Cahun's image of Jacqueline Lamba-Breton in 1939 (figure 8.6) plays for me the same role as Man Ray's many haunting images of André Breton: the beauty of the face is enhanced by the remarkable depth of the meditating pose, as if the whole look were to be turned toward the interior. The light stripes playing over her naked torso add to the corporeal texture the same sort of fascination that Man Ray's imposition of the darker stripes over Kiki's naked torso gives to his *Retour à la raison*,[9] to his repeated photographs of Miller's torso with the light and shadows of a Venetian blind playing upon it (figure 8.7), and to the startlingly white bars made by the electric lights of *Electricity* in 1931 (figure 8.8) on the naked torso, so minimal as to concentrate all energy in the contrast. In the portrait of Jacqueline Lamba the painter (at this point Breton's muse) (see figure 8.6), the darker ribbon of shadow spanning her shoulders and setting off the stripes of light gathers at her neck like a decorative puff. It lends mystery to the image, in a way similar to that of the emblems that Cornell adds at the bottom of the construction using Breton's picture by Man Ray. These two beautiful and mysterious renderings of two beautiful and mysterious beings belong side by side.

Cahun's brilliant double portrait of André Breton and Jacqueline Lamba (figure 8.9), taken between 1935 and 1936, plays on reflections to infinity, upside down, to the sides: the two faces seem endlessly reflected against the curtain

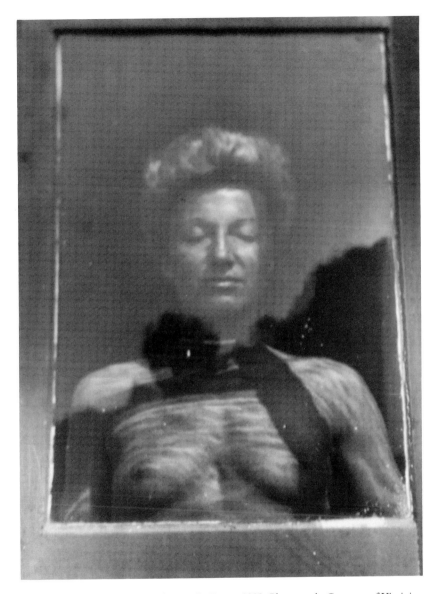

Figure 8.6 Claude Cahun, *Jacqueline Lamba-Breton,* 1939. Photograph. Courtesy of Virginia Zabriskie, the Zabriskie Gallery, New York.

Figure 8.7 May Ray, *Untitled* (photograph of Lee Miller), 1929. Private collection. © 1997 ARS, New York/ADAGP/Man Ray Trust, Paris.

and forever separated from their bodies. Compare it with her duller portrait (figure 8.10), full-length of the two, Breton looking sad, and Jacqueline, silly. Bodies do not always help. Only the faces to look at, in this willfully dramatic rendering, where the curtain shines in its folds, and small globules or dots, as if dripping light, give texture to both curtain and face, as do the stripes of light and shadow imposed on the naked torsos. We read *against* the curtain as we read against and through the mask and striped light and dark. Our reading of the

Figure 8.8 Man Ray, *Electricity,* 1931. Photoengraving, 10¼ × 8⅟₁₆ in. The J. Paul Getty Museum, Los Angeles. © 1997 ARS, New York/ADAGP/Man Ray Trust, Paris.

Figure 8.9 Claude Cahun, *André and Jacqueline Breton,* 1935–36. Silver print. Courtesy of
Virginia Zabriskie, the Zabriskie Gallery, New York.

Figure 8.10 Claude Cahun, *André et Jacqueline Breton,* 1935. Photograph.
Courtesy of Virginia Zabriskie, the Zabriskie Gallery, New York.

image must also be constructed "inside the visible," with our experience built in. This gives the texture to our looking.

Claude Cahun's pictures cause us to reflect doubly, on her, on ourselves, and on our own constructional ability, which she mirrors, reflects on, and curtains off from what we used to consider the "real world."

RENAMING EVERYTHING

It is very odd to consider oneself as Claude Cahun does. To give oneself and one's living and loving partner new names—"Claude Cahun" for Lucy Schwob and "Moore" for Suzanne Malherbe—is already surrealist. The androgynous nomenclature makes every sense. What is far odder is the chosen *aspect* of those faces. They haunt you. "Tell me whom you haunt," says Breton in *Nadja*—all the hauntings I have known have been of intent faces: Breton, in a photograph of chosen surprise, caught by Man Ray with his mouth open; Artaud with his hollow cheeks and otherworldly stare; Desnos, with his thick glasses and glazed look. Claude Cahun's look is no less mesmerizing—I mean of course in the pictures with her head elongated and shaved, in profile with her dominant nose, or straight on as if demented, or leaning against a mirror with her ear protruding.

Perhaps the most arresting photographs, those self-portraits for which she is celebrated, are the double ones, sometimes with Moore, sometimes just herself twice over. A great deal has been written about the complicities and duplicities of this self-picturing. We do not actually know whether they were made with a timer, or whether Moore was behind the camera. They are, in every case, totally unlike other people's self-portraits. Whether she is lying on the floor in a jester's outfit, or dressed as a young man, or walking over a cemetery wall led by a cat on a leash, or staring at the observer behind dark glasses with a fixed smile, there is no mistaking Claude Cahun for anyone else. She is a theatrical personality: see the work with Pierre Albert-Birot, for his *Bluebeard,* where she is the innocent, childishly dressed victim, or, in *Le Mystère d'Adam,* the devil. ("Si c'est vraiment le démon qui nous a perdus, lui seul peut nous sauver" we read. "[If it's really Satan who damned us, he's the only one to save us"].) Given these quite remarkable visual doublings of the self, she could be forgiven were she to be (1) dull in her person or tongue, (2) incapable of any other expression than the visual, or (3) a bad writer, if a writer at all. But in fact her writings, those illustrated by Moore and in the form of a prose poem, or *Les Paris sont ouverts,* political in nature, are forceful and fascinating. They are, moreover, as inclined to doubling as are her self-portraits. The prose poems are constructed in repetition, with one side of the page visually and verbally an almost perfect echo of the other.

When Artaud recommended a certain method in the theater (*The Theater and Its Double*), it concerned a pantomime mimesis, doubling the words or replacing them. It is, in his case, about *repetition*—also in the French sense of "rehearsal," the repeating or *répétition* of a role. A verbal gesture is repeated in a visual one. But Claude Cahun's self-consciousness disturbs and leaves you feeling far more troubled. In every way, she is a surrealist figure. It is fitting that she should have been a close friend, probably a lover, of the original Nadja, the dancer and theosophist Béatrice Wanger, to whom she dedicated a poem, addressing it to Breton.[10] Her friendship with Jacqueline Lamba Breton is more than fitting; Lamba was sensitive to originality, to art of all kinds, and to creative people.[11] Claude Cahun's creative genius was unique.

DOUBLE ARRANGEMENTS

One of the singular elements of reading Cahun is the difficulty entailed not just by her androgyny but by her insistence on pointing it out. The double portraits with Moore are striking enough. Her self-presentation as a man at a café table and as the princess in Bluebeard's castle is a startling case of both sides convincing. The doubleness goes past her personality and her poses into her texts. When you begin to notice that her major publications, such as *Aveux non avenus* and *Les Paris sont ouverts,*[12] feature two sides responding to each other, it becomes clear that her usual technique was this self-replication, self-contemplation, and reversal. On both sides of the page, the protagonist has a migraine and a beloved who sings and rocks him (her) to sleep, before being left without gratitude, with just a gender change here and there: "cet ami" or "cette amie."

Take the cover of *Les Paris sont ouverts:* the front and back covers correspond, surely by design. Take the way in which the episodes in *Vues et visions* respond to each other, illustrated by Moore. The narrative, if you can call it that, a sort of prose poem, takes exactly the same elements and actions on opposite sides of the page and simply changes the subject, that is, the pronoun, and the description of the setting. Pattern rules over content.

Take the rhythmic and heavy stresses in the celebrations of the eponymous *Héroines*.[13] Among them are Eve so easily taken in, Dalila the woman's woman, Judith the sadist, Helen the revel, Sappho so misunderstood, Marguerite given to incest, and Salomé the skeptical. Each is described in the same form, invoked in the same rhythmically scanned tones. The evocations are ironic, witty, chilly as they see through the myths used as a heading for each stanza.

> *Eve, too Credulous:*
>> *A Unique Opportunity:*
>>> Ask for the tasty fruit.
>>> There's only ONE left . . .

> *Judith the Sadist*
>> "People! *what do I have in common with you?*
>> Who gave you permission to penetrate my private life? to judge my actions and admire them? to heap on me (me so weak and tired, always your prey!) your hateful glory?"
>> But her words weren't understood or even heard. The joy of a crowd with a thousand mouths—and no ears.

> *Sappho the Misunderstood*
>> To create is my joy. I don't care what it is. . . . Alas! the seers have told me my womb is sterile . . .
>> When you stop creating, all you can do is destroy: for nobody can stand up—without moving—on the wheel of fate.

But Cahun is at her wittiest, and most terrible—most surrealistically available— in her depiction of Salomé in her daily indifference, forgetting whatshisname whose head she wants on a platter. Never mind, says *Salomé the Skeptical,* my father-in-law will know who I mean. And indeed he did.

Why did I ask for that? That head is still uglier now it is cut off, it looks worse than in the theater. *It seems* I should touch it, take it in my hands, kiss it! . . .

Ugh! but it's getting me all dirty with its sticky blood, less red and hot than usual . . . it's blood rather like mine . . .

(*This isn't even a good play.*)

What does it matter? It just means I was right:

Art and life, same thing

. . .

Me, it leaves me cold.

THE COLD ARRANGEMENT

Claude Cahun is known for her arrangements of objects. They are as frightening as her self-portraits. Insects creep around on a plate; spiders drip over a crib. Things stab, point, prickle. Her relation to *objects* and herself as object is terrifying. "Prenez garde aux objets domestiques," her celebrated essay for the 1936 exhibition at the Charles Ratton Gallery, published in *Cahiers d'Art,* speaks loudly: "Watch out for those domestic things!" it translates loosely. Her arrangements even with the simplest objects—a fork, a key, a knife, a bed—turn very ominous indeed. A spear protrudes through a child's head, one cupid atop a fountain has its parallel in one falling backward to the ground and one submerged in the background. Elsewhere, nature and culture combine menacingly: a pair of lips has a tiny twig hand spilling out of them while prickly flowers merge with scissors to cut them, all of this transpiring behind the cage of a mailbox whose bars reappear in some of Cahun's self-portraits: the natural is threatened by imprisonment, speech is about to be silenced, and what might flower will prick you should you touch it. Watch out, for nothing is homey about Cahun's "domestic" vision. It is anything but domesticated. Our society produces so many useless objects that our own beings lose their actuality. We have to fabricate irrational objects ourselves to tame them, to understand what we are looking at: take a little blood on a sponge looking like a brain, put it in some water and see what sorts of animal forms come forth. "Disturb the *animarium* with a stick, and the word *agitator* will impose itself on you with a start."[14]

Yet her photographs, where the objects play the role of people, I find most disturbing. Not the ones with a sense of humor—not the photograph of Moore and Claude buried up to their faces in sand, but the ones where the eye searches in vain for a human presence. Just when you would have thought yourself on safer ground—after all, the picture of an object might feel farther from the eye of the observer than those horrendous faces, beautiful in their monstrosity—you are most menaced.

Something about the human doubled by, indeed *replaced by,* the object is more horrendous than the rest. I think here of Giacometti's *Woman with Her Throat Cut* or the more obscene and therefore more disturbing ball hovering above that vaginal cavity. Cahun's object photographs feel to me like a male insult to the long nails of the female . . . If I feel elated by the different guises of her self-portraiture, I feel intensely depressed by these *arrangements.*

Cast a cold eye . . . Cahun's *look* frightens, whether it is upon herself or anything else. It is cold, whatever it concerns. It reduces. It sharpens. Take her meditation on home stuff, domestic objects, or her photographs of still lifes or the arrangements in tiny beds in a photograph in the collection *Le Coeur de pic* (1937) to illustrate the book of Lise Deharme[15] and another in *Un air de famille* (1937), with a veil of muslin draping the crib, suspended from a central pole, around which are placed various menacing objects. The very tininess of the arrangement disturbs: as if a bridal veil were to hang over a baby, or a mosquito netting. Nothing indicates rest or response here. "Here is a primary truth. You have to discover, manipulate, *tame,* even fabricate yourself some irrational objects in order to appreciate the particular or general value of those we have under our eyes."

"Only to man," we read in the essay on domestic objects, "does there belong such an upheaval of matter that his organs themselves have flowered into monstrosities and sicknesses so numerous. . . . Inanimate matter is just like the other. It is malleable however man, that irrational animal, chooses."[16] A menace hangs heavy over *all* photographs taken of or arranged by Cahun, over the portraits as over the objects pictured: a skull, ceramic hands, a doll, a fork, a clock face, bird feathers . . . none of these "upsetting objects" comfort, they rather frighten as they signal instruments of cruelty and the cruelties of time passing, diminution, deprivation. They are, in Salvador Dali's terms, "objects with symbolic functions." When, in 1935, the journal *Minotaure* paid homage to Cahun's work, in "La Grande Actualité poétique," it was for the creative freedom she had always embraced. But over that "freedom" there always hung a heavy menace.

Cahun does not want to remember what she arranges, nor do I. Take a few of the more bothersome realizations of her object-haunted imagination: a bony construction on a glass stand in the center of a mirror, holding a wildly peculiar group of objects. A little plaster church, some seashells and butterflies, moths, leaves, and peacock feathers, the face of a grandfather clock with a sword for the hands gather in profusion around a dog's head with its eyes protruding violently from its face of plaster or wood, holding a long stick between its teeth. Or the eye-vulva, a hand as mirror or mask with a single eye almost hidden but "counterfeited": "It's a kiss with its lashes meeting, it's a palpitating pupil" atop the hand, looking like a skull opened or female genitalia, surrounded by eyelashes and a central tuft of hair on top. In her drawings, she places cards in the hand, has the heart beat in the eye. Her texts are as obsessed as her drawings and her conception of things or beings in their acts. To see them is more than disturbing: it can obsess.

Watch Cahun describe, in the same essay, the act of self-mirroring and self-loving: "Take a mirror, scratch off several centimeters of the silvering at the height of your right eye; place behind this transparent spot a ribbon on which you have stuck a few small disparate objects, and look at yourself when you go by, right in the eye." She shows the imagination of a child obsessed or of a fanatic, with words as with objects. Things, people, words, all enter into what she describes in "Prenez garde" as that "chain of forced, stultifying labor." I feel exhausted just looking.

If we compare any of her constructions with those of Joseph Cornell, we are likely to see his as more controlled, more optimistic, and less dangerous— and thus in a sense less surrealist. In her work everything is on the point of danger, and we are never at ease. Hers is a sometimes playful yet serious celebration of art as life, of moments wanting to be remembered and celebrated. She does not celebrate, except through her *Héroines,* who all go against the ordinary way of seeing and doing.

Her own way of arranging can look like clutter. But—significantly—one arrangement under a glass bell like some of Cornell's early compositions, including a baby tree, a baby's head, a pansy, and on and on, features a large key at the top. The idea that unlocks it all is to be found, like Breton's "the key to the fields." I think it is probably that of freedom itself.

What is Natural Here?

Everything is so arranged, in fact, that there seems little place for the natural. Perhaps not in her art or the art with which she made, remade, and doubled herself but surely in her actions during the war, when the Germans were occupying Jersey, where she was living with Moore. We have the record of her bravery during the occupation, when she circulated statements urging the German soldiers to desert, stuck paper butterflies on the tanks, and generally undertook such symbolic and "subversive" acts that she and Moore were imprisoned and condemned to death.

Even what might seem most "natural" was difficult and fraught with danger for Cahun. Her passion for Breton was natural enough and long-lasting. While he was wary of taking someone with such a strange and changeable appearance into the group, she proved herself, like another Nadja, the kind of challenge he could not meet. Cahun caused discomfort, in both her own looks—so many of them—and how she looked at the world and presented herself to it. When, in June of 1953, she contemplated moving back to Paris and encountered, for the last time, the surrealist group including Breton, Benjamin Péret, and the artists Toyen [Marie Cerminovä] and Méret Oppenheim, she wondered about herself: "This morbid obsession: what can I do?" and returned to Jersey.

In the fall of the next year she wrote one of her last letters, to Breton: "Je me bouleverse l'esprit dangereusement pour ceux que j'aime. Avertissement: vous êtes du nombre" ("I upset myself dangerously for those I love. Warning: you are among those").[17] Everything felt like, looks still like danger around Claude Cahun, a heroine both of singular passions and of doubleness. She is the most disturbing surrealist I know. For herself, she claims that she was condemned before birth, executed already in her absence: "Avant d'être née, j'étais condamnée. Exécutée par contumace."[18]

You have to make sacrifices, says one of her more complicated texts in *Ephémérides: Extraits d'un calendrier perpétuel,*[19] in January of this perpetual calendar. I will end my look at Cahun's look with this text, dealing with circumcision. It is January, and the text—and the year with it—begins like this:

> I preach daily circumcision for the soul. . . . You have to make sacrifices. That's the only reason for writing.
>
> If we decided to eliminate from the world all the organs of showiness (luxury—lux—light), those we don't know, whose use we aren't aware of, think of the heads that would fall! . . .
>
> I feel mine swaying from side to side . . .
>
> But, frankly, has taking out an appendix ever changed anyone's heart or instincts?
>
> If Jesus's foreskin had been shaped like Cleopatra's nose, would the face of history have been altered?

What indeed changes anyone's heart or instincts? What indeed is natural? Cahun's investigations of herself and her relation to Moore, of objects, and of the world surrounding her island mix bravery with brilliance. We should watch out for this particular surrealist disturbance, exiled or self-exiled, like some before her, to the island of Jersey.

9

FASHION: MAN RAY'S MANIPULATIONS

> Pour qui sait mener à bien la barque photographique dans le re-
> mous presque incomprehénsible des images, il y a la vie à rattraper
> comme on tournerait un film à l'envers . . .
> (Whoever can maneuver the photographic vessel in the nearly in-
> comprehensible wake of images has life to catch up with, as you'd
> make a movie backwards . . .)
>
> —*André Breton, in* Le Surrealisme et la peinture[1]

To fashion an icon recognizable and memorable, you have to get a conscious
handle on the object. Among fashion photographers, May Ray, the American
who turned himself into a French fashion and fashioner, is distinguished by his
seriously postmodern intelligence and manner (figure 9.1).[2] The knowing wit
of his photographs, as well as his original conception of remaking the model
for the viewer, demands—as I have argued elsewhere[3]—a certain complicity of
the person modeling. But it also demands a *specific* reformulation of the art
of observing. We are looking, in these pictures, at an icon maker skilled in
representation; it is our own looking skill that we must refashion.

Man Ray's signature style concerns not only the pose of the model but
also, and even in particular, how it refers beyond itself. I want to examine this
reference in several images: what is so crafty about Man Ray's representations
and references, how the artful is made to look natural, and how the natural

Figure 9.1 Man Ray, *Self-Portrait,* 1924. Gelatin silver print, 8⅛ × 6¼ in. The J. Paul Getty Museum, Los Angeles. © 1997 ARS, New York/ADAGP/Man Ray Trust, Paris.

takes on an artful manner. In each case the references both implied and evident transform the pictured object into a subject of interested contemplation, representing more than it initially did.

MANIPULATIVE HANDLING

Man Ray's handling is "manipulative" in the most literal sense: hands-on arranging (*manus:* "the hand") of each image, which, as Tristan Tzara points out, "exceeds the space" it takes up. Only the first group discussed below bears any resemblance to what we think of as "fashion photograph," an enhancement of the figure via a glamorizing prop. Thus the object and person combine in one fashioned and fashionable thing.[4]

Take, for example, Juliet Man Ray wearing different sorts of headdresses or necklaces, the prop, however minimal, emblematic of beauty itself (figure 9.2). By isolating the prop and stressing it to its limit, Man Ray manages to combine simplicity with excess.[5] Juliet may be wearing a Marajo hat, her face framed by it and by the exotic flavor it imparts: the caption, probably added by a collector, explains that the headdress's straw and pieces of shell were taken from the Marajo Indians, living on an island shaped like an egg in the mouth of a snake that is the Amazon River. "The island is larger than France," continues the caption, and "These people are the greatest artists of the region." So her beauty is enhanced by the art of the *other,* representative now both of geographic region and of local art. The human is adorned by the natural, reconstructed for this specific enhancement.

In a superb picture of this type, simply entitled *Juliet with Scarf and Big Necklace* (1948), Juliet's outline is blurred and bent back on the diagonal, as if in action; we are not looking just at the photographer's embellishment of a human figure but at an emblem of beauty beribboned yet free. Streaks of light run strangely and becomingly up and down her body, and her feet are encased in beribboned sandals; yet the whole composition is so indicative of freedom that there is no sense of being tied/down, even by the glamor of the image.

In the painterly *Juliet, Nude (1945)* (figure 9.3), Juliet stands sideways to the viewer, graceful in the double drapery of the towel around her hair and the piece of clothing held in front of her, extending below her left arm. The white

Figure 9.2 Man Ray, *Juliet with Scarf and Big Necklace,* 1948. Gelatin silver print, 9¹⁵⁄₁₆ × 7⅞ in. The J. Paul Getty Museum, Los Angeles. © 1997 ARS, New York/ADAGP/Man Ray Trust, Paris.

towel is knotted loosely behind, like a gigantic ribbon whose ends fall down her back. The construction quotes Ingres's bathing nudes, turned away from us in the same way. The sight line flows from the turbaned towel down the back and behind the slight protrusion of the shoulder blade, forward to the draped cloth in front of the figure, in a serpentine sweep at once liquid and "natural," slightly swaying toward the front. Nudity, drapery, modesty knot together in a graceful twist like that of the towel. The picture reads like a classic icon of a

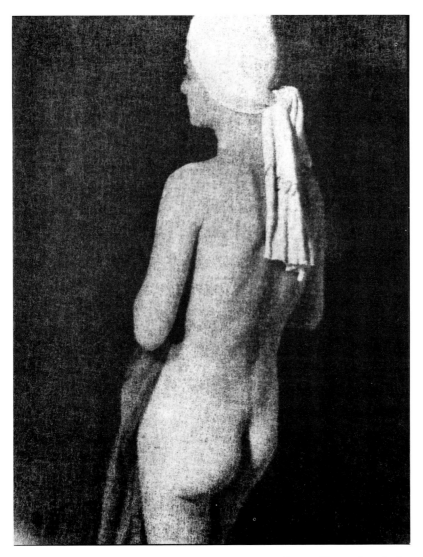

Figure 9.3 Man Ray, *Juliet, Nude,* 1945. Gelatin silver print, 13¾ × 10¹¹⁄₁₆ in. The J. Paul Getty Museum, Los Angeles. © 1997 ARS, New York/ADAGP/Man Ray Trust, Paris.

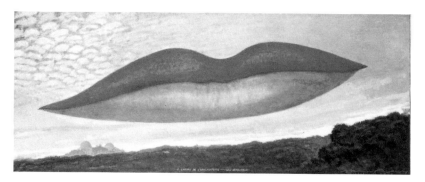

Figure 9.4 Man Ray, *Untitled* (Lee Miller's Lips), *L'heure de l'observatoire—Les Amants (Observation Time—The Lovers),* 1932–34. 39⅜ × 98½ in. Private Collection. © 1997 ARS, New York/ADAGP/Man Ray Trust, Paris.

bathing beauty. In one silver print gorgeously, richly illuminated ("treated") with colored pencils, the knot of the white towel is breathtakingly delicate, lending majesty to natural nudity. Many other photographs of Juliet pluck adornments from nature: she might wear snail earrings and a floral motif for a hat; but the toweled nude turned away serves above all as the very icon of naturalness.

High Fashioning

When the image is rendered in stark isolation, an emblem divorced from what it emblematizes, we are looking at iconization, with a high fashioning of surprise. Man Ray's signature is so highly visible in any case that in order to *do* a photograph, he has only to hint at the slightest give and take between the model and the world and the whole thing bears looking at, bearing also in itself a metonymic charge of the whole. He needs no props to bring about what Antonin Artaud used to call the "miraculizing" of what the artist touches. Again the signature is quite simply: "Man Ray Fecit." Man Ray Did This. Again.

So, for instance, Lee Miller's lips (figure 9.4) will take up an entire photograph and dominate the painting *Observation Time* (1932–1934). They exist without the rest of her, a metonymy of herself, like a body part sailing across the sky if we look long enough. In a strange but strangely predictable transformation, recognizable, they float by quite naturally, just as if some red velvet sofa

126

Figure 9.5 Man Ray, *Picabia,* 1922. Gelatin silver print, 3⅝ × 4¹³⁄₁₆ in. The J. Paul Getty Museum, Los Angeles. © 1997 ARS, New York/ADAGP/Man Ray Trust, Paris.

were to take up celestial residence.[6] From there, it goes on, famously, like the eye of Magritte's *False Mirror* (1928) (figure 1.1) floating by with clouds across it. Surrealist eroticism, surrealist vision seen as sublime.

Figure 1.1

In Man Ray's crafting of the photographic image we recognize instantly the way in which he clamps the figures to their identifying objects, welding them with bizarre overtones. He uses the wheel and its knob as a particularly erotic device, a female/male juxta- or super-position. Thus we remember his picturing Picabia and his steering wheel (figure 9.5), the knob of which he will later transpose in the glass circle overlay upon a naked female breast (figure 9.6). We see *Erotique-voilée,* with Méret Oppenheim standing nude beside her printing wheel (figure 9.7),[6] with printer's ink on her hands, as if she were printing her own figure, fashioning her own image. She is crafted by the picture maker even as she seems to be printing herself, the dark marking a sign of the image's

127

Figure 9.6 Man Ray, *Interior,* 1933. Gelatin silver print, 11¾ × 8¹³⁄₁₆ in. The J. Paul Getty Museum, Los Angeles. © 1997 ARS, New York/ADAGP/Man Ray Trust, Paris.

Figure 9.7 Man Ray, *Erotique-voilée*, 1933, uncropped version. Photograph in *Minotaure*, no. 5, 1934. 1933. Gelatin silver print, Bibliothèque nationale. © ADAGP/DACS Musée National d'Art Moderne, Paris. © 1997 ARS, New York/ADAGP/Man Ray Trust, Paris.

extreme high charge, like a kind of chosen disorder, and we compare and contrast this same erotic charge with the utter calm and order of Man Ray picturing
himself in his own studio (figure 9.8). Tzara is pictured with his monocle, Duchamp with his larger glass: all of these images with objects serve as instant
identifications.

When the observer bears in mind these instant identifications, Man Ray's
magnificent and minimal constructions of and with Kiki de Montparnasse,
Lee Miller, and Juliet Man Ray take on an entirely different mode of self-
presentation. They are already inscribed in a body, a *corpus* used to being imposed upon, read against, fashioned.

He also fashions himself. In a typically complex *Auto-Portrait* of 1944,
Man Ray reflects on his image in a mirror, where he is framed, as it were,
smoking a pipe. The latter's presence is—like that of the king and queen in
Velasquez's *Las Meniñas*—only mirrored. And he is pointing to it, that is, to his
own question about what is and isn't in pipedom: does the heavy irony make
the thing real?

FASHIONING THE NATURAL

A picture of Kiki de Montparnasse with ferns (figure 9.9) manages to *unite* the
natural object and the female body, as if they were speaking to each other. Kiki
posing nude among the ferns and grass, with the shadow of the fern against her
arm like a bracelet above the elbow, laughing, and another fern playing a fig
leaf, feathering gently over her left thigh. A protrusion of phallic rock sticks out
to the right of her head. She is a laughing Botticelli, with leaves in her mouth,
joyous.[7] This joyous outdoor Kiki embodies nature itself, or the myth of naturalness, loud with sheer animal joy. She is fashioned here in a way both primitive
and knowing, and makes a direct appeal.[8]

So far none of these images reads as an imposition of the photographer
but rather as the conversations of body and surround. Fashioned here is exactly
a union, no more problematic than that of Henry Miller and a nude posing
behind him (figure 9.10) with the outline of a leaf with its striations, transparent, over each eye, the nose, the forehead. Made into an African statue, she is
as primitive and cultured as Kiki among the ferns, bare in the forest.

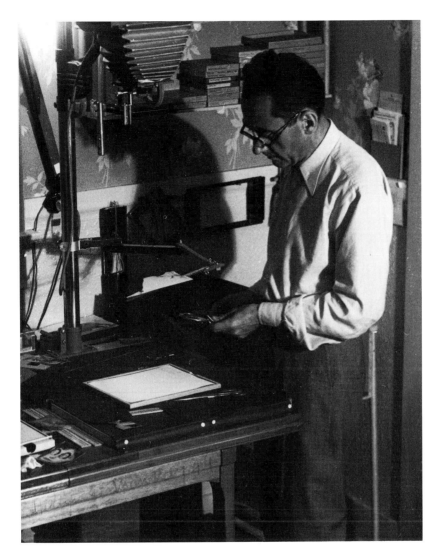

Figure 9.8 Man Ray, *Self-Portrait in Hollywood Studio,* 1944. Gelatin silver print, 9¾ × 7¾ in. The J. Paul Getty Museum, Los Angeles. © 1997 ARS, New York/ADAGP/Man Ray Trust, Paris.

Figure 9.9 Man Ray, *Kiki, Nude,* 1927. Gelatin silver print, 6¹³⁄₁₆ × 5¹⁄₁₆ in. The J. Paul Getty Museum, Los Angeles. © 1997 ARS, New York/ADAGP/Man Ray Trust, Paris.

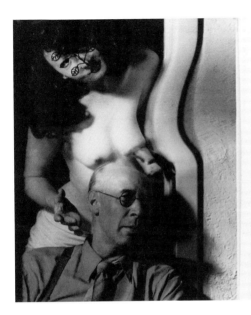

Figure 9.10 Man Ray, *Henry Miller and Masked Nude,* 1945. Gelatin silver print, 9¹³⁄₁₆ × 7¾ in. The J. Paul Getty Museum, Los Angeles. © 1997 ARS, New York/ADAGP/Man Ray Trust, Paris.

BETWEEN NATURE AND ART

Man Ray's treatment of Elsa Schiaparelli in a draped white dress with short-cropped jacket of feathers and a light cast on her short-cropped feathery hair (figure 9.11) works a transformative magic: this bird/woman is caught in profile, the feathers of hair and jacket fluttering downward to the drape upon the dress, as she looks away from the camera and into space. Like a fleeting object of cultural desire, she is so wrapped in feathers that she is about to take flight, a creator of fashion taking off into nature.

CHARGED OBJECTS: ILLUMINATIONS AND IMPOSITIONS

Entirely different in feeling is the image of Kiki posed in one of the frames for *Retour à la raison,* her bare torso striped with the reflection from the window

Figure 9.11 Man Ray, *Elsa Schiaparelli*, 1934. Gelatin silver print, 4¹⁄₁₆ × 2¾ in. The J. Paul Getty Museum, Los Angeles. © 1997 ARS, New York/ADAGP/Man Ray Trust, Paris.

curtain.⁹ The sense is both natural, like an animal—tiger-striped—and cultural, since the reflection reveals a constructed object. This woman is made animal by the imposition of the photographer's design.

Compare with this form of imposition the striking one of Duchamp with the frame of his glass placed over his face (see figure 9.17). Just as striking, in the series of photographs called *Electricité* (figure 9.12), a sharp white tubular line, its very distinctness outlined against the softness of skin, is laid over a nude

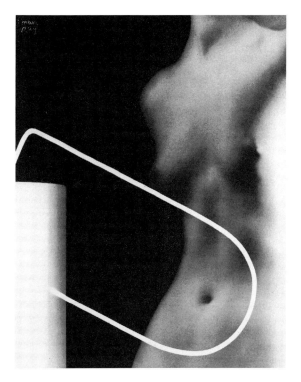

Figure 9.12 Man Ray, *Electricity—Bathroom,* 1931. Gelatin silver print, 10¼ × 8⅛ in. The J. Paul Getty Museum, Los Angeles. © 1997 ARS, New York/ADAGP/Man Ray Trust, Paris.

Figure 8.8

Figure 8.7

female. This is handling with cruelty in the sense of Antonin Artaud's "Theater of Cruelty," part of his *Theater and Its Double,* since it reads like an imposition of necessity.

Compare two other headless female nude torsos with this one. Figure 8.8 further illustrates the erotics of electricity, the body crossed by a bright ribbon of three wavy lines. Both these electrified females, their arms cropped out of the picture like their heads, are caught in a definite swerve against the edge, in a sinous sensuous nude pose, whereas figure 8.7 shows the photographer Lee Miller, half-stripped in a pose of purposeful revelation rather than simply being imposed upon, her body upright with her arms partially visible, held to the sides of her torso. Her pose is frontal, and seems as chosen as it does forceful. The evident beauty of the model's complicity is that she too can master the situation.

In other photographs Man Ray continues to romanticize the glamour of light—for example, a light bulb in the sky sheds white flakes, forming a constellation. This adornment of the natural by the electrical is charged to the limit, making icons of both body and lighting.

This universe speaks loudly and high of relations in the surrealist world and framework, of the delight at bodily exhibition, even of the bodies of objects—it is fashioned carefully and contained without scandal. There is no apparent struggle between model and fashioner or between the objects pictured. Impositions and juxtapositions are achieved without resistance.

Look back. A naked body is visible under the left side of a glass circle (see figure 9.6), part of a lamp. Again a play on illumination, although when we first look at the body, just taking pleasure in the play of glass against flesh, translucent layers against dewy surface, we do not realize that it is indeed part of a lamp. Part of the joy of reading Man Ray's sometimes complicated images is that we come to them slowly. They *develop* in our minds, their artifice becoming natural in our view.[10]

Figure 9.6

ICONS POSED AND WRAPPED

The celebration of the female image calls for multiple techniques—one sometimes has the feeling that Man Ray used them all during his periods of genius. Of which he had many.

One of the most successful glorifications of a female face and its features is the implicit comparison with the religous: thus, Genica Athanasiou is pictured with her head thrown back, her black hair gleaming against the light backdrop, for all the world like some Byzantine icon (figure 9.13). We can almost see her head outlined as with a halo, her face solemn and gorgeously turned to the side, not to face us. Worshippers do not want to, do not need to see face-on. The many photographs of Athanasiou, with head lifted on the diagonal or thrown back, capture that slightly haughty expression, sanctifying her with her own pose, as representative of art as Kiki laughing outside is of nature.

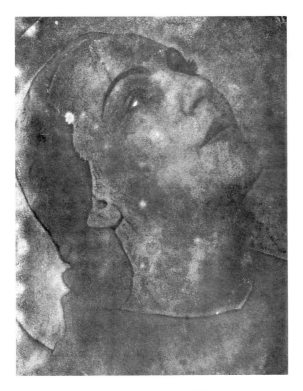

Figure 9.13 Man Ray, *Mlle. Athanasiou,* 1933. Gelatin silver print, 10⅝ × 8³⁄₁₆ in. The J. Paul Getty Museum, Los Angeles. © 1997 ARS, New York/ADAGP/Man Ray Trust, Paris.

More poses, easy to make and take. In 1935 Man Ray posed Nusch Eluard against a background so soft it feels, to the sight, like velvet (figure 9.14). A good illustration for Paul Eluard's volume of poems called *Facile* (*Easy*). Love seemed easy then, and the body was chiseled against the ground. Easy, and carved in deep. We grew used to that; such is the carry-over expectation from the lovely "easy" pose that when we see Rosa Covarrubias sitting in front of her mirror, a large spit curl perfectly in place, dressed only in her slip (itself slipping off one shoulder) and with a towel casually caught between her legs, all of the other easy and beloved images come back, with their own accessory

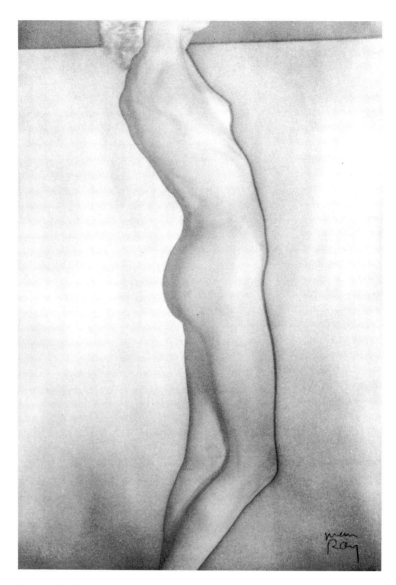

Figure 9.14 Man Ray, *Nusch Eluard, Nude,* 1935. Gelatin silver print, 8^{15}/$_{16}$ × 6^{1}/$_{16}$ in. The J. Paul Getty Museum, Los Angeles. © 1997 ARS, New York/ADAGP/Man Ray Trust, Paris.

objects. This one, however, wears nothing imposed, no stripe or feather or leaf. Eve with a scrap of a towel, just a suggestion of a suggestion. But bringing all of the others back creates a network of Man Ray images, remembrances of his eye and hand, that do the work of the narrative. Juliet even is posed like this sometimes, a blond wig over her hair, nude, with a transparent cloth between her legs (figure 9.15).

It is not all easy. A ghastly and no less iconic imposition comes from 1936, appropriately called *Restored Venus* (figure 9.16). She is just a torso, wrapped in heavy cord, packaged like something Christo would wrap, immobilized like something out of the Marquis de Sade, for beating or then sending like one of Derrida's *Envois*. The lady is very smooth; yet she has, of course, no head about her and cannot protest; no legs, and cannot flee; no arms, and cannot take revenge.[11] She is in fact a statue, which does not reconcile the female viewer to the cording of her body.

No one is posing here as a natural. The reference this time is to the Venus de Milo and the Victory of Samothrace; they are not yet restored to life, but the rope scaffolding is there for restoration. Tied up, and ready to be worked.

FASHIONING THE READER

We are led into the iconization of the image, posed and imposed on, wrapped ready to go. As happens with the model, we as onlookers are seduced into collaboration with the photographer's sight. What, in May Ray's pictures, captures the onlooker as well as the model? It is, on occasion, just the sense of the collusion and collaboration ongoing in the image itself. As an early example, take the frequent collaboration of Man Ray and Marcel Duchamp, developing in 1920.

Against the ascetic, unsmiling, and beautiful face of Marcel Duchamp is superimposed the white frame of his *Large Glass* (1917–1923) (figure 9.17). His eyes look out through the rectangular shape, as though imprisoned by his own glass. Who has chosen the pose here? Whose *is* the imposition here? It is as if Duchamp's *Glass* had been imposed upon its creator, used by Man Ray to frame him. But he is plainly willing, as he collaborates in the pose. In another shot of the same frame and framer, Duchamp is lying down, his hands grasping the

Figure 9.15 Man Ray, *Juliet, Nude in a Blond Wig,* ca. 1950–51. Gelatin silver print, 5⅝ × 4⅛ in. The J. Paul Getty Museum, Los Angeles. © 1997 ARS, New York/ADAGP/Man Ray Trust, Paris.

Figure 9.16 Man Ray, *Restored Venus,* 1936. Gelatin silver print, 6½ × 4½ in.
The J. Paul Getty Museum, Los Angeles. © 1997 ARS, New York/ADAGP/Man
Ray Trust, Paris.

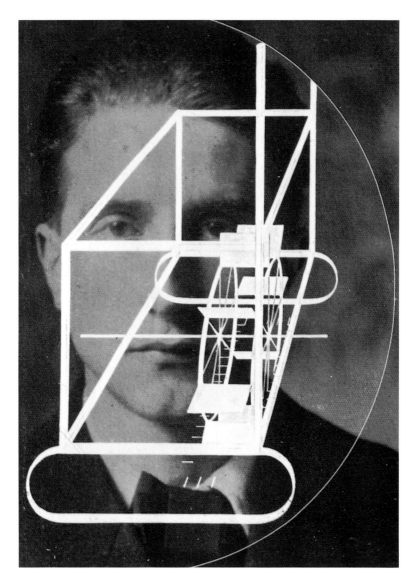

Figure 9.17 Man Ray, *Duchamp with His "Large Glass,"* 1917/23. Gelatin silver print, 6⅝ × 4⅝ in. The J. Paul Getty Museum, Los Angeles. © 1997 ARS, New York/ADAGP/Man Ray Trust, Paris.

hemisphere of the glass in repose; Man Ray then cuts out that image, carefully cutting around the hands, placing it upon a piece of paper, in a further cropping and collage.

Man Ray's well-known photograph of Duchamp tonsured, with a star cut out in the center of his hair may imply ironically that he is a star; it also says that Man Ray was here with his camera, one star photographing another. Already in Man Ray's shot of Marcel lurks a larger-than-life characterization of a figure as myth, of a great conceptual artist as subject/object.

The case is especially complicated in the doubling of the character of Marcel Duchamp in drag, physically and mentally—as Rrose Sélavy (see figure 1.3),[12] always photographed by Man Ray. All three Rrose Sélavy shots of 1920 have a lot to say. "Eros, that is life," reads her name, as she poses in various fashions, impersonated by Marcel, most remarkably as a high-fashion model behatted and perfumed, in the classic pose of *Marcel Duchamp as Rrose Sélavy.* Here as in the other pictures, Marcel EROS, THATISLIFE himself/herself appears in drag, heavy circles around the eyes, thick eyebrows, and a hat bordered with a chic design. There have not been many more seductive poses—something about the offness of the image is instantly attractive. Marcel's wig is rough, and the continuity of texture between its rough hair and the hat border is to be *felt.* The light falls on the back of the fur, and the cheek directly above gives the impression of luxury and of ease, slightly leaning to the side—as if it were not quite as seductive to be straight. The insolence of "her" gaze unsettles, beside her blond wig.

Figure 1.3

More than unsettling, this image is an icon of disquiet. Between her little finger and the others extends an erotic gap, and even the fur collar of her coat lies a trifle sideways. Things are tipped, unbalanced, insolently begging to be questioned. This is a deliberately mystifying Marcel(le), transfigured into a Rrose. Marcel/Marcelle did not, as Rrose Sélavy, have to put on special drag. She was, in *Belle Haleine—Eau de Violette,* (figure 9.18) for example, with the sultry face and necklace, with the perfume bottle opening to the right and slightly protruding erotically, sensually, already a quintessence of *eau de violette/voilette* instead of *eau de toilette,* violet-scented (*violette*) and veiled (*voilette*), like something shimmering in moiré, at once swathed in veils and subtle, cross-dressed, initialed (RS) and exclamatory: (*Eau*-Oh!). The edges of the stopper

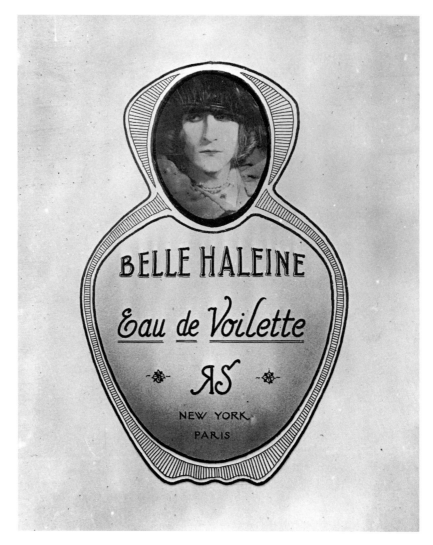

Figure 9.18 Man Ray, *Belle Haleine—Eau de Violette,* 1920–21. Gelatin silver print, 8¹³⁄₁₆ × 7 in. The J. Paul Getty Museum, Los Angeles. © 1997 ARS, New York/ADAGP/Man Ray Trust, Paris.

are striped like hair on either side, and the face looks lovingly at us. In this sultry perfumed scene, even the letters *RS* are reversed, Eros and Sélavy leaning on each other back to back, in a step from a frozen tango: to the beat of "Eros, that Is Life."

Figure 9.14

This kind of ambiguity, frozen and in movement, is characteristic of Man Ray's fashion. For his numerous studies of the body nude and clothed, masked and androgynous, are at once simple and beautiful (see the velvety nude body of Nusch Eluard in figure 9.14), complicated in their crossing, and somehow terrible (see Barbette, the crossover artist, making up, figure 9.19). His studies of masking (see *Henry Miller and Masked Nude,* figure 9.10, and the simple study of *Masks,* figure 9.20) are ultimately baroque, in the sense that crossover can easily be: they are irregular, complicated, and revealing. They transgress, like the extraordinary rendering of Lee Miller's *Neck* (see figure 2.3) made a part of *Anatomies* the next year, and resembling nothing so much as a penis.

Figure 9.19

All of Man Ray's collaborations are themselves crossovers ambiguous and gamy, hung high. In their own posed *look,* both photographer and willing subject are captured in a collaboration that seduces the onlooker, forcibly in cahoots with the pair or entirely excluded. The out-of-sight references often draw the onlooker into the picture implicitly: the myths of nature (birds and country landscapes) and art (ancient statues and Byzantine icons) and, early on, of doubleness, in gender and representation. Man Ray's photographs are not *excluding* or *exclusive*: rather they imply something beyond, in another space. Knowledgeable viewing, in cahoots with the photographer, is preferable to being cropped out.

Figure 9.10

Man Ray fashioned into icons his imagination, modeling itself through his posing figures: Rrose Sélavy is the height of a fiction *à deux,* the double creation of Marcel and Man. Man Ray created more than style—it is a whole erotics of representation, involving the observer.[13] In his associations, isolations, and impositions, he not only iconizes the subject but refashions seeing itself.

Figure 9.20

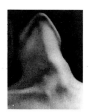

Figure 2.3

Figure 9.19 Man Ray, *Barbette Making Up*. Gelatin silver print, 8⅝ × 6⁷⁄₁₆ in. The J. Paul Getty Museum, Los Angeles. © 1997 ARS, New York/ADAGP/Man Ray Trust, Paris.

Figure 9.20 Man Ray, *Masks*, 1946. Gelatin silver print, 6¹¹⁄₁₆ × 4¹¹⁄₁₆ in. The J. Paul Getty Museum, Los Angeles. © 1997 ARS, New York/ADAGP/Man Ray Trust, Paris.

III

Setting

10

Decor: Desnos in Mourning

Un jour ou une nuit ou autre chose les portes se fermeront: prédiction à la porteé de tous les esprits.
(Some day, some night, or some other time the doors will close: anyone could predict it.)

—*Robert Desnos,* Deuil pour Deuil[1]

Of this town, important in days gone by, we see only the remains. In grief over the loss, the beginning of *Deuil pour deuil* (*Mourning for Mourning*) (1924), looks like the very emblem of nonreferential, undifferentiated absence: "These ruins are situated on the banks of a winding river" (LA, 121). The title laments a loss without revealing the object lost. I'd like to try this hypothesis: the very contents of this story whose ruins begin it are singing their own grief, like Benjamin Péret's piece on the "Ruins of Ruins" in *Minotaure* (figure 10.1). *This loss is the loss of loss itself, and its potential story, now unrecoverable.* Like a baroque *vanitas,* like a figure fingering a hollow skull—Georges de La Tour's Mary Magdalen with her rough dress (see figure 7.5), her rope belt for repentance, her fingers on a skull, the scene lit by her vigil lamp—this city is, as much as any De Chirico rendering, full only of emptiness. In its monumental buildings and underground networks, in all of its "bizarre and varied architecture," this town bears no relation whatsoever to an ordinary city, extant or extinct. It is closest to the extraordinary painting by François de Nomé ("Monsu Desiderio") called simply *A*

Figure 7.5

Photo Alvarez Bravo

Ruines : Ruine des Ruines

PAR BENJAMIN PÉRET

Cerné par mille fantômes obsédants, l'homme sort trébuchant d'un château de ténèbres inoubliables où le hantera toute sa vie jusqu'à ce que, mort, on l'enferme dans un autre château, épouvantail ridicule irrité et haï à la mesure du ver qui le ronge. Mais voici l'homme, fantôme pour lui-même et château aussi par son propre fantôme. Aussi loin qu'on le retrouve, aussi jeune qu'on le voie, son désir prend la forme d'un château : caverne disputée à l'ours ou construction minuscule dont la mémoire ne gardera qu'une image d'aventurine.

Certains indiens troglodytes de New-Mexico façonnent des poupées dont la tête silhouette un château qu'ils n'ont jamais connu et ne connaîtront jamais.

L'homme envie la félicité muette de l'huître et de l'escargot, aspire — s'il est un lamentable petit-bourgeois à la hideuse villa de banlieue, à la paillotte s'il est nomade, s'il est artiste à quelque ruine veloutée

qu'il devra disputer à la végétation et aux oiseaux rapaces, ruine qu'il transplantera dans ses terres s'il vient de s'enrichir dans le commerce des saucisses.

L'homme, pagure, ne voit de la vie que la ruine où cacher l'animal qu'il se défend d'être resté. Mais l'animal s'est transformé. De tigre, il est devenu loup et le loup s'est souvent mué en chien. Le chien issu de chien reconnaît à peine les ruines du loup, mais celles du tigre ne sont plus pour lui qu'une empreinte dans le sable, ce sable dont il a oublié les ruines, images dérisoires de celles qu'il méconnaît.

Cette sale bête d'homme n'a d'autre âme que les fantômes de son enfance qui, à son insu, le subjugueront toute sa vie. Rien de cette enfance qui soit à renier, sinon pour celui qui en est devenu indigne. Rien de l'enfance collective n'est à renier sauf pour les sociétés qui en sont devenues indignes et la glorifient afin de la mieux renier. Mussolini célèbre la Rome

57

Figure 10.1 Benjamin Péret, "Ruine des ruines," in *Minotaure* no. 12–13, 1937.

Figure 10.2 François (de) Nomé (sometimes attributed to "Monsu Desiderio"), *A City in Ruins at Night,* ca. 1625–30. Oil on canvas, 40¾ × 60¼ in. Menil Collection, Houston, Texas.

City in Ruins at Night, baroque in conception and rendering, from 1625–30 or thereabouts (figure 10.2). These monumental and noble traces represent throughout the textual lament what must matter most to a reader of surrealism: a frenetic lyricism pure even of content. The substance of the city is already signaled as absent, so that it can be reconstituted completely upon these very ruins. With the city, the constituent text has been lost.

Like some gigantic De Chirico painting, these ruins, metaphoric and metaphysical, are inscribed with a deep anxiety, pervaded by a sinister unknown. The celebration of this site at once abandoned and undone calls forth a poetry rife with a panic both past and future: "In these deserted and sunny squares, we have been invaded by fear." Under the sway of this voice coming forth from the metallic construction, fear is the constant accompaniment to characters never named but no less present from the start. That no one knows the use of the melancholy construction suffices to place the reader under the sign of a present and future ignorance, extending to the next construction.

BAROQUE SOLITUDE

Who is speaking here, spying on us from atop these deserted towers? This voice sounds forth eternal, like a voice from the dead: "I have lived infinite existences in obscure passageways, in the heart of the mines. I have waged battle against vampires of white marble, but in spite of my clever discourse, I was always really alone" (LA, 122). In fact, the entire text is as permeated with solitude as many of the most celebrated poems of Desnos, like the majestically sad "Never Anyone but You" of 1927:

> Jamais jamais d'autre que toi
> Et moi seul seul seul comme le lierre fané
> des jardins de banlieue seul comme le verre
> Et toi jamais d'autre que toi.[2]
> (Never never anyone but you
> And I alone alone alone like the withered ivy
> of suburban gardens alone like glass
> And you never anyone but you.)

The intense and lyric loneliness of those suburban gardens, no less than that of the city squares, is one of the characteristic moods of surrealism. It is the other side, and perhaps the necessary one, of the exaltation of collective thought and practice.

Desnos uses the same procedure, construction, and subsequent deconstruction of both his loves and his sorrows, always mingled in his experience. Indeed, the ideal decor of this solitude and this linguistic deconstruction, of this elaboration of nothing and of nothingness proves to be the very ruin on which *Deuil pour deuil* opens and closes. As the text takes back up what is presented as a not-knowing and an undoing, the enigmatic remains of the past successfully defeat any possibility of present or future knowledge: "These ruins are situated on the banks of a winding river. The climate is nondescript. To the Southwest there rises a metallic construction with openings, very high, and whose purpose we haven't been able to determine" (LA, 123).

For reason itself, we are in mourning here. The anxious desire to know how something is used (*l'usage*) is situated as far as possible from the surrealist celebration of the state of open and unspecified expectation (*l'état d'attente*), that expecting just of always potential expecting. Besides the material substance represented in the text, a parallel mental construction appears. The textual building itself is pierced with openings into nothingness, as is the reader's perception: ruins and holes correspond. Thence the obsession with the closure of the imagination as of its writing: "One day or night or another time the doors will be closed: a prediction any mind can make" (LA, 123).

The convergence of mysterious text and mystifying architecture, of empty gaps between the words and openings into nothingness, silence and closings-off into solitude immobilize the spectator before the unmoving spectacle. There is nothing to say when the emptiness separates us more even than words. Lost between the ruins, lacking even a city once known and then lost, the reader is likely to experience an utter desolation right in the place of those textual ruins that may seem, if only for a moment, in the duration of reading, to be more real than the others.

The Corner of the Eye

The figure coming forward looks like a fairy-tale heroine endowed with an erotic saintliness: "The woman clothed in sky-blue advances rapidly in spite of her high heels, with the double halo of Saints Peter and Paul around her naked breasts, thanks to two gaping openings in the satin of her high bodice" (LA, 124). Like another sort of opening in the textual performance, this bodice rising high but revealing what and where it must says a great deal about what to expect from the expectation, itself raised toward what gapes open.

Instead of a name, this woman will always be known by these sky-blue draperies. Yet such a celestial color does not guarantee the terrestrial perfection of the heroine, and her bizarre secret is revealed by another gap laid open in the very act of disguise: "But what about her, the woman in sky-blue? (she's always the same), I never tire of talking about her and disguising her, careful of course to dissimulate before your eyes the pincers of a violet lobster that serve as her feet" (LA, 125). A careful dissimulation indeed, pointing itself out with that typical surrealist gesture: show, tell, and say you are hiding. To this woman the secret arts seem intimately linked, and she makes a show of hiding. For now the secret is mentioned again, and repeated, whispering to be remembered: "The little snakes whistled in my ear; by chance I said two letters aloud, the initials of the woman in sky-blue with the bare breasts, with lobster pincers instead of feet" (LA, 125).

Like Louise Lame later in *La Liberté ou l'amour!* (1928) this heroine is already steeped in the mystery to the point of not representing anything other than the very repetition of her leitmotiv. When, for once, she loses her sky-blue costume, through a strictly formal exchange in the narrative arena, she can only leave. There has already been one absorption, that of the dancers in black tights by the crocodile, who then becomes a black bracelet, offering the opportunity for an anthropological exchange or potluck as a departure ceremony: "I gave this bracelet to the woman with sky-blue costume. In exchange, she gave me her clothes. I saw her leaving completely naked in the night, between the trees" (LA, 125).

This disappearance marks the end of one chapter of the novel, which is structured like a long prose poem in which the stanzas end with departures, plunging into sleep or death. Yet through some multiplying procedure, this disappearing person makes way for two completely other persons, a woman white and rose and another of Prussian blue: "The woman on the right, the woman on the left," says the narrator. Everything is in expansion: from one woman two, from one direction, two—yet in spite of the proliferation of figures, of objects, of meanings filling this poetic universe, an undercurrent of solitude dominates.

One of the most emotionally charged cries issuing forth from this solitude stands as—is disguised as—a challenge to any interpretation: "Do you have the change for my coin? No one in the world can have the change for my coin"

(LA, 128). If there is never anyone but Robert Desnos in the world of his own currency, he is nevertheless able to fill his world with what he calls "the prismatic binoculars of my imagination" (LA, 126). He will find a metamorphosis still more baroque, as if to exemplify both the imaginary and the magical ("The magic of colors which, for painters, is not yet a commonplace, was held in my little spoon" [LA, 126]).

The woman on the left, once she has become a little leg of lamb wearing a high ruffled collar, richly sliced, can nourish the entire passage that follows:

> Little streams as white as mild and still shining like diamonds were spilling out of the tender flesh, filling a champagne glass. This outdated container grew larger and larger as the liquid ran into it so that there was never more than one drop of liquid in the bottom, reflected in each one of its chiseled facets. Thanks to the sun, each of these virtual images represented my face and one foot of the woman on the right in its blue stocking. As the glass widened at the top, the whole picture grew larger without being noticeably deformed. (LA, 126)

The text wanders, lost. In the traces of this woman on the right, you can see the word *corridor* lit up, as if we ourselves were about to take that path instead of just following a woman down it, as if we were to follow Kiki as she wanders along a lonely path in the film *L'Etoile de mer* (figure 10.3), in its joining of the starfish in the title with sea, night, love, and mystery. The blur of this image of Kiki conveys exactly that blurring of boundaries and that atmosphere where nothing is clear as in daylight or sharp in profile: a setting propitious for the erotics of encounter with which this book is concerned.

POINTING FINGER

Figure 2.2

The dada/surrealist gesture picks up the age-old fascination with the pointing finger, discussed later in the case of Duchamp and his *Tu m'* (see figure 2.2) and other related pointings. Indeed, one of Desnos's most effective sketches is called

Figure 10.3 Man Ray, *Still from "Etoile de mer,"* 1928. Gelatin silver print, 9 × 11⅝ in. The J. Paul Getty Museum, Los Angeles. © 1997 ARS, New York/ADAGP/Man Ray Trust, Paris.

"In the Midst of Fists and Pointing Fingers" (figure 10.4). The figure of Bossuet raises his white finger in the air, picking up on the pointing finger in Michel Leiris's *Cardinal Point.* Further along, the words *corner of the eye* are written in capital letters, the visual and verbal indications designating something about to happen. As if the pointing finger were calling our attention not to what is pointed at but rather to the pointing itself. And it does: "My double waiting was not in vain."

But what is awaited? When these two women disappear, on the right and the left, the narrator has in front of him a blond beauty, naked to her waist as she waters her geraniums, and later, a brunette beauty with bright eyes angrily attacking the separation of physical, psychological, and grammatical elements, intertwining them: "I am and you are and still I can't say that we are. The

Figure 10.4 Robert Desnos: Original illustration, 1925, "Au milieu des poings et des doigts indicateurs" found in the manuscript, *The night of loveless nights,* by Robert Desnos. Anvers, published privately, 1930. Pencil and ink on paper, sheet: 8⁵⁄₁₆ × 11⅛ in. The Museum of Modern Art Library, New York. Photograph © 1996 The Museum of Modern Art, New York. © 1997 ARS, New York/ADAGP, Paris.

ridiculous convention of the verb separates us and attracts us. . . . I am the brunette Beauty and the blonde Beauty. The triumphal beauty without beauty. I am You and you are I" (LA, 130).

Surrealism rarely lets us lose the consciousness of the all-importance of language: a thing in itself, a substance as untreatable as a person. In every case, when the contraries meet, their union is quickly over: the whole narration, whether of presence or lack, is based on this splitting of elements, on this disquieting symmetry, baroque to a fault. Through such a love of doubling, of enigma, and of contraries as is displayed here, the baroque spirit and its techniques of repetition, anaphora, chiasmic and reversible structures enter into the very heart of surrealist vision.

DOUBLING BACK

The figure of the double presides over the astonishing text of mourning with which this chapter began. Here, the North Star is matched by the South Star, Assassination by Night, and so on. The symmetry attracts both the eye and the ear, even as it disquiets the mind: for this baroque representation progressively underlines the unreality of the text, its specular and spectacular side, frequently in spite of the "real" substance of what is said to be "everyday life."

Furthermore, at each reappearance of these doubles, the tone rises a notch, like an index finger raised—it points in *La Liberté ou l'amour!* like a deictic sign. Even when only implicit, it makes its presence felt. The phallic force of this finger attracts an equal feminine force, raising the whole construction on high, like that bodice with a gap enabling the erotics of encounter.

As in the Renaissance blazons, the celebration of each corporeal element occurs through enumerating one element after another. Desnos's poem "O Douleurs de l'amour" ("Oh Grief of Love") (1926) undertakes an identical procedure in which the entire catalogue of female parts does not succeed in convincing the reader or even the narrator that the woman can be known by the list of her parts. This is the undoing of the surrealist construction.[3] Here the corporeal elements are exclaimed rather than explained:

> And so the lovely violet! the lovely violet with
> red hair, the lovely little veil, scarlet earlobes,
> eater of sea urchins whose prestigious crimes have
> slowly deposited tears of an admirable blood
> admired by all the heavens above upon her dress,
> her precious dress. Will she strangle them with her
> diamantine fingers, she, the charming South Star,
> taking the treacherous advice of the North Star,
> the magic, tempting and adorable North Star whose
> nipple is replaced by a diamond at the very point
> of a hot breast white as the reflection of the
> noonday sun? . . .

Treacherous North Star!
Troubling South Star!
Adorable!
Adorable! (LA, 132–33)

Vanitas

Such richly baroque enumeration prepares the drama of a *vanitas* construction as a white skeleton is covered with a blue dolman jacket, life covering death. This jacket originated in the blue costume of the mysterious woman of the mourning text of 1924, well before the poems addressed "to the mysterious one," in 1927–28.

You might believe yourself in a baroque Dutch painting, such as those by Willem Claez Heda (figure 10.5), where goblets and watches and hourglasses are neighbors of the instruments of eating well. The theme is again as much death as life: a glass is overturned, a fly rests amid the meat, the peel is being cut from the lemon, like the familiar marks of mortal and artistic destiny:

> On the table are set a glass and a bottle in memory of a blond virgin who first knew in this room the disturbing menstrual wound and who, lifting her right arm toward the ceiling and her left one toward the window, could cause carrier pigeons to fly about in triangles. Over there, where the burning sands of the desert jealously hide a jacket of tender blue upon a mannequin of white bone, she kneels, beseeching the heavens to transform themselves into a scarf to cover her shoulders, truly a bit bony but quite delicate in relation to the stripes of the whip that will unfailingly fall upon her and her rump stretched out, far away from here, in the silver mines of the Baikal, in the depths of a gallery and in Czarist times. (LA, 133)

In this key passage, the glass and the bottle meet to make love, like Lautréamont's sewing machine and the umbrella, its too well-known partner on the dissection table, signs of this joyous life that will make necessary room for

Figure 10.5 Willem Claesz Heda, *Banquet Piece with Mince Pie,* 1635. Oil on canvas, 42½ × 43½ in. Patron's Permanent Fund. © Board of Trustees, National Gallery of Art, Washington.

mortality. This blond virgin, transformed into a punishable being like a twin sister of some penitent Magdalen, will go pray in the desert to expiate her sins. She is even dressed all in blue, as in the Correggio *Noli me tangere* (figure 10.6), pleading at the feet of a mannerist Christ.

When the scene is transported to the Czarist epoch, the somber colors of desert and mines are replaced by a still life ironically vivid, almost beatific after the strokes of the whiplash, as if they had already expiated what had to be:

Figure 10.6 Correggio, *Noli me tangere,* 1518–1524, Oil on panel, transferred to canvas, 103 × 103 cm. Prado Museum, Madrid.

While waiting, the blonde virgin [*la vierge blonde*] dips her hair in my coffee; it is noon, the wine becomes a dove in the liter of wine [*le litre légal*] placed on the table beside a many-sided glass [*à côté d'un verre à côtes.*] The coffee will become tea, the blonde virgin will turn a bit pale: from now on, she will sing a lovelier song than the nightingale. Someone rings the bell; in his corduroy suit [*habit de velours à côtes*] the legal doctor [*le médecin légal*] enters. He sits down. He frees the dove closed up in the liter, overturns the glass that becomes an hourglass, kisses the blond virgin on her lips. (LA, 133)

As by a magic trick before our eyes, the words transform the elements. The glass with its many sides produces the doctor's corduroy suit; the liter proclaims its legality; the wine becomes a dove, as in some new verbal communion of elements. In shifts progressively more sudden, the legal liter becomes a crown, the glass becomes a glass eye, the narrator falls asleep on a glass table, the readers become fake doves in mortal sin, and the entire deluge enters the liter on the glass table: all of that action is summed up in a glass, as in a looking glass for the reflections, visual and verbal.

Immediately afterward the blond virgin produces the military tailor called Leblond, and the story starts off again, after a pause within the drinking glass. The blue jacket finally covers the sins of the virgin and the mortal announcement of the skeleton as the cloak of flesh covers over the sins in the baroque red sonnet of Jean de La Ceppède;

> Aux monarques vainqueurs la rouge cotte d'armes
> Appartient justement. Ce Roi victorieux
> Est justement vêtu par ces moqueurs gens d'armes
> D'un manteau qui le marque et prince et glorieux.
> . . .
> O Christ, ô saint Agneau, daigne-toi de cacher
> Tous mes rouges péchés, brindilles des abîmes,
> Dans les sanglants replis du manteau de ta chair.[4]

> (To vanquishing monarchs the crimson coat of arms
> Justly belongs. This victorious King
> Is justly clothed by these mocking men of arms
> With a cloak marking him prince and glorious.
>
> . . .
>
> Oh Christ, oh holy Lamb, deign to hide
> All my red sins, twigs of the abyss,
> In the bleeding folds of the cloak of your flesh.)

The oddly corporeal costume is reflected later in one of Desnos's last and classic poems: "the cloak of your flesh, Calixto." The baroque finds its truest post-reflection in surrealism, from its early to its classic stages. Baroque blood disturbs more than any other . . .

How to emerge from this verbal/visual expansion? First of all, in a lyric crescendo. The blonde virgin suddenly completes her scene in a surreal rapidity: "While . . . while . . ." while the tone rises expectantly to the summit of each part. One after the other, these partial conclusions open on the cosmos: "And the pearl eternally fixed on the rudder will be astonished that the boat remains forever immobile under a ocean of fir not suspecting the magnificent fate granted to its equals on the civilized earth, in the cities where the bar bouncers have sky-colored jackets" (LA, 137).

The scene is then described in a faraway representation: "But the passerby passes, and the ferocious sky remains cloudless. Great sky" (LA, 144). At this distance the sleeping narrator projects his dreams:

> I fell asleep.
> He is sleeping, said the moon.
> And slowly, she began to tell her beads of stars. . . . The stars grew paler one by one and the morning whitened my temples. . . . I was sleeping. . . . Oh crowd passing in this street, respect my sleep. The great organs of the sun keep you to your pace, I shall awake this evening when the moon starts praying.
> I shall leave for the coast where no ship ever lands; one will come with a black flag aft. The rocks will part. I shall mount.

And from then on my friends, from their high observatory, will spy on the deeds and gestures of the bands of black tents spread out in the plain, while above them the moon will say its prayers. . . .

It will tell its beads of stars and distant cathedrals will collapse.

I shall return only with the blonde virgin, the lovely charming blonde virgin who will cause the moon to pale over the flowering appletrees. (LA, 145–46)

As a final curtain to the metamorphosis of the dormant scenes, the somnolent repetition: "Sleep I say . . . It's sleep, it's sleep . . . It's sleep" (LA, 158) beds down the story.

Concluding Conceit

As in metaphysical, mannerist, or baroque poetry, the perfect ending is a *concetto,* a sharp point both conceptual and verbal, a turn, a twist, a knotting and knotting up. From this text spun out of dream elements and their language the true exit forms a conceit at once baroque and consonant with the tone of the whole. An immense granite boulder with the shape of a woman's breast recalls the diamond nipple of star already evoked, now grown larger and opaque. Here the granite rests in a cemetery like a repository of this whole second text, constructed textually after the initial textual deconstruction from the ruins to the cemetery. Chiseled into a sign, it is described as "a paperweight on a deadman, perhaps himself become paper," thanks to the rotted materials used to fabricate what is written on "and perhaps even the paper on which this eulogy is written" (LA, 160). We are then caught up in the retrospective metapoetic light as a parody of all the splendid black story.

For the desired baroque and surrealist illumination, reality sheds too simple a clarity. The miracle of this prose so highly poeticized, so metatextually conscious, is that finally the fabrication of it, brought to light and to mortality, takes its full vital meaning of loss and victory in the word *éloge.* The darkly baroque *vanitas* meets the sparkling theater of words united before the "hollow

orbs" of our eyes—as if we readers were to be changed into De Chirico's antique statues, transcending our own time.

Instead of a desert weeper, of a blonde virgin in a bar, the final representation is a nameless dead man who takes the role of skeleton modeling a light
blue jacket with dolman sleeves. Such an apparent diminution of the blue dress
implies the rotting fabric of death and, as Desnos suggests, the paper on which
this whole story has been traced: "There, didn't I say so? The magnetized but-
tons of the uniforms ripped out the eyes of the blonde virgin who, blind from
then on, will take through the fields the lamentation of her body and her soul"
(LA, 140). So the story goes further than the sentimentalizing regrets of loss
and the trivialized comedy of an only verbal game, to take upon itself the "background sound of a terrible satanic burst of laughter" (LA, 160).

In this final reflection a high resplendent lyric resounds as the cry of the
great baroque modern poet Robert Desnos.

11

Painting: Artaud and Monsieur Désir

> . . . y questa vida
> Es sueño, y los sueños sueños son.
> (. . . and this life
> Is but a dream, and dreams are only dreams.)
>
> —*Calderón de la Barca,* La Vida es sueño[1]

It is like a great and complicated meeting of legends. First, three artists share this one invented name of "Monsu Desiderio," invented by B. De Dominici in 1742: the French landscape painter Didier Barra, called by the Italians Monsu (for "foreigner") and Desiderio, an Italianization of Didier; then, François de Nomé, born, like Barra, in Metz, around 1593, like Barra again, and working, like Barra, in Naples, to whom the works formerly attributed to Barra (as Monsu Desiderio) are now reattributed; and finally, Francesco Desideri, an engraver from Pistoia.[2] The resonance of this odd shifting attribution hovers over Desiderio, this monsieur of desire.

No odder than Robert Desnos, who takes dictation, during his hypnotized sleeps, from someone he calls Rrose Sélavy, whose name is celebrated by Marcel Duchamp in drag. Monsu Desiderio as Monsieur Désir and Mademoiselle Rrose Sélavy might well be stepping out together. Who is to say what they might produce?

And indeed, de Nomé's painting *A City in Ruins at Night* (1625–30) (see figure 10.2) evokes Desnos's wonderful title for his text on ruins: *Deuil pour deuil*

Figure 10.2

(Mourning for Mourning). De Nomé is celebrated for his ruins; Desnos should be. In this ruin, everything slants up toward the right, toward the statues still standing in their niches, like immortalized forms of the human figures to the lower left, of whom no experts seem to know whether they are in the subject or out, as commentators on the *vanitas* theme. Light plays against dark, sky against earth, ruins against what remains, living forms against statues, vertical against horizontal until the mind dizzies. This is surrealist mannerism, this is the baroque as modern as it will become.

The whole thing is odd, all of it heading for ruin. The most dramatic of de Nomé's paintings—thus thought of as a painting by Monsu Desiderio until recently—is *King Asa of Judah Destroying the Idols* (or *Asa Destroying the Statue of Priapus: Explosion in a Church*) (figure 11.1), based on the episode (1 Kings 15:11–15) in which the King of Israel, Asa, destroys the pagan idol as he reestablishes his people's faith in Judaism, the scene transferred from the banks of the Cedron river to a temple like a church. The dramatic destruction and tumult on stage left, with columns toppled and exploding as from some interior force, remind the viewer of the appearance of hell itself in Christian renderings. This violent scene is dramatically distanced from the calm on stage right, the heavenly side, by the central grisaille in the form of an arch, with its statues and small figures far from us. Everything works against presence: as if the action, gestures, and reasons for it all were to be silenced and distanced, like the violence necessarily occurring offstage in the corridor of some classic French drama. The overall view is thus put in perspective, with only the results gone hellish, the consequence playing out on our emotions. You might think the canvas itself would explode or implode into its own grisaille. The scene might have been painted by Bosch, although the space here is treated as by Tintoretto, with the dizzying swirl of his *Presentation of in the Temple* (c. 1552)(figure 11.2), where figures seem to stagger up the side of a pyramid against a centripetal force. You walk with them, feeling every moment as if you might fall off, or are hurled toward a space that draws the eye, the mind, and the imagination.

This is how most Tintoretto paintings work: take *The Discovery of the Body of Saint Mark* (c. 1562) (figure 11.3) set in Saint Mark's in Venice. You feel you are lying on the floor with the body, encountering some miracle or other. You are

Figure 11.1 François (de) Nomé, *King Asa of Judah Destroying the Idols (or: Asa Destroying the Statue of Priapus: Explosion in a Church.* Oil on canvas, n.d., 29⅛ × 39½ in. Fitzwilliam Museum, Cambridge.

penned into a claustrophobic space even as you are hurled mentally by the man pointing toward the bright opening at the end. He forces your attention out.

When, in this famous architectural conceit (see figure 11.1), the space is set up for explosion, we witness a reversal characteristic of the early baroque, for example those of the Renaissance poet Joachim Du Bellay. His *Songes (Dreams),* in the *Antiquities of Rome,* repeatedly portray the raising of monuments and their subsequent destruction. An elegant ship capsizes and sinks to the bottom of a stream, or a great castle blows over: in the wrecking of the constructed form, the poem itself, which builds in momentum and architectural accumulation, is razed to the ground by some chance accident. That these great reversals

Figure 11.2 Jacopo Tintoretto, *Presentation of the Virgin in the Temple,* c. 1552. Oil on canvas, 14 ft. 1 in. × 15 ft. 9 in., Madonna dell Orto, Venice. Alinari/Art Resource.

in Renaissance space are labeled *Dreams* (songes) permits us to predict this baroque reversal.[3]

This vision climaxing in ruin is comparable to Desnos's *Deuil pour Deuil,* in which the buildup is followed by a scene of ruins, itself the buildup for subsequent elaboration. In Du Bellay, we read:

> I saw, raised high on ivory columns,
> With bases of richest metal,
> Alabaster capitals and crystal friezes,
> The double forehead of a memorial arch.

Figure 11.3 Jacopo Tintoretto, *The Discovery of the Body of St. Mark,* c. 1552. Milan, Italy Brerary. Alinari/Art Resource.

On each side a victory scene,
Wings on its back, clothed as a nymph,
Seated high, on a triumphal chariot,
Most ancient glory of Roman emperors.

The work showed no human making,
It seemed created by this same hand
Forging the father's jagged flash.

173

I want, alas, no more lovely sights
Having seen before my eyes
Such a work fall suddenly to dust.[4]

Having mourned so much ill chance
I saw a city almost like the one
That the bringer of good news saw,
But its support was built on sand.

Its head seemed to touch the heavens,
Its form no less proud than fine:
Deserving above others, not to die,
Firmly founded as anything under the sky.

I was marvelling at such a lovely work,
When from the north the cruel storm blew,
Gusting the fury of its spiteful heart

On everything in the way of its coming,
Overturning, with a powdery cloud,
The weak foundations of the great city.[5]

The point here, I think, is that the building must be great in order for its down-
fall to mean anything; the city must be great, with the nobility of the antique.
So it is with an immense cathedral, symbolic with tradition, majestic in its space,
bold as a palace.

These monuments overturned then, by a baroque wind, count heavily.
Furthermore, these tempestuous overturnings themselves build on each other:
one who has seen such a spectacle, albeit in a dream, is prepared for sights to
come. This is the mood of Calderón's "Toda la vida es sueño, y los sueños
sueños son." To build anything is already to build on sand. The baroque would
know that, and the Renaissance was finding it out, through dreaming it that
way. This is the epoch of Francisco Quevedo's sonnets of riches falling to dust,
gold to powder, and to *nada,* that finally present *nothing* as the sure sign of the
splendor of the past.

MORE VANITAS

Such is the flavor of all the celebrated *vanitas* paintings like the one discussed above (see figure 7.5), with Mary Magdalene gazing at the candle, her fingers on the skull, or with the crystal broken, the lemon peeling, the fly grazing on the fullness of what will rot, in its richness undone: if it can happen to these, then it can happen to us. Mortality is everywhere.

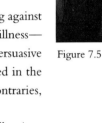

Figure 7.5

Strangely, the contraries of the baroque mentality—water playing against fire, ruin against wholeness, sickness against health, motion against stillness— accumulate in the surrealist sensitivity, to which one of the most persuasive witnesses has always been the locomotive stopped, arrested at full speed in the virgin forest. All of the *arrests* are based on this same convergence of contraries, already baroque in flavor.

What the surrealists took from the baroque mentality about this illuminative, regenerative force of the contraries clashing inspires their own poetry with a passion as memorable as it is problematic. When the elements merge, it sounds like myth: "Flame of water," ends Breton's great poem "Sur la route de San Romano," "Lead me to the sea of fire." The energy of tension here is equivalent to the baroque reversals in a flexible universe. The architectural building up and in of such paintings and poems delineates a field in which the energy of contraries is released.

If we consider the appearance of de Nomé's cathedrals or churches *before* the explosion, they appear to have a remarkably complex constructions. Take the deceptive calm of the *Interior of a Cathedral* (figure 11.4), in the Menil Collection: we might think it at first the opposite of explosion, a great, quiet sweep of space interrupted only by corridors of arches, lined with statues, to wander in, in meditation. But on examination, we see how the figures in stained glass, so carefully painted, oppose with their bright colors, each set off in a separate division, the cluster of small dark figures in the foreground. These figures are positioned in silhouette, against the clearer central nave, watching as we are. To our left, the reddish portals strangely open into the corridors of arches to either side of the nave. A dramatic play of light and dark enlivens the architectured space, somber on our left, bright in the center, and once more somber on the far right. We see, furthermore, how the careful details of the stained glass

Figure 11.4 François (de) Nomé, *Interior of a Cathedral,* n.d., 17th century. Oil on canvas, 76 × 124 in. The Menil Collection.

windows contrast with the "broader" or "painterly" passages of the sculptures, as J. Patrice Marandel points out in his introduction to the paintings.[6] The same is true another of Nomé's odd and obsessive renderings, the *Interior of a Church* in Budapest, where the small figures in foreground and background stand in silhouette against a startlingly bright central portal that seems to lead out onto the portal of another church—like one of Magritte's paintings in which the inside and outside of buildings are uncertainly differentiated. To the left, more small figures, dressed in red like the ones against the central portal, make gestures whose meaning we cannot determine. The light streaming in the left portal makes us unsure what is in and what is out. To the right, other tiny figures in red and blue are seen against the sculptures, lit by this light from the left.

Any initial calm is deceptive in any of de Nomé's church paintings. And so, still focusing on his superbly explosive cathedral painting, we feel how the cathedral of the poem or painting built up in the mind itself circumscribes the energies, holds them in, until—when the conflagration takes place, so that one side of the painting falls in ruin—the entire manifestation of human imagining catches fire.

Imagine then, how by analogy we can look at such a poem as that of Octavio Paz, beginning with a great wave of springtime water, and leading, through a powerful image of a cathedral on fire, to a final convergence of poem, conflagration, and architecture held forever in a green stone symbolizing eternity and turning forever.

Here in this early poem of Paz, a quasi-surrealist space, contrary elements determine the structure:

Como la marejada verde de marzo en el campo
Entre los años de sequía te abres paso
Nuestras miradas se cruzan se entrelazan
Tejen un transparente vestido de fuego
Una yedra dorada que te cubre
Alta y desnuda sonríes como la catedral el día del incendio
Con el mismo gesto de la lluvia en el trópico lo has arrasado todo
Los días harapientos caen a nuestros pies
No hay nada sino dos seres desnudos & abrazados
Un surtidor en el centro de la pieza
Manantiales que duermen con los ojos abiertos
Jardines de agua flores de agua piedras preciosas de agua
Verdes monarquías

La noche de jade gira lentamente sobre sí misma

(Like the green surf of April in the fields
Between the years of drought you open a way
Now the looks of our eyes are met are laced together

They weave a transparent cloth out of this fire
Ivy of gold to cover you
Tall and naked you smile like the cathedral the day of the fire
With the same gesture the rain makes in the tropics washing all
    away
The days in their rags fall down at our feet
There is nothing in the world but two beings naked embraced
A fountain in the middle of the room
Springs of origin sleeping with open eyes
Gardens of water flowers of water precious stones of water
Green sovereignties

The night of jade turns slowly upon itself)[7]

—tr. Muriel Ruykeyser

In the baroque legacy to surrealism, there is a whiff of romanticism, the movement of which, as André Breton says, surrealism is the prehensile tail. In both this baroque merging of contraries and this surrealist absorption of the explosive energies of difference, the extremes of intensity reached by the passion of the poem or the painting are of romantic appeal, as is the fascination with the ruin into which the explosion internal or external forces the art work.[8] For that ruin indicates the obsession with the incomplete, with what Thomas McFarland, in *Romanticism and the Forms of Ruin,* has called the modalities of fragmentation or "disparactions," a term he derives from the Greek: to render asunder or into pieces. Treating romanticism as "incompleteness, fragmentation, and ruin," he quotes Hegel: "The life of mind only wins its truth when it finds itself totally torn asunder." This is romanticism's great force, and this very disparactive awareness leads straight to nostalgia for a land where all will be perfect, full, and shining, as in Goethe's memorable "Land wo die Zitronen bluhn."[9]

Surrealism calls itself "the tail of romanticism, but how prehensile a tail"—and indeed the romanticism of ruins pervades the publications in *Le Minotaure* and elsewhere. "The Ruins of Ruins," runs the title of a piece by Benjamin Péret. These ruins are behind the surrealists' urge to visit the land of passion and ruin that is Mexico. They wanted a New World, and here in Central America they found it, embracing it even when they had to intensify their own vision and language to meet it.

So Antonin Artaud visits the country of the Tarahumaras, participates in the rites of peyoté, and offers himself up for sacrifice (figure 11.5). This land wherein all is written in blood—where the Solar God plays out his drama against the red earth—is supposed to teach us how to repassion the world, and poetry. For Artaud, Mexico represents "a sensibility of the flayed."[10] We moderns have, it turns out, a great attraction to such scenes: Robert Motherwell reminded me how Titian's *Flaying of Marysas* has captured the world's imagination[11] (figure 11.6).

I remember looking with Motherwell at some of those yellow *calaveras* or death skulls made in sugar dyed in Mexico to that memorably bright shade, ghastly and yet riveting. This is, I think, the attraction of such baroque overturnings of the ordinary way of seeing—say, a skull and a black cloth—such surprises in color and concept and reminders for the modern mind of its inheritance of converging contraries (figure 11.7).

Breton was particularly intrigued by Artaud's accounts of Mexico after he had returned from nine months there. In the fall of 1937 Breton was offered a series of lectures there, as he put it, "in the one country that attracted me."[12] Artaud, of course, ended up in another country of the mind . . . (figure 11.8).

The great appeal of Mexico for the surrealists can be explained by both the romantic and the baroque strains in surrealism. What we could think of as the baroque upset—overturning and destroying, undoing and making a ruin of what one sees—is in fact an intense elation, as the romantics knew so well. What gives life back its passion—that great goal of surrealism—may often pass by the sacrifice of blood (figure 11.9). To restore the myths: that was the particular emphasis of much of Péret's work, and the basis of Artaud's lyricism. "How myths are restored"—in a sense, the restoration of myth and its enabling passion is equivalent to the restoration of mystery to the European soul. Péret's *Anthologie des Mythes, Légendes et contes populaires d'Amérique*[12] speaks to this restoration. So this "Voyage to the land of speaking blood,"—as Artaud refers to it in his *Trip to Mexico* (1936)—is a quest for the unification of poetry and passion, of word and blood. "I came to Mexico to look for a new idea of man," he claims.[13]

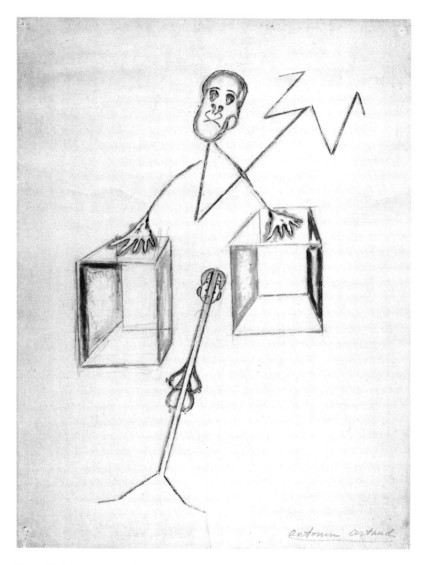

Figure 11.5 Antonin Artaud, *La Mort et l'homme (Death and Man),* c. April 1946. Graphite and wax crayon, 25⅞ × 20 in. Musée National d'Art Moderne—Centre de Création Industrielle, Centre Georges Pompidou, Paris. Gift of Michel Ellenberger, 1988. © 1997 Estate of Antonin Artaud/ARS, New York.

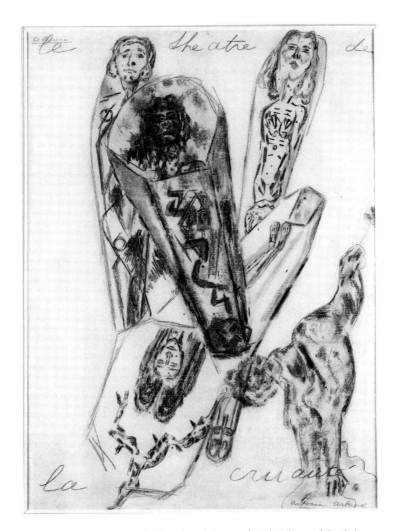

Figure 11.6 Antonin Artaud, *"Le théâtre de la cruauté" (The Theater of Cruelty),*
c. March 1946. Graphite and wax crayon, 24¾ × 18⅛ in. Musée National d'Art
Moderne—Centre de Création Industrielle, Centre Georges Pompidou, Paris.
Bequest of Paule Thévenin, 1993. © 1997 Estate of Antonin Artaud/ARS,
New York.

Figure 11.7 Antonin Artaud, *"Les illusions de l'âme" (The Illusions of the Soul),* c. January 1946. Graphite and wax crayon, 24⅞ × 18⅞ in. Musée National d'Art Moderne—Centre de Création Industrielle, Centre Georges Pompidou, Paris. Gift of Michel Ellenberger, 1987. © 1997 Estate of Antonin Artaud/ARS, New York.

Figure 11.8 Antonin Artaud, *L'Inca (The Inca)*, c. March 1946. Graphite and wax crayon, 25¼ × 18⅞ in. Musée National d'Art Moderne—Centre de Création Industrielle, Centre Georges Pompidou, Paris. Bequest of Paule Thévenin, 1993. © 1997 Estate of Antonin Artaud/ARS, New York.

183

Figure 11.9 Antonin Artaud, *Les Corps de terre (Earth's Bodies),* 3 May 1946. Graphite and wax crayon, 25¾ × 19⅞ in. Musée National d'Art Moderne—Centre de Création Industrielle, Centre Georges Pompidou, Paris. © 1997 Estate of Antonin Artaud/ARS, New York.

A firm belief in the force of analogy lies, of necessity, just behind such a quest. The cycle of nature from birth to death to rebirth must correspond to that of the human body, but also to that of the human mind, rejuvenated by observing the ritual of seasons, or more abruptly by the violence of sacrifice, whether psychological or architectural. The texts of Artaud, increasingly mad, illustrate the energy of signs and symbols, understandable or not (figure 11.10). Already, in *The Theater and Its Double,* natural forces permeate his highest and most vivid drama. Here he speaks of Lucas van Leyden's *Lot and his Daughters* (figure 11.11), found in the Louvre:

> Even before one has had a chance to determine what is going on, one senses that it is something of great importance, and one almost feels that the ear is moved at the same time as the eye. A drama of high intellectual significance seems to have been concentrated here like a sudden gathering of clouds which the wind or some much more compelling force has brought together to measure their thunder. (A, 228)

This is exactly the dramatic *high* toward which the quite considerable force of *The Theater and Its Double* is directed. Dazzling light, dazzling sound: like some super sound-and-light show, precisely, in some French chateau set up to appeal to the jaded senses, renewing them by a shock of what is other, foreign, most deeply *unheimlich*. This is how he sees it working in the Van der Leyden. His description itself hits a high and highly provocative tone[14]:

> Sometimes while we are watching a display of fireworks it happens that, through the nocturnal bombardment of shooting stars, sky rockets, and Roman candles, we suddenly see revealed before our eyes in a hallucinatory light, standing out in relief against the darkness, certain details of the landscape: trees, tower, mountains, houses, whose illumination and whose appearance will always remain associated in our minds with the idea of those earsplitting sounds. It is impossible to express better this subordination of the various elements of the landscape to the fire manifested in the sky

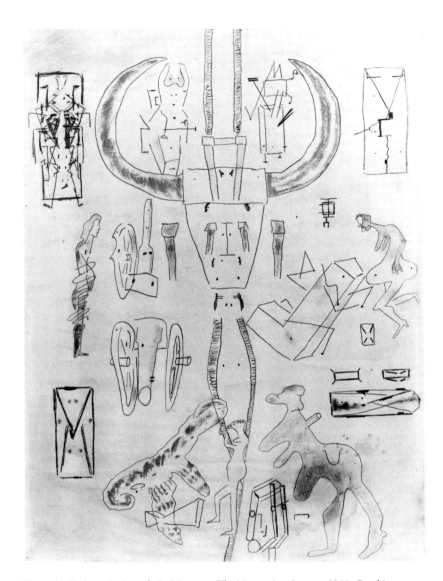

Figure 11.10 Antonin Artaud, *Le Minotaure (The Minotaur),* c. January 1946. Graphite and wax crayon, 24⅞ × 18⅞ in. Private collection. © 1997 Estate of Antonin Artaud/ARS, New York.

Figure 11.11 Lucas van Leyden, *Lot and His Daughters,* 1609, Louvre, Paris, France. Giraudon/Art Resource, New York.

than by saying that although they possess their own light, they nevertheless remain like so many muted echoes of the fire, like glowing points of reference born of the fire and put there to permit it to exert its full force of destruction.

There is, moreover, something terrifyingly energetic and disturbing in the way the painter presents this fire, as an element that is still active and mobile in an immobilized form. . . . This fire, which no one will deny, creates an impression of intelligence and malice, serves, by its very violence, to counterbalance in the mind the physical solidity and weight of the rest.

. . .

In any case, I submit that this painting is what the theater should be, if the theater knew how to speak the language that belongs to it. (A, 229–30)

This language is not just of light and fire but—and truly—the language of blood. It is this theatrical and illuminating language that Artaud sought, and found, in Mexico, with the Tarahumaras. One of his texts from 1936 speaks of the forces of an "old science."

There are in life three kinds of force, as taught by an old science known to all antiquity:

repulsive and dilating force,
compressive and astringent force,
rotational force.

The movement which goes from the outside in and which is called centripetal corresponds to astringent force, whereas the movement which goes from the inside out and which is called centrifugal corresponds to dilating and repulsive force.

Like life, like nature, thought goes from the inside out before going from the outside in. I begin to think in the void and from the void I move toward the plenum; and when I have reached the plenum I can fall back into the void. I go from the abstract to the concrete and not from the concrete toward the abstract.

I call poetry today the understanding of this internal and dynamic destiny of thought.

Poetic understanding is internal, poetic quality is internal. There is a movement today to identify the poetry of the poets with that internal magic force which provides a path for life and makes it possible to act upon life. (A, 362)

The path from this internal force to the external force upsetting the architectural stabilities is illuminated by those fire signs: the action, from abstract thought to concrete building upon thought, and its upsetting, is luminous. We have to see.

In 1947 Artaud sings of Indian culture in that odd voice of his, totally unlike that of any other writer or actor. A voice as intense as his face in those silent films, like the priest in Carl Dreyer's *Jeanne d'Arc.* This is 1947: "I came to Mexico to make contact with the Red Earth/and it stinks the same way that it is fragrant;/it smells good the same way that it stank" (A, 537). "Here lies," he writes in *Ci-gît Antonin Artaud:* "I, Antonin Artaud, am my son, my father, my mother, and myself" (A, 540). He ends, dancing, wrong side out, a baroque-romantic-surrealist hero, frenzied and free, impassioned and bloody, with a conviction about himself and what matters, that calls on baroque sensitivity as on modern vision: "and this wrong side out will be his real place" (A, 571).

I want to return to the signs that fascinated and held him with their energy, like the Cross of Palenque that he describes in a text called "What I Came to Mexico to Do": Here, inscribed in stone, is the hieroglyphic representation of a single energy passing through the four cardinal points, moving, as he says, from man "to the animal and to the plants."

That energy links the surrealism that Artaud incarnates with the legends and the truth of Monsu Desiderio. There are other reasons: Artaud did not want his true name linked to these Tarahumaras, to this trip, wanting it to emerge from some unnamed source. And so "D'un voyage aux Pays des Tara-humaras" was originally published with three asterisks instead of a name, and "La Race des hommes perdus," a part of it, was published in the journal *Voilà* (December 3, 1937) under the pseudonym John Forester. When it was repub-lished in 1945, Artaud withdrew part of it, called the "Supplement," only added again later. In short, a very problematic text.

The story is problematic and here, as elsewhere in the rite of the peyote, he is, in his body and mind, to be thought of as crucified: "I was ready for all the burns, and I awaited the first fruits of the fire in view of a conflagration that would soon be generalized" (A, 391). It was soon to be.

When the fire spread from the individual and his imagination to the ar-chitecture that others had created, when his outside energy was called upon to second the inside one, the rite was fully realized.

In a remarkable cohesion, Artaud's drawings between 1945 and 1948, particularly those of 1946 in Rodez, convey the torturous self-anguishing of this ardent sacrifice by the holes and deformations of the picture surface, as he dug his colored pencils into the paper. In the opposite mode from the still life— *vanitas* paintings present elsewhere in this book, here Death strikes like lightning (*La Mort et l'homme*) and corpses are everywhere, laid out in their coffins, low-ered into or rising from the ground (*La Machine de l'être, Les Illusions de l'âme*). In the mode of cruelty Artaud called for and found (*Le Théâtre de la cruauté*) the power of pointing and self-designation as the creator of all this high drama is strongly felt—a red hand reaches out in the bottom of *Les Corps de terre,* while to the left, the right, and at the top, fingers—marked by spots as by the plague—continue to point at and point out the simian bodies with their lightning-jagged stick figures. Even the (unconscious) conveyance is clear: in *Les Illusions de l'âme* and *Le Minotaure,* envelopes and coffins exchange their forms—each forming a kind of *envoi* or sending to some other place.

Le Minotaure and *L'Inca* give the power to the mythical and the ritualistic; even his own self-portraits have the look of a spell being cast (figures 11.12, 11.13). And all of this is overhung with the strongest possible sense of the erotic. In Artaud's *New Old World,* the rituals of death and creation interact with the

Figure 11.12 Antonin Artaud, *Self-Portrait,* 17 December
1946. Graphite, 24¾ × 18⅛ in. Collection Florence Loeb.
© 1997 Estate of Antonin Artaud/ARS, New York.

primitive and the erotic, and the obsession intensifies the experience of art as
of life: both are repassioned and it is to this repassioning that all the fingers
point. Moreover, all the scenes of suffering and exaltation are to be regarded
with suspicion, askance or askew, like the *Machine de l'être, ou le Dessin à regarder
de traviole* (figure 11.14). The surrealist look here is precisely a look askance.

In Benjamin Péret's imagination, we see through one thing to another.
Péret translates the Mayan books, like the *Livre de Chulam Byamel,* into an impassioned language, associating poetry always with the primitive and placing
bright colors and sounds at the origin.[15] In his mind, we imagine as we see, and
the ancient myths of Mexico have seen it best. ("Bird flies, fish swim, and

Figure 11.13 Antonin Artaud, *Self-Portrait,* December 1947. Graphite, 25½ × 19⅝ in. Musée National d'Art Moderne—Centre de Création Industrielle, Centre Georges Pompidou, Paris. Bequest of Paule Thévenin, 1993. © 1997 Estate of Antonin Artaud/ARS, New York.

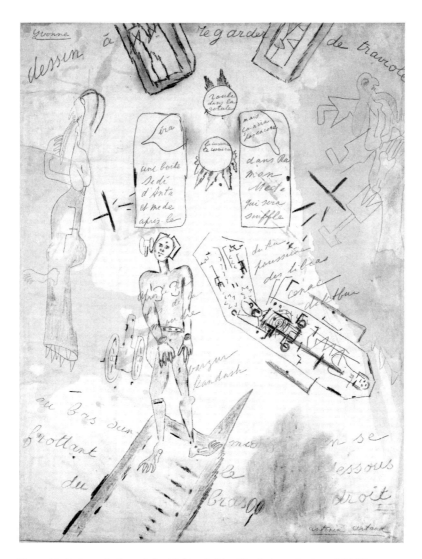

Figure 11.14 Antonin Artaud, *La Machine de l'être (Dessin à regarder de traviole) (The Machine of Being [Drawing to be looked at askew])*, c. January 1946. Graphite and wax crayon, 25½ × 19⅝ in. Musée National d'Art Moderne—Centre de Création Industrielle, Centre Georges Pompidou, Paris. © 1997 Estate of Antonin Artaud/ARS, New York.

humans invent,") because they are alone in nature to have an imagination on the lookout, always stimulated by an always renewed necessity, against barbarian society, "which treats people like jars of jam, and has them live like jam in jars," he declares in his *Anthologie des Mythes, Légendes, et contes populaires d'Amérique*.[16] The wind of the baroque blows through these myths, through the surrealist mind and what it eventually may overturn, as surrealism does all those years later.

Péret's imagining of an *amour sublime* or sublime love, beyond bourgeois categories, corresponding to Breton's concept of the "sublime point" where all the contraries meet, calls upon myths that impassion. Where the contraries energize each other, the full spread of meaning, both of mad love and of the convulsive beauty that underlies it, comes into its own.

> The word 'convulsive,' which I use to describe the only beauty which should concern us, would lose any meaning in my eyes were it to be conceived in motion and not at the exact expiration of this motion. There can be no beauty at all, as far as I am concerned— convulsive beauty—except at the cost of affirming the reciprocal relations linking the object seen in its motion and in its repose.[17]

The metaphors attached to such a concept, already energized by their own inner contrariness, are in general highly visual, from the convulsive dance (figure 11.15) to the image privileged by Breton of a "speeding locomotive abandoned for years to the delirium of a virgin forest." Erotic in its charge like the locomotive, intense in what it captures of movement stilled, stalled, and held, this image seizes forever a movement of *saccage* as intense as that explosion named desire, inward and outward, whether on a riverbank, in a church, or in the ruins seen at night in their melodramatic lighting (see figure 11.1). Drama, violence, passion: these mark the baroque and the surrealist upheaval, the psychological and physical upheaval of a storm entering an erstwhile stable place.

Figure 11.1

Just as surrealism knows of its own stable places, once the imagery of destruction takes over they cannot be rebuilt. They can be guarded from ultimate removal but not from interior struggle: the meditation that Mexico summoned the surrealists to undertake is built on the passion and the pyramids of

Figure 11.15 Man Ray, *Juliet Dancing,* 1945. Gelatin silver print, 13⁹⁄₁₆ × 9 in. The J. Paul Getty Museum, Los Angeles. © 1997 ARS, New York/ADAGP/ Man Ray Trust, Paris.

epochs piled atop each other. Based on blood, these myths survive in their "internal magic force," as Artaud puts it: "Poetic understanding is internal, poetic quality is internal" (A, 362).

To cherish the contraries on the inside as well as out, to rely on one's own myths and their own contradictions, accepting the necessary faults and the always impending destruction, is the object of a baroque, romantic, and surrealist reading, of the old world and in the new.

12

CONSTRUCTING: JOSEPH CORNELL'S
METAPHYSICS OF MEMORY

Breton—surrealism "saving my life"
Breton—same feeling then & now for him and so
—*entry in Joseph Cornell's diary, 1966*[1]

CONSTRUCTING A CONTAINER

Of all of the constructors of magic boxes to contain and nourish the imagination, the odd American genius Joseph Cornell (figure 12.1) is the most celebrated. "On the very margins of any stereotyped life," Breton says of him, "he
meditated experiments that completely overturned the usual conventions of objects."[2] His boxes, made of wood frames and glass fronts, have many sources of
inspiration: the window of a bank, where compasses and other disparate objects
were accumulated, Duchamp's *Green Box,* and the thought of "those boxes sail-
ors make for the long trip home." Insulating the experiences of his memories
and dreams from any outside context, these are "philosophical toys" for an
adult poetics.

Constructed in part to amuse his invalid brother Robert, they contain
within them the material for play. Sand can be poured slowly into a glass in the
Sand Fountains (figure 12.2), a lyric invention at the opposite pole from Duchamp's urinal spoofing a fountain. The act measures out time like a baroque
memento mori, like a *vanitas* at once grim and playful. There are little hoops
you can roll along wires by shifting the box from side to side and little balls you

Figure 12.1 Hans Namuth, portrait of Joseph
Cornell, 1969. © Studio Hans Namuth.

can insert in a hole at the top so they will roll down the slopes, visible through
several holes: this is a series evocatively called *Forgotten Game* (figure 12.3) like
a childhood experience recaptured. It is the way one would imagine a collection of Breton's *faits-glissades* (sliding facts) or *faits-précipices* (falling facts) a slope
down which the imagination can slip or slide, at varying speeds depending on
the willing strength of shock. All of Cornell's accumulations of objects move in
the mind within the atmosphere of a dream, held in a scene of mysterious
depth. Some read as *Homages to the Romantic Ballet,* with their memories of
ballerinas and singers and actresses; some are part of a *Hotel* series, an homage
to the ephemeral with their feeling of absence and temporality; some are part
of a *Bird Box* series, with some of the birds wounded, others tranquil in their
forest surroundings, and still others already flown from their perch, as in the
tribute to the poet Emily Dickinson, *Toward the Blue Peninsula,* with only the
perch remaining and a window open on the space of a blue evening.

Figure 12.2 Joseph Cornell, Untitled *Sand Fountain Series,* 1956–59. Box Construction, 14¼ × 8 × 4¼ in. © The Joseph and Robert Cornell Memorial Foundation.

Figure 12.3 Joseph Cornell, *Forgotten Game,* c. 1949. Mixed-media construction, 53.3 × 39.4 × 10.2 cm. Art Institute of Chicago, Lindy and Edwin Bergman Joseph Cornell Collection. © The Joseph and Robert Cornell Memorial Foundation.

In one of Cornell's boxes, some seashells remind us of Giacometti's response to Breton's question:

What is art?
It's a white shell in a glass of water.[3]

This kind of suggestion and understatement perfectly captures the atmosphere of Cornell constructions, collages, and boxes. They contain the space of imagination.

FIRST TRANSGRESSION: INVENTION

"The crisis of the object"—this is the expression Breton used to describe the extraordinary atmosphere in which the surrealist manifestoes and writings of all sorts flourished in such abundance. In this critical state, the customary limits of things—objects, ideas, texts—are altered, disturbed, expanded. The outlines of individual elements, stirred up and troubled by the incessant questioning of their natures and essences, permit the extension of those natures and essences past the special fetishisms attaching to them in their customary context. They exemplify the transgression of limits that concerns me here, a transgression I want to defend as the central link between surrealism and the baroque, both of which depend on the interpenetration of contraries for their way of seeing, meaning, and being, on their way to ruin.

It was the genius of this so strangely American and un-American spirit called Joseph Cornell, with a remarkable sensitivity of the Old World of Europe that he had never seen, this genius so deeply admired by the surrealists, to place a certain kind of marvelous boundary around the meeting of and the interpenetration of objects. He would set up an unlikely encounter and frame it in wood and glass as if in a theater of objects; in some, as in *Taglioni's Jewel Casket* (figure 12.4), the story is *given* as a text, inset into the box itself, whereas in others the observer has to intuit or even invent the plot. These are spaces for the imagination to construct. With all of the appearance of a true containment, the sides of his box are nevertheless extensible for the spirit—the substantial boundaries can be psychologically transgressed. Such a pushing past the rational ones of the

Figure 12.4 Joseph Cornell, *Taglioni's Jewel Casket,* 1940. Wood box containing glass ice cubes, jewelry, etc. 4¾ × 11⅞ × 8¼ in. Museum of Modern Art, New York. Gift of James Thrall Soby. © The Joseph and Robert Cornell Memorial Foundation.

mind is again baroque, in the sense I am giving to the term: the sense of extreme transgression elsewhere interpretable as the sense of ruin.

ARCHITECTURE OF A MENTAL THEATER

Matta will speak of the architecture of these boxes, delighting Cornell, whose joy at first hearing himself called an architect fills a whole page of his journal. This kind of architecture envisions and makes possible the perfect encounter, on a small scale, of mind and space, where both the set and the elements within it are mobile and recombinable as well as easily extensible by analogy. They are themselves a mapping of the mind: see the map-box called *Object: (Rose des vents)* (figure 12.5), which opens into a whole world. These boxes are particu-

Figure 12.5 Joseph Cornell, *Object (Rose des vents)*, 1942–53. Wooden box with twenty-one compasses set into a wooden tray resting on Plexiglas-topped-and-partitioned section, divided into seventeen compartments containing small miscellaneous objects, and three-part hinged lid covered inside with parts of maps of New Guinea and Australia, 2⅝ × 21¼ × 105⅘ in. Mr. and Mrs. Gerald Murphy Fund. Museum of Modern Art, New York. Photography © The Museum of Modern Art, New York. © The Joseph and Robert Cornell Memorial Foundation.

larly suited to combinatorial experimentation and to the theory of fractals. These are games of chance on a small scale, imaginable on a larger one. Like the oddly pitched photograph called *At the Eden-Casino* (figure 12.6) in Breton's narrative of chance in *Les Vases communicants,* the world opens precisely onto the imprecisions of chance.

Skilled at neither painting nor drawing, Cornell nevertheless constructed spaces for an interior theater of the mind resembling Mallarmé's mental theater, for which his great *Coup de dés* was written. Repeatedly, Cornell's diary shows how he is haunted by the memory of Mallarmé and his interior constructions,

Figure 12.6 *At The Eden Casino,* photograph, 1932, in André Breton, *Les Vases communicants*. Paris: Gallimard, 1932.

as he is by the thought of Breton—haunted in the same strange way that Breton is haunted by the memory of, the idea of, Nadja and her supreme (and inimitable) madness.[4] And as we may well be by Hans Namuth's pictures of Cornell and Cornell's constructions about Man Ray's pictures of Breton: hauntings are extensible.

Breton admires Cornell's invention of what he thinks of as a new space, this three-dimensional frame capable of keeping these hypnagogic images and having them bloom in gardens at once quotidian and prophetic. He waxes particularly enthusiastic about Cornell's *Soap Bubble* series, where you see a pipe through which to blow bubbles and can easily imagine those fragile globes about to burst, like those glasses broken in the baroque still lifes or *vanitas,* to show mortality's invasion of each object and life. As well as contemporary visions of vanity paintings, they are celebrations of an architectural meta-imagination, placed in a house of glass or crystal, exactly the house in which Breton would choose to live, as we read in his "Eloge du cristal" ("I dream that the house I live in, my writings, would be like a house of glass").[5] The dreams would be visible from the outside, like the life that Breton contemplated. But such dreams are, even as dreamed by Du Bellay in his *Songes,* likely to be overturned, in fact, to overturn themselves. So Breton himself was not "up to" living such a life, as he avowed himself not "up to" the experience of loving the madwoman Nadja. Who would be?

Cornell represents the glassed-in architecture of surrealist creation—the *passage*—as no one else did or could have.[6] "He could keep that crystalline representation and its idea intact, naive as he so wonderfully was and chose to be. This is surrealism's innocent stage, its American counterpart. Among Cornell's constructions that Breton describes and pictures in *Le Minotaure* are diverse objects collected on a shelf in a glassed-in container, a *Pharmacy* (figure 12.7) or a shadow box as theater, or assembled under a glass bell, which *isolates* them, protecting them as would a soap bubble from the secular interruptions of the unmagical world outside.[7] Under Cornell's glass bell pictured by Breton, a hand holds a fan between its fingers, the hand itself pictured as seeing with an eye in the center of its palm. These are constructions about vision, the concretization of *passages* in their own right and at their best.

Figure 12.7 Joseph Cornell, *Pharmacy,* 1950. Shadow box, 15⅞ × 10½ × 3⅞ in. The Menil Collection, Houston. Gift of Alexander Iolas. © The Joseph and Robert Cornell Memorial Foundation.

Like the cork-lined room of Marcel Proust, of whom Cornell so often writes in his diary—Mallarmé and Proust being his two heroes of literature—Cornell's boxes and spheres are homages to time lost and recaptured. They are rooms for creation and re-creation, for a work of nostalgia and of preservation of a world otherwise lost, kept here outside the ravages of time, even as they are reminders of it, these moving and memorable substitutes for skull and book and candle. The memory and the prophecy are not different: *we must remember to remember.*

About Cornell's extraordinary and yet limited *mise-en-espace,* this setting for his mental theater, surprising particularly to the French imagination, the French critic Alain Jouffroy once asked: "What is this prudent silence around his work?" Jouffroy comments of the *Hotel* series (figure 12.8) that in this space "where we have the fortune and misfortune to live, we are forbidden to take the marvelous away in our suitcase, except hidden." He continues: "The idea of reducing the whole world to a glass-fronted box, where little symbolic objects are placed on metallic wires or in wooden cubbyholes, is a child's idea." Yet they are totally "*new readings of the world.*"[8] These mentally immense, physically condensed constructions permit objects to *have their play* and to make love, like words.

Within these boxes of wood and glass a theater of the marvelous is performed for the benefit of grownups persuaded of the poetic efficacy of encounter and transformation within their small format. In this metaphysical theater of "shadow boxes," as Cornell called them, a gamut of unthought possibilities come into focus. To reassemble in this way the emblematic signals of a real but different world was the equivalent of inventing a whole new one. Participating in that state of expectation characteristic of surrealism, Cornell would wander the streets, bookstores, and libraries of New York in search of elements from which he could invent and construct the magic assemblages that were at once traps, experiments, and poems.

FIRST TRANSGRESSION: INVENTION

To invent is etymologically to come across: *in-venire.* It may imply finding or constructing a scene you will want to preserve. The discovering of the

Figure 12.8 Joseph Cornell, Untitled *(Grand Hotel de la Boule d'Or) (Hotel des Quatre Soeurs),* 1952–54. Box construction, 17¼ × 11¾ × 4¼ in. The Menil Collection, Houston. © The Joseph and Robert Cornell Memorial Foundation.

marvelous in everyday life is the most positive enactment of surrealist faith. So invention considered from the surrealist point of view is overdetermined: it is produced by something all of a sudden, the object you have come across, yet it is already expected. Wonderfully dis-closed.

So a mad love for the object found, given, dis-covered, invented, like a retrospective desire—finding something in the exterior world for which you realize you were searching all along—will be the linchpin of surrealism's passion. Joseph Cornell's gift was not just for finding and disclosing the mystery at the heart of the everyday experience but for figuring out how to keep what he had invented. He constructed a mystery of meetings and determined the way to share it.

THE RHYTHM OF MEETING

One of the most challenging certainties about surrealism is the astonishing contrast between its rhythms of creation as of reception, from the very rapid to the very slow. Already in the automatic writing that Breton did with Philippe Soupault, *Le Poisson soluble,* there are notations of the speed of writing. A rapid transcription of the automatic dictation that the surrealist hand felt it was taking down was supposed to release the mind from its ordinary logical constraints, breaking down the resistance to this flood of expression.

It takes a slow reading here to capture the sense and the insight of all of these different emblems. In surrealism, anything slow astonishes, in view of the often-noticed rapidity of its inventions, its revelations, its showy side much in evidence. Listen to Louis Aragon, a really flashy writer in this period:

> A revelation, this intellectual stroke of lightning, can't be measured in terms of the duration of the love borne from it, nor from its ravages.
> What is admirable depends on this imaginative continuity, in which it seems that the mind draws from itself a principle which hadn't been placed in it. A trace of the generalization of a discovery, its so-called value, however unexpected, always remains just beneath this sudden flash of thought.[9]

What we fall in love with, in the surrealist universe, whether a person or text or object, is a singular entity revealed by the instant lightning flash—it is never an abstract idea. The surrealist inventor and the invention both still wear "the tousled hair of dream and this mad look, ill adapted to the real world." Take a look at Joseph Cornell, the supreme dreamer (figure 12.9). Before the law and outside of it, the transgressive and found object—*la trouvaille*—is always individual. The moment of discovery, Aragon continues in a romantic vein, will be like the glimpse of dawn. "Nothing," he says, "is further from abstracting than inventing. There is no invention except of the particular." One particular image is enough to remake the world, says Aragon, always refusing to separate philosophy and poetry.

For him, all surrealist inventions retain the traces of the different moments through which they have passed, including the real and its negation, its conciliation and the absolute mediator including them. That is to say: the real, the unreal, the surreal. The logical mind, troubled by such bizarre inventions, may attempt to make the discovering into a sort of game only, ruling out the love affair between memory and invention that Cornell's boxes contain.

These are not games, says Aragon of these arranged encounters that Cornell frames in specially adapted boxes, "these are philosophical acts of great importance."[10] The limits placed around the encounter by the wood frame keep the newly found or invented object from dissipating itself. The object remains secret, even when it is exhibited, whence its beauty. Love, like invention, is localized.

SECOND TRANSGRESSION: FETISHIZING THE ANDROGYNOUS OBJECT

As for the personal relations between the surrealists and Cornell, Breton admired him greatly, and Cornell's diary testifies to his having "the same feeling then and now for him"[11] and to his regret at having destroyed a letter from Breton. That destruction I read as part of the transgressive side of Cornell's relation with surrealism and its charismatic leader, with the charismatic face Cornell found so unforgettable.

What Cornell rejected in surrealism was simply a certain tendency toward what he considered "the dark side." But he cared so about Breton and his face

Figure 12.9 Hans Namuth, *Joseph Cornell in his garden, Utopia Parkway,* 1969.
© Studio Hans Namuth.

that he used, over and over again in his diary entries of 1966, his photographic portrait by Man Ray, framing it in several different boxes, surrounding it with different emblems and giving it a totally different feeling. On one occasion he surrounded the collaged picture with curls (*Laundry Boy's Charge*) (see figure 2.1), placing below it a piece of coal on a rock in a square, a pitcher of water in a circle, both on the left, and a prismatic diamond shape and other circular play, as with a compass or a globe on the right. The photo-fetish has the same remarkable androgynous charge as Marcel Duchamp's picture of himself as Rrose Sélavy on the *Belle Haleine* perfume bottle (see figure 9.18) or the other pictures of Duchamp as that surrealist heroine by Man Ray, who himself, like Robert Desnos and Duchamp, wrote in her name. These are, for me, the most interesting heroines of the surrealist movement: Rrose in her various disguises as seen by Man Ray, Duchamp, and Desnos, on one hand, and Breton in his curls, seen by Joseph Cornell. These transgressions last in the mind, like the transgressions of love.

Figure 2.1

Figure 9.18

ENCOUNTER AND UNFOLDMENT

It was through the mediation of Susan Sontag's review of Maurice Nadeau's book on surrealism that Cornell renewed his acquaintance with the writings of Breton, the author of the destroyed letter. That destruction is fully significant in the baroque context I am claiming for surrealism. This renewed contact was, as Cornell put it, a *risorgimento,* bringing again to life the image of "the midnight sunflower." It was not only Breton's face that appealed to Joseph Cornell but certain images associated with him. These had, like his face, a certain talismanic appeal: see, for instance, the diamond, standing for Breton's dream of the crystal.

Two things associated with Breton had special meaning for Cornell. First, Breton's image of communicating vessels, with the marvelous interchange of one thing and another, this baroque interpenetration perfectly emblematized in the scientific experiment of the same name. In a sense, this imagined communication of elements compensates for the radical enclosures of his shadow theater boxes, as if between the boxes a link could be perceived. The midnight sunflower refers to Breton's poem "Sunflower" ("Tournesol"), in which he recounts the discovery or marvelous encounter of his love, inspiring Cornell's box *Tournesol,* itself an encounter, like all of his boxes. On this particular box, he worked repeatedly in January and February 1966: Cornell's Breton period. About this poem-encounter with its "secret appeal," Cornell wrote to Susan Sontag, without whom his own box "would not have come into being" and to whom Walter Hopps had proposed doing an exhibition of Cornell in Pasadena. Cornell opposed Hopps's "flushing out old catalogues of gallery exhibitions" and equally opposed too much elucidation of any image, any thought, any word, any encounter. This was urgent for him, and we should take it as that. So his shadow boxes retain their part of obscurity, leaving the marvel intact.

Cornell's attitude toward mystery and the marvelous is exactly that of the surrealists and those poets often or at one time associated with the movement. I am thinking particularly of René Char, who insisted on the silence around things of any importance: "Do not violate the mystery at the heart of the rose," he said. Never speak what is important *as mystery, as marvel,* into satiety. So Cornell wrote Sontag (see my edition of his diaries, where he drafts this):[12]

> I am against interpolation if it is going to even ripple the clear stream whence emerged the *objet donné*—in a winter of discontent the Breton *tournesol* with "secret drawer"—there is a better yield there than retrospective rummaging around (I don't like to see my name so much in print any more than you like to see Genet's scattered through Sartre.
>
> I do not like to say one syllable about "tournesol" so inviolate should it remain "after the order of Malchizadek (without father, without mother etc.)"—and yet . . . *objet donné* it is—*objet donné.*

At the heart of the surrealist faith, with its own talisman, resides the found or discovered object, chanced upon. Cornell's annotation of the reading of his Bible lesson in his diary two weeks after this last notation ends with an extraordinary comparison of Breton's poem and textual flower with the mystical and religious *turning* to the light. This use of the natural-textual image, like many of Cornell's diary entries, illuminates his faith as a Christian Scientist:

unfoldment   Breton "Tournesol"
doing Bible Lesson 3/8/66
"Christianity causes men to *turn* naturally from
darkness to light"—458:32[13]

Here invention, transgression, and refusal have their own marvelous meeting. The invention in this case consists of finding what has been given by chance— *l'objet donné*—and surrounding it with walls of silence, with a shadow box that will keep the shadow intact so that the marvelous can flower unimpeded. This boxed invention fulfills the conditions that Aragon set in his salute to the inventor and to Cornell in particular: the encounter must be like convulsive beauty, like a baroque-surrealist lightning flash, a sudden revelation like the sun at midnight, or like a sunflower turning. This is precisely the white magic on behalf of which Cornell refused what he thought of as the black magic of a certain limiting and limited surrealist attitude. We may consider that it was, by extension, this attitude that he attacked in destroying Breton's letter. He got one message—the icon of the face and hands—and refused the other.

Of course, it is up to Breton's and Cornell's readers to make their own distinctions and choices between kinds of magic, forms, objects, all having their own invented boxes in which their readings and imaginings take their transgressive and transformative places. Any secretly impassioned reading and seeing *contains* its private privilege of remaining private. Each personal encounter is set up *as a particular transgression* against a general public law and space. Each is by its nature a useless thing, partaking of a passion for dream and a poetry of the particular that are the essence of invention.

What is reinvented in this night of discovery and transgression is an encounter-event. It is mediated through the singular memory of the sunflower through Cornell's reading of Sontag's reading of Nadeau and the theorizing of Aragon and Breton about the object found or given and the frame constructed around it. This private yet collective love story, at once singular and shared, forms a shadow theater of potentialities whose inner laws must remain silent and whose obscure heart will survive untouched. Cornell's very particular vision of the particular and the framed detail, this love—say, of a flower which, in baroque fashion, *contains the sun toward which it turns*—lights up the marvelous game, like the penny arcades of which Cornell was so fond.

A METAPHYSICS OF MEMORY

Revelations, as we know, are produced by mysterious chance moments that remain unexplained, although they are best welcomed by the constant state of expectation, the *état d'attente* of the surrealist attitude. What was offered Cornell by the city of Manhattan, which he would reach by subway, or the beach or woods to which he could bicycle, in his constant and consistent wanderlust, he would try over and over to recapture in his imagination, framing it in his boxes larger and smaller, each a memorial to a moment. He was determined to preserve forever what had been given or come across by chance one day. In his own creations, remembering such unequaled richness, he had to keep every object-moment as a treasure, grouping other objects around it in associations he would term "explorations" or "constellations." The latter echoed the term Mallarmé so cherished and Breton after him, in his poems on Miró's "constellations." Everything was remembered, inscribed in a network of relations. Nothing was to be seen in isolation. In Cornell's studio, box after box of associated objects bear witness to his varying explorative passions.

His silent efforts and motions of construction, invention, and association in his shadow boxes relate to the *trompe l'oeil* encounters set up by Cornelius Harnett and John Frederick Peto, in which the patina of an instant is flattened upon a surface. The boxes differ also from the ordered chaos or the compositions of decomposition proposed by the canvases of the memento mori or the *vanitas* masters (see figure 10.5), where the skull and the cup turned over encounter, upon a table, a half-peeled lemon and a fly settled upon a rotted apple, signifying a life on its way to death. If the surrealists recognized in the juxtaposition of an umbrella and a sewing machine on a dissecting table a perfect surrealist meeting, it was perhaps also because they found therein implicit modern reference to the Dutch and Flemish meditations on mortality even amid abundance. The symptoms of fate accumulate in such conjunctions and layouts, bearing witness to the human condition. So the erotics of surrealist encounter encounters the memory of mortality.

Figure 10.5

215

A Cornell box is at once a meditation on what is and was, on what it means to keep all of the toys and games from a childhood or a present age rich in meaning. The gaming table or the theater of a philosophical game condenses the metaphysical power of desire in the movement both suggested and arrested. When in a Cornell box the rings slide along a bar when the box is tipped to one side or the balls roll down the slopes of a penny arcade (see figure 12.3), an aleatory process is set in motion, stopping the movement of the movement and thus restoring by a childlike marvel the past of a person or a city or a civilization. Innocence mingles with desire, invention with collection, holding an oxymoric revelation within the creation of a singular inventor. Such a surrealist impulse toward confrontation meets a symbolist will to suggestion and a romantic nostalgia for what can only be the past. All of those desires converge in Cornell's absolute passion for meetings arranged and moments preserved. What he found was a way to keep.

Figure 12.3

His sand fountains and deserted hotels, his night constellations and framed birds and ballerinas produce an eroticized and remembered vision in accord with a metaphysics of presence and absence. His philosophy of the daily, to which they bear sufficient witness, mingles a high sensual enjoyment of elements with the gravity of a memento mori. His boxes and collages invent a way to hold memories and to respond to constellations. They explore desires, believing in memory and in magic, in construction as in collection. Cornell invented the way to keep invention fresh.

Necessity and the Game

Breton speaks with nostalgia and affection of the epoch when the surrealists played the games of *petits papiers,* the ancestor of the "exquisite corpse," when newly born surrealism was in a state of innocence like the beginning of the world. In this permissive time you could "have the mind run . . . its maximum of adventures" (SP, 288). In short, you could play. The sense of game now restores to us, Breton says about himself and his friends, the fervor of former times but with an increased sensitivity. Like those games the surrealists refreshed by rethinking them, reinventing the relationships between objects and themselves, Cornell's boxes witness that interior necessity that motivates vision on a small scale, carrying it forward into the wider analogical understanding of the universe.

Finally, that Joseph Cornell should have refused to proffer a single syllable about what he found to marvel at in Breton and in his poem of encounter coincides with his admiration for surrealism's leader and his own mystery, as with his regret at having destroyed Breton's letter. So he preserved and represerved Breton's face, and his spirit too. The destruction of that letter can be seen as part of his refusal to probe or invite others to probe the heart of what was most secret, by simply *not looking*. "Je ne vois pas" (figure 12.10)—"I do not see," runs the caption of the famous image of the surrealist men all with their eyes closed, making a frame around (and for) the nude female body in the center upon which their closed eyes are meant to reflect.

I maintain that this refusal itself is surrealist and claim that honorific title for the great American artist Joseph Cornell and for his look. For it seems to me that Cornell's *look,* in all senses, the way he looks and the way he looks— is the most surrealist of them all. Cornell (figure 12.11) looks out a window from a room in which the dresser holds a framed picture of Jeanne Moreau, facing us directly beneath his face reflected in the mirror looking out, like the two sides of his personality: another Rrose Sélavy, in both genders. In another picture, he is outside, looking into the window (figure 12.12), in which again he is reflected. It makes every sense that he is seen only in reflection in all three images, first, the one in the chair, where his interior meditation or reflection illuminates him under the light ray as the Magdalen is illuminated by her candle and her thought: he is here the annunciate. In the second, the mirror, and in the third, the window, serve to reveal him to us, as he is looking elsewhere. Unrecognized for so many years as the genius he was, Cornell, who left his house on Utopia Parkway in Queens only for his explorations to furnish his mental adventures, had, in a sense, a very long trip home.

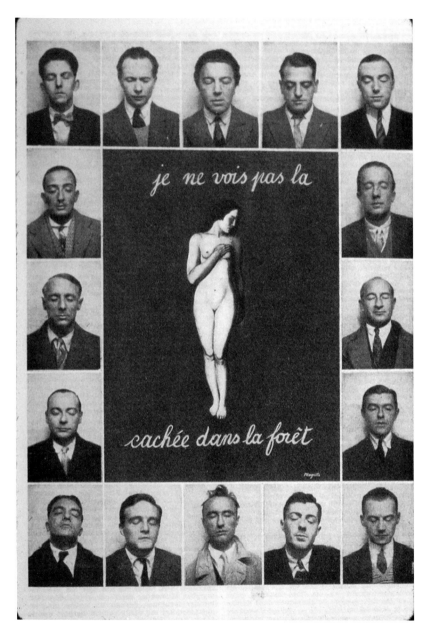

Figure 12.10 Surrealists around a painting by René Magritte, *Je ne vois pas la . . . cachée dans la forêt*. (Painting entitled: *La Femme cachée*). Published in *La Révolution surréaliste*, 1929.

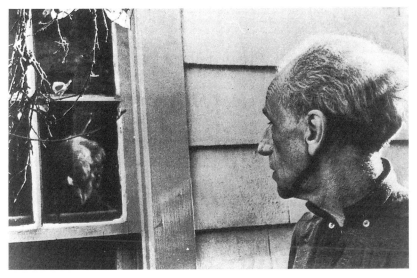

Figure 12.11 Joseph Cornell in his house on Utopia Parkway,
with photograph of Jeanne Moreau.

Figure 12.12 Hans Namuth, *Joseph Cornell looking into his window,* 1969.
© Studio Hans Namuth.

IV

OBSESSING

13

GAME: EXQUISITE EXCESSIVE CORPSE

La clé de l'amour, que le poète disait avoir trouvée, lui aussi, qu'il cherche bien: il l'a.
(The key to love, that the poet claimed to have found also, let him look: he has it.)

—*André Breton,* Second Manifesto of Surrealism[1]

THE HISTORIC CORPSE

What an odd contraption. One of those children's tops, for spinning, with a teacup for one ear and two birds for the other, heads up a torso made of a shoe placed on one side of a cylinder between two plates, balanced upon a pair of dainty child legs, one raised, one lowered to stand upon the base, which is itself, appropriately enough, a paid of scales. This odd and historic balancing act was one of a set of collective creations made by Yves Tanguy the surrealist artist, André Breton, the founder and theoretician of surrealism, and Breton's then wife the artist Jacqueline Lamba. It was a game the playing of which had historic importance, as did the players gathered around the birthing of one more of the historic corpses, to whose *experiential* value we are paying tribute, both in their continuance and their reincarnation. These experiments combined communality, performance, and personality. They took the measure of the collective mind (figures 13.1 to 13.4).

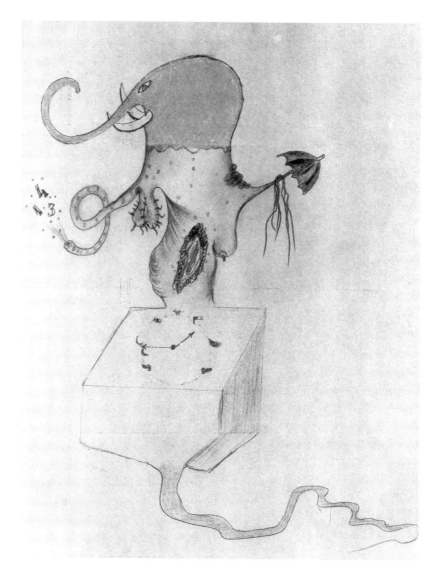

Figure 13.1 *Cadavre exquis.* André Breton, Max Morise, Jeanette Tanguy, Pierre Naville, Benjamin Péret, Jacques Prévert, Yves Tanguy. Private Collection.

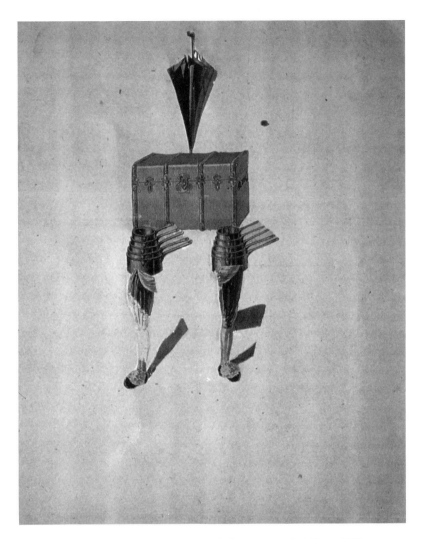

Figure 13.2 André Breton and Yves Tanguy, *Cadavre exquis,* called *Figure,* 1928.
Collage, pasted papers, 11⅜ × 9 in. Private Collection, Liège, Belgium.
Giraudon/Art Resource, N.Y.

Figure 13.3 *Cadavre exquis* (from *La Révolution surréaliste,* nos. 9–10, October 1, 1927).

Figure 13.4 *Cadavre exquis,* collective unsigned (from *La Révolution surréaliste,* no. 9–10, October 1, 1927).

The game involved a group of persons (generally three or more) and their successive contributions to an eventual collective figure of which the players only knew, until the final outcome, their individual part. It was usually verbal, as in the first one, which gave its name to the entire process, or visual, but occasionally it was both, with a double play back and forth. As a proof of the value of automatism and chance, it had to be taken seriously. Here are the rules, if you are playing in French, as those surrealists were. The first person takes a piece of paper, writes a noun upon it, folds it so that the second person cannot see what is written; that person then writes an adjective, folds it over, and passes it to the third person, who adds a verb, and passes it on if there are more than three players. The fourth player adds a noun, folds the paper over, and the last person, assuming there are five, adds an adjective and unfolds the paper to read the sentence. The same procedure is followed with the visual game: the first person drawing a head, with two lines protruding as the paper is folded so that the neck will fit upon the head; then the torso, folded and lines protruding for the legs, and so on for the feet. Adjustments are made for the number of players, but in both the verbal and visual cases, the final result is usually felt to be, from its surprising aspect, more than the product that those players would have arrived at otherwise, separately, or together in a conscious collaboration. The point of the play is both collective and automatic: the unleashing of the marvelous or the irrational in a group, with each individual effort working toward the final result greater than the sum of its parts.

The history through which this most alive corpse traipsed to get to us today is now old history. There was a time when the surrealists were dada(s) . . . Tristan Tzara, as surely the papa-dada from 1916 to 1922 as André Breton was the Pope of surrealism from then on, had once recommended his own system for liberating the pent-up unconscious poetic forces in the self. The players (the "writers") would simply cut up and out several expressions from a newspaper, drop them in a hat, and then each person would pull out at random and arrange the expressions *in the order in which* they had been found. These were the findings or *trouvailles,* the witnesses to the marvelous of chance in everyday life to which the dadas and surrealists were addicted, from Duchamp to Breton. This text, said Tzara to the players, his tongue firmly where it usually was, in his cheek, "will resemble you."

So all the experimental corpses were made of *slips*. The first corpse, as the story goes, was born in late 1925, in the house of Marcel Duhamel, at 54, rue du Château in Paris: Duhamel, the poet Jacques Prévert, and the painter Yves Tanguy sat down to play the game just described, which was in its origin a children's game. "You just put down anything," says Prévert, and it works. As the story goes, the first sufficiently striking sentence that emerged said: "Le cadavre exquis boira le vin nouveau" ("The exquisite corpse will drink the new wine").

There they are, first the dadas and then the surrealists, in the actual and mental pictures we have of the groups, all huddled around, waiting, watching whatever experiment is on the boards or the table. They are gathered in the equivalent of the surrealist moment of grace, the *état d'attente* or state of expectation: Salvador Dali, later despised by the surrealists, who called him Salvador Dollars but who could wield a mean pen as he could a brush, giving us a vivid picture of one of these small groups in willing collaboration. The game is other than the paper one, but grasps the scene of both:

> All night long a few surrealists would gather round the big table used for experiments, their eyes protected and masked by thin though opaque mechanical slats on which the blinding curve for the convulsive graphs would appear intermittently in fleeting luminous signals, a delicate nickel apparatus like an astrolabe being fixed to their necks and fitted with animal membranes to record by interpenetration the apparition of each fresh poetic streak. . . . Meanwhile their friends, holding their breath and biting their lower lips in concentrated attention, would lean over the recording apparatus and with dilated pupils await the expected but unknown movement, sentence, or image.[2]

This is, allowing for a bit of Dalian melodrama and opacity, the way it was, when they gathered around the corpse, in their communal aspect.

It was a joyous affair. "André shrieked with joy," says his wife, "seeing immediately one of those sources or natural cascades of inspiration he loved to find. Suddenly everything was unleashed."[3] Immediately, suddenly, rapidly, right now, look: the transcription was not just automatic, it had to be quick. The instantaneous was able to abolish a mental censorship that would have been the death of the lively corpse. Breton himself was to comment at length about rhythms and their importance: when he and Philippe Soupault wrote their famous *Poisson soluble* (*Soluble Fish,* like the man "soluble in his thought")—they carefully recorded the rate at which each wrote. Verbal inspiration could be relied on, at least for the beginning sentence. Longer texts proved problematic, even in theory: for conscious judgment might sneak in a sequence of sentences, so that transitions were not without dangers. The advantage of the single-sentence collective corpse was its spontaneity.

Just so the visual equivalent, which followed closely on the heels of the verbal experiments. Breton recounts, in *Communicating Vessels* (*Les Vases communicants*), how he gave the map of France as the head of "one of the hybrid beings we wanted to form" and, later in the same text, describes an object he conceived of, which combines the verbal and the visual. The description is of capital importance, exemplifying the most interesting original construction and his obsessional force, when *possessed by his imagination*. This is his own one-person cadaver writ large:

> This phantom object, which I have never ceased to think of since then as constructible, and whose real aspect I expected to be rather surprising, can be described as follows (I sketched it in the game more or less as a bust, on the second third of the paper; this drawing was reproduced in *La Révolution surréaliste,* no. 9–10) (fig. 2): an empty white or very pale envelope with no address, closed and sealed in red, the round seal without any particular imprint, perhaps a seal *before* any imprint, its edge bordered with eyelashes (*cils*) and a sideways handle (*anse*) to it. A rather poor pun, which had nevertheless permitted the constitution of the object, furnished the word *Silence* (*cils-anse*), which seemed to me to be able to accompany it or designate it.[4]

Breton insists on the freedom of "procuring any emotion I like" through the image and also upon the fact that anyone who wants to share it is free to. The poetic here is a matter of collective interpretation. Freedom, as construed in this game and all that it entails, is essential; the moral does not enter into the poetic, which is the point of the essentially joyous experimentation with words, images, cognition, and recognition: "any emotion I like."

THE HOLIDAY AND THE SERIOUS

Many of the dada and the surrealist techniques aimed at liberating the unconscious from rational restrictions: from Max Ernst's various *frottages* or rubbings (paper, soft pencil, and planks) and Hans Arp's tearing of papers (see figure 5.1) to the hypnotic sleep writings and conversations practiced in the surrealist group, especially by Robert Desnos. What might, to the outside eye, have seemed disorder proved able to free some remarkable hidden ideas and longings into a visible and above all, dynamic form, like the games of chance in Joseph Cornell's *Penny Arcade* series—see the magnificent and complicated *re-Autumnal* version (figure 13.5), with its cubes and magical forms, with index fingers pointing out the details one by one. What you point at you can play with: part of the game is the stress, implicit or explicit, laid on the complications of choice and chance. Precisely because it depends on chance, you have to point it out, as if you were choosing it. Here, something gets pointed at and out, whereas in Desnos's drawing with its finger uplifted ("Among the fists and pointing fingers") the sign is, as it were, pure of any explicit reference, and nothing gets pointed out or at. It is just about pointing.

Figure 5.1

André Breton, founder and chief spokesman of the surrealist movement, wanted, at all costs, to avoid a deadly and stultifying static world whose normality and balance would be taken as a virtue by rationalists, those beings diametrically (and forever) opposed to the surrealists' "lyric comportment." His praise for "the art of madmen and of children" was undying—the results of *cadavre exquis* have, at their very best, the feeling of both. Reason is, says Breton, sent on holiday, to set the writing and drawing mechanism in free play, each enabling the other. But the holiday was serious, and as Simone Collinet, Breton's first wife, commented, this collective play was "a method of research, a means of exaltation and stimulation, a gold mine of findings, maybe even a drug."[5]

There is a side issue in this particular manifestation: in the matter of the corpse just described and in others of the same set or series. Breton, nothing if not serious in all things, saw to it that the rules were followed, as befitted the

Figure 13.5 Joseph Cornell, *Penny Arcade (re-Autumnal),* 1964. Collage, 12 × 9 in.
C. and M. Arts © The Joseph and Robert Cornell Memorial Foundation.

head of the group. He exulted, like the others, in the *idea* as in the fact of surrealist group work and play.

But there remained a problem with naming this play. Jacqueline, his second wife and the heroine of Breton's most famous poem, "Sunflower," as well as his lyric meditation on *Mad Love,* subsequently changed her name on the exquisite corpses in which she had participated to Jacqueline Lamba—for she was, after all, an artist in her own right and refused to be just "Jacqueline Breton." This anecdote is crucial: it is about what we sign, when we work together, and in whose name we sign these figures. In this collective, it was important that the participants sign their own names: they had to sign in, and to sign off.

The players we often recognize, with a start: in the later years of the game, take the sensual composition of Frieda Kahlo, the friend of Trotsky and wife of Diego Rivera (whose double play with Lucienne Block—a friend, who stayed with them in Detroit—is something to behold); Victor Brauner, whose blindness in one eye had been foreseen by Breton; Yves Tanguy, the surrealist artist of all those desert spaces, married to the talented Kay Sage. These personalities all willing to be part of something communal—the text was often signed by three or four, but the play depended, as Tzara said, on the personalities of the signers. We *know* who did what. We *know* that, for instance, Méret Oppenheim, creator of the fur teacup, was obsessed by chair-corpses: *The Chair in a Waterfall* (figure 13.6), where the spirals above sink into the swirls below. Who else would do that?

We recognize, in many cases, the style of the signer. But what we mainly know is how it mattered to them, this play between several persons. It was, in part, a generous letting go of self as well as of rationality, indeed as surrealism was supposed to be. That too was the state of grace that the exquisite corpse gathered around itself, with its various ways of interrelating persons and ideas under the surrealist sign of the marvelous invention or *trouvaille.*

AUTOMATIC ENERGY

Indeed, Breton had doubts about automatic writing as such: his definition of surrealism had early been connected with it, but then, in his "Automatic

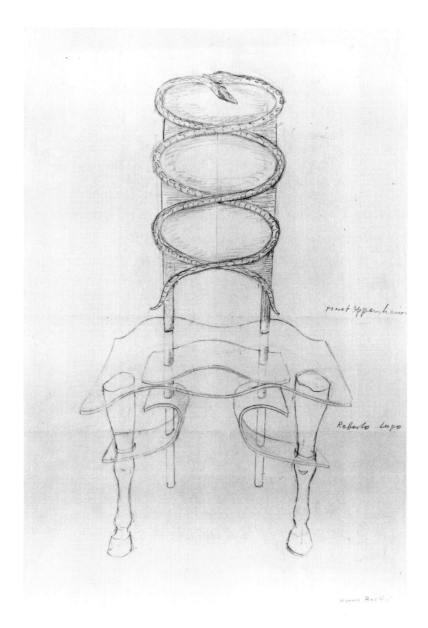

Figure 13.6 Meret Oppenheim and Roberto Lupo, *Chair in Waterfall (Cadavre exquis)*, 1975. Photo: Roland Aellig, Berne. © Meret Oppenheim Archive, Berne. Courtesy of Dominique and Christophe Burgi.

Message," he spoke of its continued bad luck; and in another revision, in an interview of 1951, he again revised the tale: "Automatic writing, and everything that comes with it—you can't imagine how precious it is to me."

What is its problem? Why does automatism focus such self-questioning? What is it that automatism goes against? For one thing, the ordering impulse; for another, the smug assumption that things around us, especially the ones we create, have *significance*. Belong where we put them. Are marks of what we care about. To create something automatic(ally), we have to be detached from outside and inside, "from the solicitations of the external world, as well as from individual cares of a utilitarian or sentimental nature, etc." This is the advantage of Oriental thought, says Breton, which Westerners can, nevertheless, learn. Those who can would be finally convinced that the land of the free-from-rational gesture is not, finally "*elsewhere,* but *in themselves*." They would learn to discard the heavy baggage of Western thought, "so that their step would be light enough to cross the bridge leading there."[6]

The exquisite corpse cares not a fig for order, for how we fit in, for what we sound like and look like. It disorients: it devalues the singular imagination. It is antiestablishment in the crudest sense; it exults in the antisentimental, the anti-individual, the antilogical. It is in no way Apollonian, being strictly Dionysian in impulse. Ah, but it is about relations: about the one between the mind and its objects, the mind and chance, the mind and "what it will never reach."[7] No single mind can grasp the relations set up, so arbitrarily, in principle, between this thing I find and set down, and this next thing the two of you are finding and setting down, separately. It is like the "sublime point" of surrealism, a spot on a mental mountain, where all contraries impossibly meet—life and death, up and down, yes and no—about which Breton tells his small daughter: I can point to it, but no one can ever dwell there. You can look at the convergence in one of these exquisite bodies, be it visual or verbal, yet you could not live there. For, says Breton sadly, "It would . . . from then on, have ceased to be sublime and I should, myself, have ceased to be a person."[8]

These corpses are far from sublime and don't stand in the way of humanness. They don't look like anybody you've ever seen or wanted to, isn't that right? Sort of like the stuff of dreams. That this technique should have elicited such enthusiasm, over such a long period, in so many diverse places and in so many diverse players, both poets and artists, is at least partially explained by this conjunction of highly charged elements. They converge, in the gaming moment, and in its subsequent revelation, to produce a dazzle whose dynamics are equivalent to that of the surrealist image itself, where elements are deliberately chosen from fields as far apart as possible for the maximal energetic force.

COLLECTIVE CREATION

The collective lyrical comportment that Breton defined at the heart of the movement found its perfect antibourgeois statement in these willingly modest materials, this paper and these crayons and pencils, in this careful unindividualized stating of the case for the game. Here, where collective composition is the point, the idea of *playing together* and its result makes an effective demonstration—always taken as miraculous—of the mental affinities among the three or four persons playing the game and between the exterior world and themselves. In this, as in much of Breton's thinking and writing, he proves his own dictum about surrealism being the "tail of romanticism, but how prehensile!" Goethe's notion of elective affinities or strange and wonderful correspondences between persons of which they are not always aware provides the willingly mysterious background for the unspoken, unanalyzed communication between the players of this singularly important game.

Against the pride of personal possession, the group-manufactured sentence or drawing makes a maximal effect from the simplest sources, like the child's game, the found object, the fragment. As for the meeting of fragments, the encounter of elements in the marvelous whole, Isidore Ducasse, called the Comte de Lautréamont, is responsible for the meeting of these elements in the beginning, with his explosive encounter of the sewing machine—female—and his umbrella—male—on the bed of the dissection table. "Poetry," he had said, "will be made by all." And indeed the *cadavre exquis* gatherings were just that, several making poetry together. Like Breton's own idea of word games: "Words are not playing," he said, "they are making love." These communal gatherings had something of the erotic to them, no doubt about it.

Speaking of umbrellas, one of the more remarkable corpse figures from 1928, composed by a relatively large cast including André Breton, Benjamin

Péret, Max Morise, Yves Tanguy, and Jacques Prévert, shows an umbrella balanced on a trunk, doubtless closed upon some secret, above two rather mismatched legs with saucepans, their handles fluttering like so many feathers, cooking up the link between the trunk—here the verbal and the visual wonderfully merge, with the trunk where the trunk should be—and what comes lower down. The outflying handles are visually echoed by ribbons protruding from the "legs," so that the whole thing, top to bottom—umbrella, trunk, legs, ribbons—pans out into something that works. No need of a sewing machine to tie it all together. The mind does it, with the eye. Instead of a dissection table, we have a contraption that works like a construction. (See figure 13.2.)

Figure 13.2

These collage figures were formed by each player picking a dictionary or encyclopedia illustration from among those in a basket at the center of the table. They picked their contribution, that is, from among what had already been predesigned and precontributed, into and out of an ironic *play* on the notion of passing the basket to solicit generous spirits. The generosity here is collective. The play becomes the work, the layers of reference here involving the collective work of the great *Encyclopédie* and then of the great ancestor Lautréamont and his umbrella opening out to this visual poetry made by all.

It isn't just the corpse that returns: so does the umbrella. Imagine the 1935 figure made by Valentine Hugo, Breton, Tanguy, and Nusch Eluard (the beloved wife of Paul Eluard, who had succeeded Gala when she left with Salvador Dalí—Nusch was later killed in a tragic accident). The left leg strides along upon an umbrella replacing its foot, and the umbrella casts a shadow before itself, with a certain delicacy of premonition, under the awkward wing-shaped forms at the center of the body. The corpse won't be taking off very quickly, but it is prepared for whatever weather, give or take a little inversion. This is one of the more heavily humorous corpses, whose return we salute with our own umbrellas at the ready: umbrellas abound (see figure 13.1).

Figure 13.1

As for the verbal equivalent of the visual, listen to what it sounds like, at its best, rhyming strangely, as in the first verbal example given in the October number of *La Révolution surréaliste,* (no. 9–10, October 1, 1927): "La vapeur ailée séduit l'oiseau fermé à clé" ("The winged vapor seduces the bird locked away").[9] Impossible, you may say, to have such an echo: that the *é* sound should occur four times (*ée, sé, mé, clé*) in an eight-word text by several hands is

peculiar, to say the least, whereas the statement is already imbued with a remarkably imaged lyricism. Agreed: but this not atypical example is precisely the
sort of discovery that was to be exulted. Lautréamont had said, "Poetry will be
made by all," and here it surely is.

Later, the idea of the collective hope and the automatic gesture would
have its influence on the New York School, and Matta—some of whose exquisite corpses were the best in the corpse business—would transfer the energy of
the *initiating gesture,* through Robert Motherwell, to the other painters
of spontaneity. The hand would trace, freely and "arbitrarily," some strokes
(doodles, said Motherwell) to the page, and the inspiration would take over:
the subsequent abstract expressionist gesture would will itself large, heroic even.

BODY FRAGMENTS AND THE WHOLE CORPSE

Surrealist objects of any kind were "precipitations of our desire," said Breton,
speaking for the collective body of the surrealists. If his poem-objects were, as
their name indicates, a combination of the verbal and the visual, just so the
exquisite corpses drawn, quartered, and given their titles by the same folded
paper procedure, were mixtures. That each participant only supplied a part yet
that their tripled or quadrupled or even quintupled imaginations should have
led to a whole more intense in effect than any of them could have imagined
singly was proof of the continuing *marvelous* of the discovery. Here the automatic met the erotic, for the partial creations merged in an explicit substantia-
tion of group desire for the body entire. Each part imagined refers, in the long
run, back to the whole. That umbrella, wherever it is found, can be seen opening in and out.

More often than not, this *charge* is felt, like an electric energy surging
through the folds, pleating itself like so many reserves of individual longing,
until the unfolding, unpleating of the body, of words and images, extends from
head to foot. Breton claimed that this work of art, like all the others, must
"refer to a *purely internal model* or will cease to exist."

We hear in this dramatically formulated faith the same wording, feel in it
the same spirit as in the famous statement about the aesthetic revolution surrealism meant to be, among other revolutionary desires. Listen to the conclusion

of Breton's *Nadja*—"Beauty will be CONVULSIVE or will not be"[10]—and to his reiteration and expansion of this faith in his period of *Mad Love:* "Convulsive beauty will be veiled-erotic, fixed-explosive, magic-circumstantial, or it will not be."[11] Those convulsions shaking the corpse link, marvelously, the collective faith and the automatic individual gesture, in the idea of and the realization of the game. This is just the way it is, says the collective image: take me on my own terms, as they are folded up into each other. Otherwise, individually, they cannot be. Each time, the unfolded whole body was greeted—as the repeated documentation insists—to the amazement of the participants, as something they *re-cognize*. Like a group dream, like a fantasy owned up to, by more than one possessor and possessed, this collective creation speaks loudly for more than itself and even past the creators to observers of these traces of belief.

The technique of the exquisite corpse was part of this experiential conviction in its many manifestations, from the historic source experiments of the 1920s to the present (re)flowering by invitation, into a rejuvenating force far beyond itself and not to be decomposed. We might see it as an expression of faith in what we can do in small groups, if invited, still now. In what we can do, finally, together, situating ourselves on the very edge of the by now traditional postmodern gesture, with its revolutionary reliance on the fragment and the part (figure 13.7). We can look now, all of us, toward the whole of this art/act, at once behind us and still going on, determined never to lose that sense of play that works at a constant renewal of our "hunger for the marvelous," as we carry on with such exquisite exultation at collective discovery and with the life that it intensifies.

Figure 13.7 Roy Dowell, Tom Knechtel, Megan Williams, and Lari Pitman, *Cadavre exquis,* 1992. © Drawing Center, New York. Courtesy of Anne Philbin.

14

FACE: STILL ENVISAGING ANDRÉ BRETON

Above all I could not detach myself from another detail . . .

—*André Breton,* Mad Love[1]

I opened this book with a contemplation of the surrealist and the baroque. Among their major links is the one between the representation of the part and the whole, between what is isolated to be fetishized or iconicized in admiration or desire and the entire body of the person, thing, or concept represented. I am above all thinking about how an icon is constructed, what our response to it is likely to be, and to what extent desire depends on distance.

Specifically, I have been thinking about what it is to contemplate a person not in bodily form but facially, as it were. This seems at once singularly appropriate and inappropriate for a surrealist, given the immense and gloriously selective celebration of body parts: just imagine how we so often see, of the woman sung in poetry or art, many isolated elements, so that each body part has its separate distinction yet something is lacking in the whole conception. One of the best-known examples is the partializing eulogy of André Breton to his *femme,* that is his wife, woman, companion, entitled "Free Union," where diverse parts are singled out and described in succession, in accord with all of those familiar deconstructive tendencies so profusely and familiarly illustrated in the surrealist work of painting and photography.[2] The single elements are eroticized, straight (as it were) or then in slippage. "Ma femme à la taille . . . à la bouche . . . Aux dents . . . A la langue . . . aux cils . . . aux sourcils . . . aux épaules . . . aux poignets . . . aux doigts . . . aux bras . . . aux jambes . . . aux mollets . . . aux pieds . . . au cou . . . aux seins"—that is, her waist, mouth, teeth, tongue, lashes, eyebrows, shoulders, wrists, fingers, arms, legs, calves, feet, neck, breasts, and so on, like a renaissance *blason* indeed, a celebration of parts before arriving at the concluding repeat, six-sided like a star, a stunning litanic eulogy of her eyes, which sum up in themselves all the natural elements:

Ma femme aux yeux pleins de larmes
Aux yeux de panoplie violette et d'aiguille aimantée
Ma femme aux yeux de savane
Ma femme aux yeux d'eau pour boire en prison
Ma femme aux yeux de bois toujours sous la hache
Aux yeux de niveau d'eau de niveau d'air de terre et de feu

(Woman of mine with eyes full of tears
With violet-panoplied and magnetic-needle eyes
Woman of mine with eyes of water to be drunk in prison
Woman of mine with eyes of wood always under the axe
With water-level eyes the level of air earth and fire)[3]

These parts can seem in their fragmentation both brusquely thrust at you, as happens in many of Magritte's images, and conspiratorial, since they seem aimed at the male imagination—or deforming, monsterizing, if I can put it like that. Or they can be, as in some of Man Ray's images—such as the torso sheathed in moiré silk, discussed in an earlier chapter—images of sheer deprivation. Without heads and legs, only the torso: there is nothing to think with, walk with, handle with. These are images of total passivity, like Magritte's woman's middle part, sheathed in a mirror frame, called *Representation* (see preface, figure 1). That Magritte should have *signed* this woman represented on her thigh skews the representation of representation to the side, just as the body is, in fact, in a skewed position in the mirror. This is not a straight representation, says Magritte, his reflection mirroring our reader-thoughts.

Figure 1

If we compare this mirrored representation of representation to Claude Cahun's self-portrait in a mirror, we see the difference between her complex mirroring of her intelligent face, and Magritte's pretended mirroring of our female middle part. In his heavy framing, this handling, I feel as a woman the heavy *manus* or hand upon me, putting me in my place for *his* representation of me. I know I am being manhandled by these very expert manipulators of the Magritte and Man Ray stripes. They can do fashion, they can fashion and defashion my body, and—as a surrealist speaker, upon occasion—I could in principle do the same thing with the male body. But it is just not interesting to me. We know that André Breton never wanted to be seen without an erection; in any case, this was not my concern. In a very long interview I had with her in 1973, Jacqueline Lamba described to me how he never wanted to be seen without his socks on, or even in stocking feet. As opposed to that, we imagine her walking along the beach naked with David Hare, both of them totally gorgeous and André heavily behind, fully clothed. In one film in which he appears, he seemed to me clumsy, high-voiced; as a friend of his once said to me, he always seemed to waddle.

Here is the thing, though: I have always been smitten by his face. I wrote my thesis on Gaston Bachelard and Breton because of falling in love with Bachelard's beard and Breton's face. What more can I say? I love his face, from the dada moment on. I love it in glasses, I love it surrounded by a cardboard outfit. I got my first Breton sweater because I saw that wonderful face of his next to Paul Eluard, both of them with those sweaters, on the Ile de Sein. This is quite as serious as falling in love with someone's language—in this case, it was both.

Figure 2.1

I want for a moment to think how you frame someone you want to make into an icon, summoning three examples. In *La Révolution surréaliste* we see Georges Bissière's Proust depicted as just one eye in front of that marvelous mind (figure 14.1). This is iconization by separation, as the surrealist treatment of the woman's body might seem to be, upon occasion. Breton, in his essay "Le Merveilleux contre le mystère" ("The Marvelous against Mystery"), installs Mallarmé's head directly in the middle of a text, so that it presides. But my favorite is Joseph Cornell's series of 1966 constructions about a Man Ray iconization of Breton in 1931 (see figures 2.1, 14.2).

Figure 14.2

How do you set apart an icon? Cornell's settings of Breton are based on a celebratory centering, a technique that seems always successful in his hands. Take his bird boxes: each bird is perfectly framed like Cornell's owl in the forest,

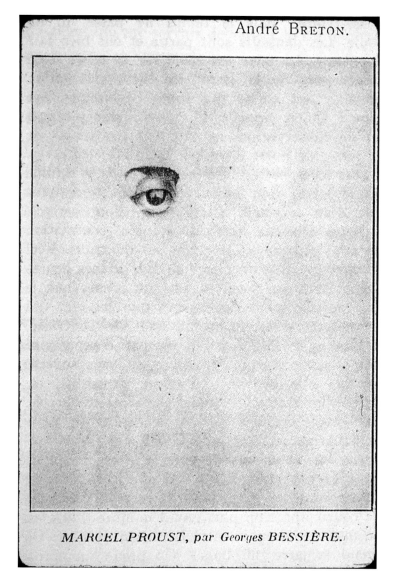

Figure 14.1 Georges Bessière, *Marcel Proust,* in *La Révolution surréaliste,* no. 2, January 15, 1925.

Figure 14.2 Joseph Cornell, Untitled. Construction/collage, with portrait of André Breton by Man Ray, 1966. © The Joseph and Robert Cornell Memorial Foundation.

placed against the bark he went out on his bike to find. Take some forgotten Medici prince or princess like the boy painted by Pinturicchio (figure 14.3), some singer or ballet dancer, some Giuditta Pasta or Carlotta Grisi or Nellie Melba he has remembered. They may be framed by upright columns, with emblems about them, set in a recess of deep and dim-colored space, often blue and mysterious, as if in the night sky like one of the constellations Cornell loves to meditate. His *Caravaggio Boy* is set in midnight blue with the double crossed vertical line in front of the young boy's astonished face (figure 14.4), just visible in its blue surround, his astonishment preserved forever. Or just a head is apparent against the empty space. Cornell's haunting rendering of *La Bella* (1950) (figure 14.5) poses her like one of the ancient Roman tomb figures, her grave and beautiful face and the upper-left part of her body down to her hand across her waist held against a wash of faded red, with the trace of a HOTEL sign beneath, its lettering significantly backward, and balanced, to the right of her head, by the letters ARCHE, below them, TOILE, like the end of *étoile* (star). Celebrated like a star and set apart, she will no more be dwelling in a house than in a hotel or a tomb. As with the other figures whom Cornell divorces from any ordinary context to make a setting of space and timelessness, she has the surrealist look of the ages.

This is the way also with his *Penny Arcade*. Take the one with Lauren Bacall (figure 14.6): her sideways look inflects the position, both spatial and psychological, of the entire work. All the *Penny Arcades* are richly mental and delight in their own presentation, often abounding in elements. Animals and coins and bright colors compound the feeling of marvelous potential. Sometimes a finger, or several, point at some of the parts with childlike glee, like an adventure or *encounter* about to take place. I cannot imagine a better example of the openness to chance, that state of expectancy that surrealism wanted itself to be, concretized in the cadavre exquis (see figure 13.4).

The surprise of encounter is just what Cornell's frame wants to celebrate. In all his celebratory imaging, as in his construction of a box around Man Ray's portrait of Breton, each element in the figure or the surround plays a decisive magical and enlarging role. Below the face of Breton as pictured, whether with light streaks or curls, Cornell changes the symbols: there may be a glass, as in the communicating vessels he came to know through Susan Sontag, or a crystal,

Figure 13.4

Figure 14.3 Joseph Cornell, Untitled (*Pinturicchio Variant*), 1950s. Menil Foundation.
© The Joseph and Robert Cornell Memorial Foundation.

Figure 14.4 Joseph Cornell, Untitled (*Caravaggio Boy*), c. 1953. Box
construction, 14⅛ × 10⅛ × 5¼ in. C & M Arts. © The Joseph and
Robert Cornell Memorial Foundation.

Figure 14.5 Joseph Cornell, Untitled, 1950. *La Bella*. Box construction, 18¾ × 12⁷⁄₁₆ in. C & M Arts. © The Joseph and Robert Cornell Memorial Foundation.

Figure 14.6 Joseph Cornell, Untitled (*Penny Arcade Portrait of Lauren Bacall*), 1945–46. Construction, 20½ × 16 × 3½ in. Art Institute of Chicago, Lindy and Edwin Bergman Joseph Cornell Collection. © The Joseph and Robert Cornell Memorial Foundation.

or a cube. These are often alchemical symbols, as in surrealist magic. Never mind that he turned against surrealism because of its adoption of what he called black magic, and, as an always faithful practicing Christian Scientist, preferred white magic, positive change.

Yet is it not true that surrealism practiced not looking at what was evident, centered? "Je ne vois pas le . . ." (see figure 12.10) reads the caption of Magritte's painting of a naked lady, standing for the nude as an apple stands for New York. Around her, the surrealist men are closing their eyes, presumably with the meaning: I don't want to see; I close my eyes to what is so evident. This is the place to admit how I love this face that will never be looking back at mine. He will always be not just recognizable but iconizable because he will look past me, away, or in admiration at someone else.

Figure 12.10

For the Breton whose face I now love is not the one about which I used to care, the face Man Ray captured with its mouth open in ecstasy. The face that wears a monocle in its dada guise or looks at the typewriter and his wife in the center, the face laughing alongside Eluard, or sober alongside Louis Aragon, or surrounded by the other members of the group in the café, or with the other surrealists in exile. Not the noble Roman face, glamorized theatrically by Claude Cahun and made part of the famous surrealist couple: André and Jacqueline, doubled against each other in a continuing reflection, or then, against a curtain (see figures 8.9, 8.10).[4]

Figure 8.9

No, the one I now love is another face (see figure 2.1). It wears curls, as if Breton were doing his Rrose Sélavy number Andrée-Andrée! (Figure 14.7) It doesn't just cross-dress, it acts toward the other faces it admires as the passive, traditionally female admirer: look at Breton looking up at Max Ernst. Look at Breton looking at an object. This is, it seems to me now, the real Breton: the one who knew how to admire, the one whose face you can confront straight on because it will never look back at you. It will always be in profile, or in admiration—this is a face belonging to a body that sees itself split as in "Rideau rideau":

Figure 8.10

Les théâtres vagabonds des saisons qui auront joué ma vie
Sous mes sifflets
L'avant-scène avait été aménagée en cachot d'où je pouvais siffler

Figure 2.1

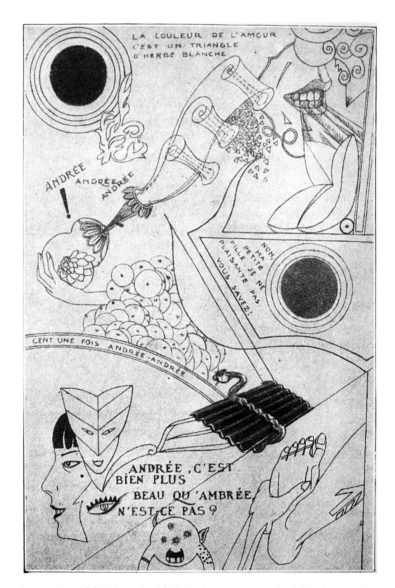

Figure 14.7 *Dédé Sunbeam*. *La Révolution Surrealiste,* no. 9–10, 1 Octobre, 1927.

. . .

Liberté de chasser devant moi les apparences réelles

Le sous-sol était merveilleux sur un mur blanc apparaissait en
   pointillé de feu ma silhouette percée au coeur d'une balle

(The vagabond theaters of the seasons which will have played out
   my life

Under my catcalls

The forestage had been set up as a cell from which I could
   prompt

. . .

Freedom to chase real appearances before me

The basement was marvelous there appeared on a white wall my
   silhouette fire-specked and pierced with a bullet in the heart).[5]

This is a face, finally, that I can stare at because, precisely, it will never face up to my love. This face—in its combination of the feminine, whether or not surrounded by curls, and the masculine—does not believe in equals, and so I find it unequaled. If this loving in nonreciprocity says something about me as a reader or a looker as onlooker that I am trying not to face, so be it. Perhaps I want not to see, as those others did not: "Je ne vois pas . . .". Looking isn't, after all, always seeing.

V

PHILOSOPHICAL CROSSINGS

15

POINTING: WITTGENSTEIN AND DUCHAMP

Put it *here.*

—*Ludwig Wittgenstein,* Zettel[1]

Of all dada and surrealist gestures, the act of pointing is one of the most characteristic. Surrealism insists upon insistence; the pointing finger is the most insis-
tent image of all. As baroque as it is surrealist, the pointing gesture calls attention
to itself and to the observer. It is the equivalent of a shout in a manifesto, of
WRITING LARGE in a text. The attention it gets, it means to keep.

A PHILOSOPHICAL POINT

The surrealist point, made already by dada, enters a long tradition of hand gestures: literally, of the manus, so relating to mannerism in its purest sense. It
takes a good deal of its charge precisely from being prepared by, pointed to, by
that tradition.

Always, the act of pointing is highly charged. It may lead by the extension
of a divine finger toward a figure of importance to the presentation, as in the
angel's gesture toward the child Saint John in the Louvre version of Leonardo's
Virgin of the Rocks (figure 15.1). The difference between this Louvre version and
the nonpointing version in London's National Gallery conveys exactly my
point. This is the one in front of which Dante Gabriel Rossetti wrote his poem
of place, for

Figure 15.1 Leonardo da Vinci. *The Virgin of the Rocks,* c. 1485. Oil on panel, 75 × 43½ in. Louvre, Paris, France. Alinari/Art Resource.

Our Lady of the Rocks
by Leonardo da Vinci

Mother, is this the darkness of the end,
    The Shadow of Death? and is that outer sea
      Infinite imminent Eternity?
And does the death-pang by man's seed sustain'd
In Time's each instant cause thy face to bend
    Its silent prayer upon the Son, while he
      Blesses the dead with his hand silently
To his long day which hours no more offend?

Mother of grace, the pass is difficult
    Keen as these rocks, and the bewildered souls
      Throng it like echoes, blindly shuddering through.
    Thy name, O Lord, each spirit's voice extols,
      Whose peace abides in the dark avenue
Amid the bitterness of things occult.[2]

The angel's sweet face here is quite simply turned toward Saint John the child, with the entire atmosphere shadowed by the "gloomy, dark enigma of the landscape, the complex background with its structures of rock, water, and occluded access to distances," as John Hollander writes of the painting.[3] In the Louvre version, the young angel's face is as *knowing* as it is sweet, and the remarkable trinitarian and vertical lineup of hands on the right—the Virgin's hand stretched downward above the angel's elongated pointing finger just above the holy baby's two pudgy raised fingers—seizing our attention as much as the looming background. Had Rossetti written his poem in front of this version, with the emphasis on the pointing, would it have been a different poem? Could he have mentioned only one hand? I think not. To a present-day viewer, I submit, the drama of the three hands with the pointing so centered is inescapable and all-consuming.

The divine gesture always summons our attention to things not of this world, away from things human and up toward somewhere higher, like Correggio's Christ (see figure 10.6). A more earthly usage is equally inviting to our

Figure 10.6

Figure 15.2 François Clouet, *Diane de Poitiers Emerging from Her Bath,* c. 1571. Oil on panel, 36¼ × 32 in. Samuel H. Kress Collection. © Board of Trustees, National Gallery of Art, Washington.

look, as in François Clouet's *Diane de Poitiers* (figure 15.2), or any of the Fontainebleau School's versions of the lady emerging from her bath, thinly veiled or not, to signal with a delicate finger the items of her toilet. We are supposed to react to this pointed look, and we do. These are the earthly erotics of encounter on a mannerist scale.

In all these cases, someone, we observe, is trying to persuade someone of something by a gesture designed to attract attention, in the direction of which we play no part. Pointing seems to be, more than others or at least initially, a noninteractive gesture: it can be perceived but not participated in. It is a one-way sign.

Were there a philosopher of gesture, that philosopher might well be Wittgenstein, whose own often disquieting mental gestures were ever directed against closure. What he says in one of his *Notebooks* he could have said in every place and of any topic he treats. It is worth pointing out that the sentence typically begins with a deictic or verbally pointing gesture: "In this work more than any other, it is rewarding to keep on looking at questions, which one considers solved, from another quarter, as if they were unsolved."[4] His lifelong circling about the subject position and the kinds of wording that position all relations valuably complicates our own concerns with the language of gestures. His *Philosophical Investigations* study the grammar of our "mental activities," how we phrase our sense data and how we think about what we are given or persuaded to see, when it is pointed at.[5]

His meditation begins: "Put it *here*"—indicating the place with one's finger—giving an *absolute* spatial position. And if someone says that space is absolute, he might produce this as an argument for it: "There is a *place: here*."[6] And again, he says, if I say "'Only what I *see now is really seen*,' or 'Only *this* is really seen,' I am assuming a privileged position which determines the visual field."[7] But then, he admits, that is like weighing down one of the hands of the clock by subjective concern, so that we really never know what the "real time" is.

Now "ostensive definition," as in the deictic "this is. . . . ," entails an arresting view of hereness and thisness, of the moment when we choose to stop and punctuate our frenetic processing of sights, like the finger pointing in a dada manifesto. This signal of a stop, this pointing to a moment made from a place of privilege, whether as creator of a work of art or as observer, can convey an intense feeling or desire. It is highly charged, and as such, impassions its own readings, from Renaissance, High Renaissance, and baroque into surrealism.

The pointing mechanism appears to consist of four, sometimes five, primary parts: the artist behind the pointing gesture; the outside observer of the gesture, in this case, us; the pointing person or object designating (Christ and his pointing finger in the Correggio); the person, thing, or place designated, pointed out or at (heaven in Correggio's case); and the included observer, if there is one (Magdalen in this case) (see figure 10.6).[8]

Figure 10.6

Although the pointing gesture in a work of art indicates either enthusiasm or an estimation of importance on the part of the pointer: this is what I see, am interested in or passionate about, and want to show you; it generally refuses possession on anyone's part.[9] What it shows, it does not keep, does not live in, at least for the present, or take away for private consumption.[10] Nor do we excerpt anything for our own use by pointing toward the picture thus on display. I see the pointing gesture, then, as more generous than grabby: "Look!" "See with me!" or sometimes: "Come hither" or "Come with me." Surrealist pointing is usually of this sort, insisting on including the observer.

POINTING OUT

Figure 11.2

Any pointer, visual or verbal, reveals intention, supposes relevance, and invites the gaze. In a painting, the finger or hand pointing is often stressed by an echo somewhere in the background: in Tintoretto's *Presentation of the Virgin,* (see figure 11.2) for example, the gesture of the presenting hand as the Virgin is led up the stairs is echoed by the pointed steeple behind. Or again, the finger or pointed object may point to a source of generation, such as a lily pointing to the lap of the Virgin, as in Rossetti's *Annunciation,* or may stand in for something less presentable, more obviously erotic, as in Cupid's dart aimed at Saint Teresa. Or the whole thing may be held in ambivalence, when such a pointed and illuminating object as a candle flame substitutes for the finger itself, shines through it, as in Georges de La Tour's *Education of the Virgin,* or the centrally important *Repentant Magdalen* (see figure 7.5). In every case, the pointed object focuses the sight of observers within and without the picture. These pointings

Figure 7.5

are paralleled in verbal text by grammatical deictics such as "this" or "that," exclamations such as "Look!," or designating and limiting expressions such as "only" and "nothing but" that demand close attention and posit the object's relevance.[11]

From pre-Renaissance to baroque art, the pointing object, often the index finger, indicates, like an address or apostrophe to the reader in literary works, what is to be seen close up and contemplated. This is part of the dramatized *appeal structure* of *ostension,* defined as the sort of showy "behavior which makes manifest an *intention* to make something manifest."[12] In Christian art, for example, the designator often appears to be saying, in his smaller stature or modest demeanor and in all humility: "I am nothing, look at what I designate."[13] The finger of a saint points to the iconic object, often the body of Christ, as in Masaccio's *Holy Trinity* (figure 15.3), where the finger shows the crucifixion in a clear, self-effacing statement: "I am an index pointing to Christ," and the eyes fix us: "Have you understood?" Here, nothing is left to chance: we *know* what we are seeing and how we are supposed to be seeing it. This is a perlocutionary, even propagandist act, for we are supposed to comport ourselves just as the figure points out, reflecting on the sacrifice.

Often the painter guides the reading straightforwardly, just as Alberti would have it: "I like to see in a painting a figure which admonishes us and designates with its finger that which is taking place inside the picture."[14] Nothing is wasted in such pictures: they are for our moral and aesthetic good. Everything that is "happening between characters is shown and designated as ornament or lesson." The reading is implicit, and we are at ease, even if we are rarely fascinated by what is so obvious.

In some invitational pointings and gesturings, we observers feel ourselves summoned to join in, as Christ himself gestures to us with a beckoning open hand to share a meal with him in Caravaggio's *Supper at Emmaus.* Here again, our focus is forced on what the painter intends us to see, Christ as the center, with the gesture echoed by the other hand extended. The structure of faith controls the system of gesture. We have no choice but to *see* that we are invited; we can accept or not. In all such iconicized presentations, the gesture within the work of art is of far more importance than its result.

Figure 15.3 Masaccio, *The Holy Trinity with the Virgin and St. John,* c. 1425.
S. Maria Novella, Florence, Italy. Alinari/Art Resource.

Because of the different spaces *from* and *toward* which the gesture is directed, and the stance or attitude of the designator, we may sense a certain unsettlement or disproportion. This is the point at which the reading becomes interesting. For example, in Tintoretto's *Discovery of the Body of Saint Mark* (see figure 11.3), according to Rudolf Arnheim, there is a conflict between the designator and the designated, between the observer and the spectacle, and the "viewer's position is made to be at odds with the structure of the world he is facing." Saint Mark's narrative and visual prominence and his off-center position cause an impossible situation, an "uncontrollable extension of his composition, which will make it ambiguous, self-contradictory, unreadable."[15] We are off-balance, as is everything else. As readers of the gesture, we like to know from where we are supposed to be seeing and toward what we are looking—*this* stage, however, is one we are not invited to enter, unwelcoming as it seems to any willed participation. Like Parmigianino's celebrated and ubiquitous *Self-Portrait in a Convex Mirror* (figure 15.4), such works exercise a permanent fascination for those of us who like ambivalence and love to read unreadability.[16]

Figure 11.3

MAKING THE POINT

The delicate balance of faith and art can lend a splendid ambivalence to the signal. Take the odd smile of Leonardo's *Saint John the Baptist* (figure 15.5), with its come-on: "Look, I can show you something." We look at the smile rather than at what he might be indicating: thus the discomfort of the situation, in which the intrigue of the designation itself breaks the frame as convincingly as any modern Brechtian playwright: "I am showing you that I am showing you." It verges on the erotic.

Since the pointing gesture is so often knowingly erotic and eroticizing, this *act of showing* can make a great stage play. Religion rarely rules out eroticism in art: they can, as we know, strengthen each other. They generally strengthen each other, in fact, whether in the pre-Renaissance, Renaissance, or baroque and mannerist stagings or the symbolist ones that follow. One of the most highly eroticized pointings, as I read it, is verbally represented by Rilke's "Annunciation to Mary," where the last line, isolated and pointed, points visually and verbally like a dart and figures the act of engendering by its breaking into the

Figure 15.4 Il Parmigianino, *Self-Portrait in a Convex Mirror,* 1524. Oil on panel, diameter 9 5.8 in. Kunsthistorische Museum, Vienna.

Figure 15.5 Leonardo da Vinci. *Saint John the Baptist,* c. 1515. Oil on panel, 21¼ × 22½ in. Pinacoteca Ambrosiana, Milan, Italy. Alinari/Art Resource, N.Y.

Figure 15.6 Jacopo Tintoretto, *The Annunciation,* 1583–87. Oil on canvas. School of San Rocco, Venice.

sacred space: "It was then the angel sang his melody."[17] Here, the point is the point. I have analyzed elsewhere the convergence between this engendering enunciatory line and the various annunciatory gestures of Titian, Tintoretto, Poussin, Rossetti and others (figures 15.6 to 15.9). These are spectacles about an enclosure, a *hortus conclusus* or enclosed garden, and the highly charged act of a pointed *breaking* into it.[18] In a glorious overdetermination, one Titian *Annunciation,* in the Scuola di San Rocco in Venice (figure 15.10), presents three designating objects: a finger, a lily stem, and a light ray, all darting in.

Speaking of darts, the well-known conjunction of pointing and the erotic works exactly like this. Take, for example, Cellini's *Salt Cellar,* a small and sumptuous theater of privilege. Its dart is as well-aimed, if with a less divine purpose, as that aimed at Saint Teresa, in either the Bernini or the Seghers renderings.[19]

Figure 15.7 Jacopo Tintoretto, *Annunciation*, 1570–80. Oil on canvas. Staatliche Museen, Berlin.

No matter how self-enclosed the drama may seem, the moment it is placed on the stage of art, onlookers are to be persuaded. An aroused response is built into the view, as in the viewers Bernini placed in the chapel to view his Saint Teresa taking her pleasure, in front of everyone, from the pleasurably painful, accurately pointing dart (figure 15.11). This is the metaphysical poets' favorite metapoetic instrument, with the erotico-religious poem as the result, as in a famous Richard Crashaw poem based on the Seghers *Saint Teresa* in Brussels (figure 15.12). The audience can be built into the painting, as in the Seghers, but whether inbuilt or outbuilt, through the surrogate viewers, this other-directed erotic aims along the same lines as those pointed dramas in which we are aimed at, stared at directly.

I am thinking of *The Beautiful Gabrielle d'Estrées and the Maréchale de Balagny* (alternate titles for this figure read "Her Sister" or the *Duchesse de Villars*)

Figure 15.8 Nicolas Poussin, *Annunciation,* c. 1627. Oil on canvas, 75 × 95 in. Musée Condé, Chantilly, Laros-Giraudon.

Figure 7.4

(see figure 7.4), where the court ladies are in their hot water of trouble, their bath or theatrical box, thus doubly their *baignoire,* with its dramatic curtain.[20] The fingers point out the pregnant nipple even as the fingering eyes look straight at us. We sense that the king is looking through his peephole at these ladies in their bath, the brunette and the blonde, whose nipple is getting the action, even as the trousseau is being prepared.[21]

As I read a latter-day surrealist single version of this double bath, a Magritte nude caresses her nipple in the shower/ocean. As we look on, she looks away, knowing we are looking. She is making waves, but her caress is pointed.[22] Like many surrealist gestures, this refers back to the baroque one.

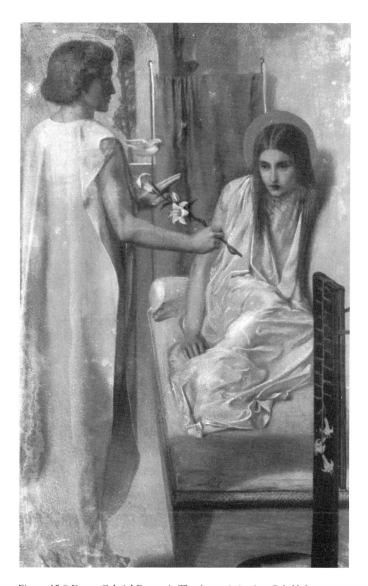

Figure 15.9 Dante Gabriel Rossetti, *The Annunciation* (or: *Behold the Handmaid of the lord*) 1850. Oil on canvas, 72 × 4.3 cm. The Tate Gallery, London, Anderson-Viollet.

Figure 15.10 Titian, *The Annunciation,* c. 1540. Oil on canvas, 166 × 266 cm. Scuola di San Rocco, Venice, Anderson-Viollet.

POINTING INWARD

This kind of handling, fingering, and staging of a mannerist mind-set depends on a necessary convergence of contraries, the verbal equivalent of Saint John's gesture of ambivalence in the Leonardo painting, calling attention to itself by a double reading. Mannerist poetry spells out the ambivalence as a delight. See Quevedo's poetic definition of love as "a freezing fire, a burning ice, a wound that hurts yet is not felt . . . a carelessness that gives us care" or Camoes's "a long contented discontent . . . it is to never be content."[23] This ambivalent drama takes place at once out, yet more importantly, in. Wittgenstein speaks of the "inward pointing" as an "act of attending," calling attention to something inside: "When I write: I have *this* feeling . . . it seems that I am pointing out to

Figure 15.11 Bernini, *St. Teresa in Ecstasy,* 1645. Sculpture. S. Maria della Vittoria, Rome.
Alinari.

Figure 15.12 Gerhard Seghers, *St. Teresa in Ecstasy,* 17th century. Koniniklijk Museum voor Schone Kunsten, Antwerp. Courtesy of A.C.L. Brussels.

Figure 15.13 Caravaggio, *St. Jerome,* 1605. Galleria Borghese, Rome. Photo: Il Gabinetto Fotografico Nazionale.

myself what I am feeling, as though my act of concentration were an 'inward' act of pointing, one which no one else but me is aware of."[24]

But, of course, this inward pointing can also be signaled on the outside, particularly in the baroque meditations on the convergence of outer and inner picked up again by the surrealists, and is the basis of what I call the *surrealist look.* Caravaggio's moving Saint Jerome (figure 15.13) meditates on a text while his outstretched arm reaches across other books to point with a writing instrument at another. In close proximity to the pointing, a skull eats away at the page of another book on the same table, mocking both learning and life. This baroque drama is marvelously enfolded in the same cloth that the repentant saint is wearing, draped under the books and across the whole table, like a great curtain woven into the act that it contains, presents, and underlies—the *tissu* of the inner and outer text. Such inner thought and concentration is illuminated

Figure 15.14 Georges de La Tour, *Repentant Magdalen,* c. 1640. Oil on canvas, 44½ × 36½ in. Ailsa Mellon Bruce Fund © 1996 Board of Trustees, National Gallery of Art, Washington.

in all versions of de La Tour's *Repentent Magdalen,* the image around which the chapter on René Char already circled, taking into itself the poetry and translations of William Carlos Williams: the Magdalen concentrates attention upon herself.

In the version owned by the National Gallery (figure 15.14), the flame, blown upon by her breath, slants away in a precise extension of her fingers so lightly touching the skull. Thought is here lit up. As in the *Education of the Virgin,* the flame completes the gesture of holding, showing, casting light, in an extension not only of the hand's agency but of the mind's working. In her supremely *meditative gestures,* the Magdalen fingers the skull, contemplates the sharp flame of the candle, her breath causing it to flicker, as she rests her cheek in her hands, in the traditional inturning attitude, observing in the mirror her own penitential meditation.[25] Inner and outer pointing converge in such a meditative gesture, inviting our own contemplation as the extension of our gaze. Although her meditation relates to her repentance and not to us, our own repentance is in a sense mirrored yet neither required nor pointed at. This inward pointing that her flame enables relates to an inner discourse and an inner perception totally at odds with any neutral demonstrator.[26] As in the *Education of the Virgin,* the flame lights the hand gesturing and the mind behind it.

One last pointing gesture takes one further step inside, toward Rossetti's Pre-Raphaelite Neoplatonic envisioning of the *Beata Beatrix* (figure 15.15), whose own inward visionary contemplation under her closed eyelids is signaled by the pointing finger of the sundial: *look what seeing is.* She cannot see what her seeing is, and precisely because she cannot, we can. She will never stare out at us, and so we are, ironically, all the more involved in her gesture. There is no breaking the frame.

She is, says Rossetti, in speaking of this picture,[27] his other half, his soul behind whose entranced figure appear Dante/Rossetti on one side and love on the other: they look at each other in the light of death. "The bird," says Rossetti about this painting, "messenger of death, drops the poppy between the hands of Beatrix." Since Elizabeth Siddal, the model for this and many Pre-Raphaelite works, was soon thereafter to commit suicide, the picture can read as a prolepsis, a prefiguring. Her visionary look is signaled by the pointing finger of the sundial, gesturing to the interior. Here the inturning gesture demands a

Figure 15.15 Dante Gabriel Rossetti, *Beata Beatrix,* 1862. Oil on canvas, 34 × 26 in.
Tate Gallery, London.

prolonged attention and training of our sight, not for a trance but for an energetic *inlooking*. Her looking in a trance is not negative, Rossetti insists, because she is conscious of "a new world of the kind that his story "Hand and Soul" presented twenty years earlier, less deadening than life-giving, enlivening to the spirit. Yet hand allied with soul may, after all, designate; it does not manipulate.

One of the more detailed points matters. We can choose to overlook the finger of the sundial, for it points neither at us nor at anything visible. Thus its gesture is, I would maintain, all the more powerful, once we learn to see it. The strongest pointing gesture, in my eyes, trains us how to look, without doing the work for us. And that is what philosophy does, pointing us not outward but inward. That is at once its privilege and ours as readers. Over time we learn to read such designations, which, if we know how to look at them closely, train us to *attend* without usurping our agency. We are left with all of our potentially ambivalent uncomfortable alternate readings, as various as they are, and we are.

FINALLY, DUCHAMP'S GESTURE

The way in which all of these famous and already emblematized pointing gestures and so many others like them accumulate in our minds is, as I see it, as a sort of library of gestures, in which we tend to read those that draw our particular attention.

Among all visual dada and surrealist gestures, by far the most pointed, to my mind, is Marcel Duchamp's enigmatic, erotic, and problematic *Tu m'* (see figure 2.2), that finger pointing at nothing in particular and so at everything, or rather, pointing at pointing itself. That is just the point I want to make about the strongest gesture being the unsolved: unclosed, unspecific. I would take this finger as the direct and positive image of dada/surrealist pointing at pointing itself, of the insistence on insistence. All we know of points and darts enters into our reading of this one point about pointing.

Figure 2.2

Its troubling nature arises precisely from our not knowing at what it is directed. This is the surrealist gesture par excellence, as dada points at it and leaves it unspecified. The relation between Wittgenstein's minimally expressed yet major notions of pointing and this deliberately inconclusive gesture is as clear as something pointed at in this way can be. It says, "This is," and that is enough.

Here is my point about the surrealist gesture: what it says, finally, is that and no more. It is as *unrepresentational* as possible: it simply is and says so.

DEFINING THE POINT

I want to end with Wittgenstein's act of attending and its possible extensions into our seeing of seeing and pointing in and out. Strangely ironic and paradoxically efficacious, his kind of pointing away from the central element manages to point at it most clearly. Sending his "Blue Book"[28] to Bertrand Russell, Wittgenstein says: "I don't wish to suggest that you should read the lectures; but *if* you should have nothing better to do and *if* you should get some mild enjoyment out of them I should be very pleased indeed. . . . As I say, if you don't read them *it doesn't matter at all*."[29] Wonderfully, he underlines the expressions "if . . . if" and "it doesn't matter at all," showing how much in fact it does matter, "if." The deflection underlined calls for attention, since the matter is central precisely because so heavily marked as being *to the side*.

That is, finally, my point about pointing. The attention that it demands centralizes and focuses the pointing itself, just as contemporary notions of framing call attention to the frame and not to what it contains.[30] More than what it gestures toward, the act of pointing itself, however ambivalent its manifestation and its effect, demands our attention even as it involves us in its own outwardly manifested theatricality and the often attendant discomfort. When I look, in the unforgettable double portrait just observed, at those two ladies looking out at us to see if we see, as we return their unsmiling stare, pointedly uninvited into their *baignoire,* we don't know where to look. When Duchamp points his finger at . . . we know even less. We feel signaled out, aimed at, and disappointing. Perhaps also disappointed.

Figure 7.4

Just as modern notions of and readings of the frame focus on the act of framing as process rather than on what is contained therein,[31] such an act of pointing calls our semiotic awareness to its complexities and to our own (see figure 7.4). The theatricality of outwardness, as in the unforgettable uncomfortable stare of the double portrait of Gabrielle d'Estrées and her sister, may serve as an invaluable comparison with and intensifier of an eventual and more subtle inlooking, in an energetic contemplation, perhaps even a rereading of that closed-eye trance.

Here, in last place, I want to stress the *generous act of attention*. We can, I believe, participate by our willing redirection inward, in the kind of luminous rereading of some texts visual and verbal and above all philosophical, in relation to which an outer-directed ungenerous first reading, an unreflective first gesture, will not suffice. Saying "this is" or "look here" without having a specific object to behold or define is a gesture so deeply dada (see figure 2.2) that it can only be its own definition. Unless we pay attention to it, and to all the preceding gestures that it sums up and references, we cannot make, cannot handle, cannot even see the most pointed of points.

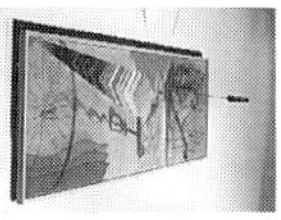

Figure 2.2

16

MEETING: THE EROTICS OF ENCOUNTER

On crée . . . une forte image, neuve pour l'esprit, en rapprochant deux réalités distantes dont *l'esprit seul* a saisi les rapports (You create . . . a strong image, new for the mind, by bringing together two distant realities whose relation only the mind has grasped.)

—*Pierre Reverdy,* "L'Image"[1]

Breton says words have finished playing and started doing something more serious, making love. It is exactly these now serious games of erotic encounter that attract our attention; otherwise we'd have long since left, just as Breton did, left the waiting room (*la salle des pas perdus*) and gotten on with it. But I sense there's something about risk that's missing here, something about too much control.

Wait a minute, wasn't it Breton who refused all the railings over the abyss in honor of madness, wasn't it Breton who loved Nadja? Yes, but. This is what has been sticking in my throat for ages about him and surrealism: he didn't want to play Nadja's game about not looking when he was at the steering wheel. That's where the slippage is: when she wanted to block his sight so they could die together in a highly romantic movement, an accident where foresight would have replaced just plain old sight. He wanted to see, with both eyes. So he was the one who stopped the car that could have taken off for a gloriously unbourgeois death as in *Jules and Jim* or *Thelma and Louise*.

And so Nadja slips away from him to the asylum, causing that dreadful space in the text, a sign of his falling short, just before the blank statement:

"They came to tell me Nadja was mad." Then he goes toward the one who "was not an enigma for me."[2] I find this the saddest space in surrealism. Breton, who didn't want to be interrupted when he was eating artichokes[3] and who didn't want to be seen without his socks,[4] wasn't so very eager to slip into the abyss after all. None of those slippery facts—because they weren't, after all, *faits-précipices,* precipitous facts that would send you right over the cliff—was going to keep him from the obligatory group meetings at the café.

No, it's words that did the slipping and not life, which he held on to— as he did to the fact of looking, which he had an absolute need to control. Both hands on the wheel and both eyes on the road.[5] The point of view is understandable, of course, like the joy of eating artichokes: it just may not seem very surrealist.

As for the gaze and the look,[6] he's fascinated but frightened: what if one were *not able to see?* In the surrealist montage of the whole group arranged, each with eyes closed, around the central figure of a naked woman, with the caption reading, "I don't see the nude hidden in the forest" (see figure 12.10), the avoidance has a specific object. This collective refusal to look halts the passage of her body to consciousness but rivets the reader's attention, staring at this odd thing: a group of men refusing to see a lady. It's perhaps a little bit impolite for her. There she is, after all, in her natural state, and no one wants to see her. Like the privileged image of the train stopped in a virgin forest or vibrating in the Gare de Lyon, ready to take off—one of surrealist eroticism's great moments—this is an ultimately visible, imaginable sight: not one you would think had to be blacked out.

Figure 12.10

Maybe the picture is of them shutting their eyes in imitation of Breton. In the car, he would keep them open, but here is a different matter. Maybe can choose not to control *wordplay* in surrealism, yet you have to control *eye play,* its reactions, the domination by perception. Nothing gets in here, or gets seen, that isn't wanted.

By that process he calls "perception-reaction," Breton is repulsed.[7] He advocates the possibility of a tactile art that would react against anything "too tyrannical and too decadent in the reign of the *eye*" (SP, 59). You can go right on celebrating psychological openness if you like, but the surrealist gentlemen who were thought to be celebrating it also are now closing their eyes. This lady doesn't have any luck if she's hoping for something from their male collectivity. That's my view, and I'm looking right at her.

Now isn't there a slight problem about spontaneity, even on an individual level, if collective looking is such a terror?

LET'S SEE . . .

Surrealism believes in "the constant temptation to confront everything existing now with everything that could exist, to summon forth from things never yet seen what could best render the things seen less blatantly visible" (SP, 105). Anything that can undo "the bourgeois mentality of order and luxury" is supposed valid in the domain of surrealist art: nothing to do here with when-you-are-eating-artichokes at a well-appointed table. In Picasso's work, red and white stickers on the heaps of cigarette packets illustrate the kind of mysterious construction possible to the human imagination. His objects hint of some gestation taking place elsewhere, in some woods where, for the moment, Breton is not closing his eyes upon the naked woman; nor is he worrying about the intellectual's dilemma expressed in his *Communicating Vessels:* What should one make of the others who have the same rights to the wild strawberries there, even if they are the kind who have made their peace with life in a couple, its furniture and its arrangements of bourgeois comfort, perhaps even worse than the consumption of artichokes?

In Picasso's studio Breton fixes his attention on an extraordinary little canvas that he describes with its large blotch in the center, quite like the excrement of children who've eaten cherries with the pits in them. Picasso was going to put a few flies on top to show it was really shit, a word that Breton prefers not to write down, of course. But then later Breton, thinking about the remarkable lyricism the flies would have added, finds himself taking a particular interest in this representation of the relation between what is assimilated and what is not, that is, "the special taste of these pits in this place" (SP, 114). But precisely, the excrement is itself necessarily the unassimilated thing that Breton has assimilated in his aesthetic system: what he likes he takes in; what he doesn't like he leaves out, obsesses about and sometimes takes back in, albeit with a difference.

285

His fetishistic passions—for paintings, for some kinds of representations and ideas—also permit him not to reject the pits on which others might choke. So his very special fixation makes him as chirpy as a child playing with his own excrement, forming a masterpiece from it. Passages like the following confirm just this feeling, where freedom has the same sparkle as the irridescent wings of flies perched on a pile of shit: fixation and freedom are the two poles of Bretonian desire.

> I was surprised to find myself thinking about those flies all new and shiny as Picasso would have made them. Everything felt joyous. Not only did my gaze not remember alighting on anything disagreeable, but I was in a place where it was always fine weather, where it was a delight to be alive among the wild flowers and the dew: I penetrated deeper and deeper into the woods. (SP, 114)

The phrasing is in itself more than revealing: his look rests or alights on the heap of stuff into which he sinks ("je m'enfonçais librement"). If he penetrates something with such joy, it isn't just the woods. It is very exactly, just as he says, his look that doesn't remember the primary matter.

I like Breton this way, as a great forgetter, in Apollinaire's tradition: "Où sont les grands oublieurs?" ("Where are the great forgetters?"). His look knows how to choose what it remembers, where it alights, what it penetrates: "There are things I have only seen very rarely and that I haven't always chosen to forget, or not to forget, depending" (SP, 1). Breton is wonderfully *possessed* by his idea, to the nth degree: "There are things I never dare to see in spite of looking at them, which is exactly what I care about (in their presence I don't see anything else either)" (SP, 1). As always, his love of the paradoxical spurs him on to his most memorable writing: "There are also things I see differently from others, and even that I begin to see *when they aren't visible*. And that isn't all" (SP, 1). This whole list opens on the idea of enumeration—*il y a, il y a*—again like Apollinaire's lists beginning: "Il y a, il y a . . ." and Breton's own response in a genial moment: "Il y aura une fois. . . ." Here the listing finishes by starting over: "And that isn't all."

Whether his eyes are open ("It's broad daylight") or closed, as they are upon the woman in the forest, he knows exactly how to look for something not yet specified in the everyday world, through his silent contemplation. He's the one in control of himself and us during this time: speaking of the moment when he is staring at some image in some book, he will never say that he is seized by the image. Rather, he sees himself arresting his own gaze, at which point the world outside him is of no account: "Nothing keeps me, in such a moment, from fixing my gaze upon some illustration in a book, and suddenly the things that were around me are no longer" (SP, 2). He will not be taken or taken in, either by the illustration or by anything in his surroundings. Breton keeps a clear head, even as his eye is arrested upon his obsession. *He gives himself his obsession, willing it,* just like Stendhal's Mathilde de la Môle, who wanted to "give herself a great passion." The vista may stretch in front of him as far as the eye can reach, but he will not be lost in it, neither in the woods he imagines himself penetrating, like the pile of stuff, nor in the painting on the wall or the illustration in the book. He will control, as through a window frame, what he sees, even through the verbs expressing it, verbs of looking and thinking, knowing, liking and loving: "So it's impossible for me to consider a painting as anything other than a window about which I need first to know what *it opens out upon,* and I love nothing more than what stretches out in front of me *as far as the eye can see*" (SP, 3).

He takes pleasure, he says, in this immense and measureless spectacle (*inside the frame,* like this remark between parentheses). Precisely because, or so it seems to me, he won't be getting lost inside this framework—defined, measured, opening out like a window frame—he can take his pleasure from it. Breton cares about control. Inside he can give way to a certain chosen folly, "going like a madman through the slippery rooms of museums." These slopes are allied to those *faits-glissades* that Breton extols in *Nadja:* they cause you to slip outside normal time and space. They are the key moments of opposition to the staid world of the "seated" or bourgeois dullards. He sees things differently from others, which he will do by choice until he feels "his imagination only coinciding with his memory."

WHAT IS SLIPPING?

Our thought is an eye . . .

—*Xavier Forneret*[8]

What makes those museum rooms so unstable is the quavering of these assembled canvases and their gathered emotions, enough to drive any susceptible person mad. Breton's sensitivity is for me the most appealing thing about him, whether expressed between the walls of the museum, in an artist's studio, or out in the world, where a chance encounter can set you trembling. If Picasso leaves a rope hanging from his paintings so he can climb up into them or down from them in his sleep, the way Breton imagines it, Breton knows how to locate and use it for his own mental adventures. Opposing the very notion of the eye as a passive mirror, as in a banal conception of the world and of art as mimesis, he defines two powerful ideas about seeing, both of which actually affect the ways we can learn to see more fully. First, the vision that lays down a conducting wire like an analogical link, perceptible only to the mind, between objects outside, preferably from different fields, and second, an "interior perception" where certain ideas meet in another marvelous encounter, according to an *interior model* in the mind able to insulate itself from the outside world of banal perception.

It is not, of course, only in the notions of painters that Breton finds the lyricism he needs in the things, ideas, and persons he chooses: "What I love, what we love" (SP, 23), the way in which he slides from the first person singular to the plural or collective (is this the surrealist group, or just those with his sort of perception?) is itself a slippery grammatical fact: a *fait-glissade*. Here is what I read into this: even the persons most insulated from the world and each other will not find themselves alone at the height of surrealism. At that point what they care about, they care about collectively, including the work of a few poets. Or at least, this is what Breton would choose to be the case.

He cites a line from one of Hugo's poems, of which he says he has forgotten the rest, great and willing forgetter that he proves, perhaps even wills himself to be. The words *botte rose blanche* (bunch white rose) give him a feeling of pleasure that he associates for some reason or other with the paintings of Victor Brauner. The unconscious power that such paintings hold over him provokes his own energy: the verb *provoquer* is essential to him, suggesting the same power of irritation as the *frottage* techniques of Max Ernst or Jean Arp (see figure 5.1), bringing forth all of the vigorous potential of the matter provoked. Just so, what counts in poetry is such a power to arouse the reader's energy. The arousal proves the authenticity of a work of art. Its erotic potency serves as its guarantee.

Figure 5.1

This is where the pile of excrement fits in, and its representation is so convincing as to permit Breton's gleeful penetration of the forest—this time as a fly and not as a train in convulsive speeding—and everything else the train/ forest image might signify. Potent among the wildflowers, drunk with energy like any fly grazing on such richness, transcending what he considers the "normal" criteria for judging the work of art, he finds his way toward that lyric behavior that urges surrealism toward its creative and vivifying tone. Here normal vision passes over into the visionary, and what might have seemed waste matter, into power: it is, as always in surrealism, the passage that is all-powerful. So the links of excrement with expression are clarified.

CREATION'S CARD GAME

Imagination is not a gift but an object of conquest *par excellence.*[9]

"When Max Ernst came. . . ." Everything had to be rethought at that point. Breton uses the image of the labyrinth whose pieces, he says, Ernst brought with him in order to accentuate the heroic nature of the arrival and prepare the outcome of the narrative or creation myth: someone had to show the way. The implicit allusion to the myth of Theseus in the labyrinth and to the thread that Ariadne gave him is also a clear thread leading to the conducting wire that the surrealist eye knows how to detect between elements trying to rearrange themselves, on the exterior or the interior. They will be revolutionized in their relations that used to be so simple. As for the appropriate atmosphere, Breton calls on a mise-en-scène as murky as can be, situated at the beginning of the world: "A diluvial rain, soft and certain as dusk, was beginning to fall." There in that liminal situation between night and day, the objects that were thrown

Figure 16.1 René Magritte, *La Maison de verre (The Glass House)*. Wash on paper, 35.5 × 40.5 cm. Museum Boymans-van Beuningen, Rotterdam. © 1997 C. Herscovici, Brussels/ARS, New York.

into an imaginative crisis, like some material and symbolic revolution against the bourgeois way of seeing and doing and arranging, will find new ways of being: see the photographer Claude Cahun's lesser-known but remarkable piece on the object and Breton's essay "Crise de l'objet."

René Magritte manages, says Breton, to keep his eyes half closed and half open to control the "precise instant when oneiric representation switches over into the waking state" and when the waking perception is just on the point of shifting into dream (SP, 402) or, in other words, his attempt, as in *The Empire of Signs*, "to extract from shadow what is clear, and from clarity what is shadow."[10] The hypnagogic moment at the very threshold of dream encourages

Figure 16.2 René Magritte, *La Réproduction interdite (Reproduction Forbidden)*. Oil on canvas, 81.3 × 65 cm, Museum Boymans-van Beuningen, Rotterdam. © 1997 C. Herscovici, Brussels/ARS, New York.

such a questioning of the state of things and of the mind, of the idea of boundary. In fact, Magritte is a great crosser of boundaries, of the image facing both ways. What we think we will see, we do not see, as the man whose head is turned away stares back at us, in *La Maison de verre* (figure 16.1), or its exact opposite, *La Réproduction interdite* (figure 16.2): a man looks into a mirror; so we would expect to see his face reflected back to us, but instead it recedes into the depths, still turned away, with the mysteries of Poe's *Adventures of Arthur Gordon*

Figure 16.3 Sir John Everett Millais, *Christ in the House of His Parents ("The Carpenter's Shop")*, 1849–50. Tate Gallery, London, Great Britain. Foto Marburg/Art Resource, N.Y.

Pym on the mantelpiece to his right. Poe, of course, of course. The difference in our modern/postmodern gaze toward a picture of Magritte, already accustomed to seeing differently, to being stared back at as in the paintings of the baroque, can be clearly seen when we compare our reaction to Sir John Millais's *Christ in the Home of His Parents ('The Carpenter's Shop')* (1849–50) (figure 16.3) with that to Magritte's *Le Mois des vendanges* (figure 16.4). In the former, a flock of sheep and a ram in the middle staring through the window at us occasions no particular surprise on our part and only marks the difference between inside and out from the carpenter's shop perspective. So much is going on inside that the outside is only a pastoral backdrop. But in surrealism, take Max Ernst's famous spanking of the baby Jesus with the onlookers in the window, for example, or this Magritte image where the room is empty and the faceless anonymous faces in their identical costumes and bowler hats, precisely like a flock of black sheep boringly tamed stare in, we are startled by the inlookers. Something is watching, and we are watching it watching. Its onlooking can be funny, as in the Ernst, or highly disquieting, as in the Magritte, when it is looking at us, into our own private space, through just the opening that we use, usually, to

Figure 16.4 René Magritte, *Le Mois des vendanges,* 1959. Oil on canvas, 51½ × 63¾ in. Collection Claude Hersaint, Paris. © 1997 C. Herscovici, Brussels/ARS, New York.

look out. We are rendered nervous by the intrusion, just as in his *Chambre d'écoute* (figure 16.5), where the apple enters our room. This is boundary crossing, as surely as Duchamp's taking over of the Mona Lisa in a waistcoat, with a moustache (figure 16.6), with a play on her erotic desire: L.H.O.O.Q (figure 16.7). His posing as Rrose Sélavy or as the Mona Lisa crosses genders; his posing of himself around a table in many positions always the same crosses identity boundaries (figure 16.8). He is a great crosser. That this last multiple position report recalls the futurist Umberto Boccioni's multiple self-portrait around a table, testifies to Marcel's and Rrose's memory as to their wit.

The creators Breton admires most employ a wide range of techniques, different every time, to prolong every visual and mental uncertainty, to cross every possible boundary between what is real and what is imagined, between

Figure 16.5 René Magritte, *La Chambre d'écoute,* 1952. Oil on canvas, 17⅝ × 21⅝.
The Menil Collection, Houston. ARS Art Resource.

public and private space, between one gender and one perception and the other.
Breton admires most what turns out to have been prophecy. Reading the future
by the potential of the present can prove a dangerous act. A self-portrait by
Victor Brauner in 1931 depicted the artist as blind in one eye. When subsequently he lost that same eye in 1938, by intervening between two quarreling
men, he became a prophet-victim at the limit situation of day and night,
stricken by the fate his self-portrait had predicted. Perception led to blindness.
The eye, as Pierre Mabille says in a piece on Brauner called "L'Oeil du peintre,"
is a part of man's female nature, as in the old images of an eye in the place of
the female genitalia—an image Brauner himself had used in a canvas of 1927.
But the story is still more unsettling, according to Mabille: before the famous
accident, Brauner was "self-effacing, timid, pessimistic, and demoralized,"

. . . she is without malformation."

Figure 16.6 Marcel Duchamp, *Mona Lisa.*

Figure 16.7 Marcel Duchamp herself! with a moustache, *L.H.O.O.Q.*, 1919. Replica from Box in a Valise, 7⅝ × 4¹³⁄₁₆ in. Philadelphia Museum of Art. © N.Y. Art Resource, N.Y. © 1997 ARS, New York/ADAGP, Paris.

Figure 16.8 *Marcel Duchamp around a Table,* photographer unknown. New York, 1917.

whereas afterward he was "certain, deliberate, affirming his ideas clearly and authoritatively" and working with a new energy toward the goals he would set for himself.[11]

Now if it is deemed useful to lose something in order to become more self-assertive and less feminine, perhaps it is time to take another look at such a surrealist attitude. Claude Cahun, through shaving her head, was able, in her self-portraits with their elongated hairless skulls, to take on the oddly self-assertive consciousness of the masked, the monstrous, and the deformed. Whether she blindfolds herself and walks over the cemetery wall leading her cat, as in *The Path of the Cats,* or splits herself into two hairless heads, or faces off with her companion Suzanne Malherbe (Moore), femininity is not her problem. Her act is strong.

Brauner's act was not willed, but his response is equally strong. He maintained his good temper, continuing to play practical jokes in his paintings. Breton points out how the figures in them "are doubled or fade out." These tricks have a kind of humorous lyricism, which Breton compares with two lines of the Breton poet (and victim of the Nazis) St.-Pol Roux. These lines have just the mysterious tone that Breton is apt to detect in the texts of a poet, to project them subsequently on the paintings of the painters he chooses:

> Personne avec toi n'est entré?
> Personne que ma chevelure. (SP, 124)

> (No one came in with you?
> No one but my hair.)

The threshold of such a lyrically strange room, both architectural and psychological, has to be marked in such fashion, as it often is in the poems of Breton and Eluard, so that the poetic games, decontextualized from the ordinary world and eroticized by the look, can work and play themselves out. The slippery perspectives of the surrealist imagination turn in the opposite direction from the rectangular and the rational. The "ardent look of poets" (SP, 396) becomes the erotics of the surrealist stare. The break is as crucial as the one that Apollinaire signals in his poem "Zone," his modernist manifesto in verse, as Breton calls it:

> A la fin tu es las de ce monde ancien
> Tu en as assez de vivre dans l'antiquité grecque et romaine

> (At last you are tired of this old world
> You've had enough of living in old Greece and Rome).

Those lines open "the greatest collection of poems in our century," says Breton, violently separating the past from the material and spiritual point of view, as from the ocular. It is a radical break; as Duchamp will put it, down with painting for the retina.

Crossings

After having looked for a long time at certain aesthetic inventions, like that experimental excrement of Picasso, we surely have every right to find our eyes crossed by this obsessional sight. A great lover of games, Breton believes in this joyous childlike source of the revolution of the gaze. Like the young Rimbaud "écrasant son oeil de darne"—pushing down on his eyeball to discover his interior visions—Breton finds other ways to see what we usually miss seeing: he knows how to stare hard at things until they switch their usual paths, detached from their context, decontextualized like the surrealist games, diverging from their primary essence. He takes these visual plays seriously, even erotically. Breton takes things hard and high: "we are very high up, and not at all in the mood for coming down."

Surrealizing art—in its most active and ongoing sense—finds all sorts of ways to go past ordinary ways of doing things. Collage for Max Ernst, *frottage* for Jean Arp (see figure 5.1) provoke new ways of seeing, like Esteban Francès scraping with a razor; colored inks are dripped onto a white sheet then rotated, or blown on; there is Kurt Seligmann's way of petrifying time; and those automatic movements of the arm or the hand with paint or pencil: the list of techniques is unending. One of the most fruitful is described in an exceptionally lyric-erotic passage about one sheet of paper pressing down amorously upon

Figure 5.1

another:

> To open your window whenever you like
> on the loveliest landscapes of
> the world and elsewhere
>
> Spread out with the broadest of brushes some black gouache rather diluted in spots, on a sheet of smooth white paper that you cover immediately with another one, pressing down rather hard with the back of your hand. Slowly lift this second sheet by its top edge as you would do for a decal, dropping and raising it until it dries. What you have before you is perhaps nothing but Leonardo's old wall with its paranoiac visions, but it will be this wall *carried out to perfection*. (SP, 129)

In such a paranoiac delirium as it is knowingly provoked, you can see certain mistakes or flaws in the wall developing as you stare, developing a "passionate attachment" to them (SP, 130). This obsessive desire, this erotics of everyday analogical life is no longer the same. The strength of your increasing emotions repassions the world, just as Artaud would have it. This is what he originally desired to do, through the bloody rituals of old Mexico; this is what Nadja would have wanted to do, through the games of the true madness she knew. That madness risks everything—and that Breton did not risk. Oh, says Breton, but she should have known just to turn her head away when the national flag was passing, implying—how can we read it otherwise?—that she should have moderated her madness, lessened her passion, increased her politeness or neutrality. You know, those paranoiac games shouldn't get you incarcerated. Unless, of course, you take madness seriously. Or are really mad.

On this thorny topic, the whole odd story of Aragon's poem "Front rouge" is sadly instructive. Insulting everything and everyone in this violent poem (particularly a luxuriating society with everything wrapped in tissue paper and sipped through straws), Aragon was accused by the French government of sowing the seeds of revolution. Ah, said Breton to the authorities, thinking to get Aragon released this way, it's just poetry. You know, just a poetic way of speaking. Ah no, says Aragon, it's real. Poetry, says Aragon, can be real like everything else. This is also Claude Cahun's point of view, in *Les Paris sont ouverts*. This debate, which went far in its implications, is in no way outdated. Art and life, say Claude Cahun's heroines: the mix may be deceptive. Beware the mistruths of myth: what business is it of theirs? thinks her Judith after stabbing Holofernes: it's not their affair, it's mine alone. What an ugly bloody thing, says Salomé, of Herod's head. What did I want that for? Ugh.

Undeniably, there are moments when Breton's eye wanders, instead of taking a hard look at what is going on, in poetry and elsewhere. Words haven't finished playing at this point. We can of course talk about transcending the moment on behalf of something else, possibly, events sometimes go past games. But we are speaking here of what happens in the very heart of the surrealist movement.

VI

Summing Up

17

A Haunting Look

Among the things in which surrealism has faith, language ranks highest, as the agent of transformation, including all of the techniques worked out so laboriously and with such comings, goings, steps false and true. The proximity to the language of the baroque enables it to traverse and to transgress the boundaries between times and spaces. Its willed largeness of gesture calls attention to itself, as the drama of the manifesto provides its primary genre. Its major mode of interpenetration permits seeing through, one thing to another, as characterized by the shape-shifting tenets of the baroque and the transformative powers of Mélusine, the chosen model of the surrealist movement. Here, within the object so deeply metamorphosed and so stared at, we learn the rhythm of a slower moving language, conducive to inreading or perceptive meditation.

In the involved and much-debated problematics of surrealist representation and its feminist readings among others, the particular look taken by the other or the self upon the body occupies the central role. The various representations of the female body, and the androgynous one, have to be seen in their setting, within and against surrealism's dramatically explosive, undoing or self-undoing, and undone decor. In this very singular way of looking, the stress laid on seeing is itself already strangely baroque. The ruins look back.

Yet the collective adventure of surrealist games—the exquisite corpse experience—implies an attraction to the power of the small, a condensation in the play of words and images. Spatial limits enable unlimited metaphorical explosions, in which the surrealizing mind exults. Paradoxically, the most adaptable and *positive* frame for the surrealist experiment is the Cornell box, analogically and actually a perfect example of ambiguous containment and of the necessarily ambiguous *play* that it represents: the play among elements and with the participatory spectator.

The Play of Fractals

From the other side of the lake, a loud clear laugh answered
him . . .

—*Benjamin Péret*[1]

According to the geometric theory of fractals, the form of any part, no matter how small, of any entity reflects in itself the entire structure. For example, to see the structure of a Bach invention, you can jump over or disregard several notes, condensing the composition, whose underlying construction will appear intact. Matta's essay "Sensible Mathematics—Architecture of Time"[2] concerns surrealist relationships specifically. The analogy often used to illustrate how fractals work is the opening of a chess game, upon which the most gifted players can predict the whole structure of the coming game. Constantin Brunner uses the word *fictivism* to speak of the belief system based on the *analogon,* converting this relativity into an absolute, at least a "fictive absolute."[3]

Such fictional spaces, or condensed creations, can be located in the work of certain painters, like the sources of a future still to be experimented with. Breton says of the spirit of Frida Kahlo, for example, that it is like "a geometric space: a whole series of conflicts are set up so as to find their most vital resolution." She is "placed, preciously, at this intersection of the political-philosophical line and the artistic line, where *they may, we hope, be unified in one revolutionary consciousness that will not confuse the differing motives running through them with their different essences*" (SP, 144). From this geometric place any number of roads could be seen as starting out for a so far unimaginable future.

THE PLACE OF OCCULTISM/OCULISM

Could we not, at last, recognize this as a nourishing place, from which all the condensed and intensified resources of fractal geometry may spread out freely? Could we not envisage a fruitful encounter between the woman-child of surrealism, a border entity as she is, and the borderlines of fractal geometry? Like Breton's recurrent emphasis on the thought not yet thought, the sight not yet seen, such a free future is yet to be imagined.

Still, that is more or less what seems to happen in the reading of the stones you can find along the rivers in the Lot or elsewhere, those stones that Breton celebrates under the name of mental agates and associates with Matta. Of the latter, he says: "Matta is the one who *hurled himself at the agate*—I do not just mean by that name such and such a particular mineral, because I include in that term all the stones containing that 'exalted water,' that 'soul of water' dissolving the elements that, according to the testimony of the occultists, 'give off real sulphur or real fire'" (SP, 184).

This water dissolves things entirely, leaving nothing conventional in appearance. This occultist working on the appearance of objects can transform himself into a knowing oculist, bringing about a change of sight. The concepts: view/vision/visionary: these correspondence of the marvelous are still playing before our eyes. As for the word *correspondence* itself, Breton comments: "It seems to me absolutely essential to say it: the time of Baudelairean 'correspondances' has gone by. As for me, I refuse to see in them anything other than the expression of a transitional idea—moreover a rather timid one—which no longer takes account of any current poetic and pictorial tendencies. Dream values have definitely won out over the others."[4]

"The resource of the eye. . . ." For Breton, Arshile Gorky is the first painter to whom these secrets were uncovered, so in relation to Gorky Breton formulates his definition of the eye in its surrealizing functions, against all of its former tendencies, when it used to be, presurrealistically, a simple mirror, before our erotico-analogical times. The *analagon* is the key to seeing, and also to the fields of writing. We know how the eye lays down that famous conducting wire between the most heterogeneous of objects, encouraging the ardent relations that are suddenly perceptible. Might not Gorky's implicit understanding of the principle of geometrical fractals work proleptically, preexisting their recent discovery? For in the mode of lyric comportment and analogical vision that surrealism makes possible, indeed insists on, we project our perceptual networks outside ourselves, in the lively erotics of our imaginations. Again by analogy, the condensation of structure in a box by Joseph Cornell teaches us about relations, about their essences and our own.

The ardor of the surrealist look as projected eroticizes in its turn, penetrating further in each moment, eternally active. There will never be any way to settle down in surrealism. If that's what you turn out to want, you will have to find other ways to look. The painter Le Maréchal, Breton says, knows "that visions are still another gauze scrim, behind which there are other visionary scrims, and so on and on" (SP, 264). Part of the point of the erotic look is that veiling and penetration of the veil, even toward another illusory potential. What is potential is future, and surrealism points toward that. In the fractal theory I call on here, we can envisage other futures, like a Cornell box housing the essence of all new possibilities. Everything is part of a series of *latencies,* of projected potentialities.

The object of desire increases, as does the potency of the look. Sometimes, in surrealism, you might think that the love of objects and potentials takes precedence over the love of any person, that the expectation expects too much. Nadja, says Breton, "didn't bring me anything that particular day." His expectation was always high, deliberately in excess. Between lovers, what is brought and exchanged in the erotics of the glance, the gaze, and the look may be symbolic or material, may be fetishized: a canvas, a glove, some lines of poetry, or the potential of a box given, or exchanged, as Lewis Hyde brings it to us, or as Cornell and Breton would have constructed them,[5] one materially and the other metaphysically.

The box—perfect example of the fractal project—does not limit or begin; it focuses the passionate gaze and then extends it improbably, through its original interior model. Its extreme condensation manages to increase this convulsive-compulsive ardor, never losing its energetic acuity. "Our world has lost its passion," cries Antonin Artaud, demanding a return to the universe of blood and fire. When we change our look at things, in this universe to be reinvented, we refind our passion and ourselves.

PLAYING THE PIPE

For some time now, the look of two Picasso paintings has haunted me (figure 17.1). One reflects on the baroque in the deepest sense of the word. In an early still life found in the Moscow Museum of Western Art, a skull sits on a studio table, between a bowl of fruit and some books, piled up, atop them, a pipe.[6] Behind the skull is the artist's palette with brushes protruding from the thumbhole; around the table and palette paintings stack up, as in one of the great atelier paintings of the nineteenth century: an artist's studio. We remember how, in Georges de La Tour's *Repentant Magdalen* (see figure 15.14) and in Caravaggio's *Saint Jerome* (see figure 15.13), skull and books are wedded in an eternal challenge by death not just to life but to knowledge. The pipe, smoked or not, an emblem of dreaming and of contemplation, here signals the centrality of the artist's tool or stand-in just behind the skull, its stem pointing directly to the palette. Whatever pipe dreams you might have had, whatever delights of palate or flesh you might have enjoyed, whatever art you might create or knowledge you might acquire, the skull is at the center of things, right alongside the pipe. In a 1914 collage entitled *Pipe and Sheet Music* (figure 17.2) in the Museum of Fine Arts in Houston, a pipe is horizontally figured against two pages of a musical score, drifted over by the sand of the background, both vertically and horizontally, so that the boundaries of the collage itself are crossed by the backdrop, binding figure and ground. The collage casts a shadow on the ground, lest we should think it all of one piece. This construction is itself set in a deliberately crude and childish wood border with the artist's name upon it in large letters and then in a frame with fruit and leaves, itself set in another frame to hang on the museum wall, against which, of course, it has to be labeled with name and artist. Still, the pipe itself leaps to view, radiant in its own position, with the drifting sand as contained and controlled as in one of Cornell's sandboxes. That moment "when the interior of sight will have become at last its exterior"[7] (figure 17.3) would be a perfect conclusion to a movement based on an interior model. Cornell's magnificently blue-hued box called *Métaphysique d'ephemera* (Metaphysics of the Ephemeral) (figure 17.4) contains a gold watch, a feather, and a newspaper. And much more, in our projection. We feel the heaviness of the gold watch against the lightness of the feather, the way its

Figure 15.14

Figure 15.13

Figure 17.1 Pablo Picasso, *Still Life with Skull,* 1907. Oil on canvas, 115 × 88 cm.
Pushkin Museum of Fine Arts, Moscow, Russia. Foto Marburg/Art Resource, NY.
© Estate of Pablo Picasso/ARS, New York.

Figure 17.2 Pablo Picasso, *Pipe and Sheet Music,* 1914. Gouache and graphite on pasted papers, 27¾ × 34 in. Museum of Fine Arts, Houston. Gift of Mr. and Mrs. Maurice McAsham. Photo Allen Mewbourn.

working is *on hold,* only potential, awaiting human intervention. It is perfectly matched to the ephemeral announcements of the newspaper folded in the right corner, and equally an indication of the brevity of life. The instant that the conception is set in motion, the watch is wound, and the instants will tick by (as with Man Ray's metronome with which I started), the news of the day will be readable, relevant or not. Like a baroque *vanitas,* this box is a mind set, with its encounter marked by temporality on all sides. It takes reading.

In 1935, Man Ray makes an object that is, in a sense, a pipe; in 1963, he replicates it. It is a clay pipe with its soap bubble fully in place, the pipe marked "Ce qui manque à nous tous," *What We All Lack* (Galleria Schwarz, Milan).

Figure 17.3 *The Red Sand Box, 1960.* Construction with sand. © The Joseph and Robert Cornell Memorial Foundation.

Figure 17.4 Joseph Cornell, *Metaphysique d'Ephemera,* Nordis, 1941. Box construction: feather, newspaper. © The Joseph and Robert Cornell Memorial Foundation.

What is lacking, perhaps, is that kind of pipe we can blow bubbles with, the sort of pipe that Joseph Cornell found he had, and could pass on to us in his *Soap Bubble Series,* as a serious gift. We should take it.

But in Picasso, the pipe points to something real about perception: it is not just the instrument of dream. It is not just a pipe, although it is, also, one, like the other one implicit in our looking that does not need to be named, titled, framed, or commented on. It is the setting of these Picasso pipes that sets off the observer, whose look is fashioned by surrealist and baroque looking. Nothing better responds to Cornell's clay pipes in the *Soap Bubble* series or to his boxed-in dreams of how encounters open out. On those pipes, he was the best player of them all.

Along with the surrealist texts of Breton and Desnos, in the long run Cornell has taught me the most about playing, reflecting, and condensing energies. So I end with this response, maybe just a pipe dream after all, to his boxes from Utopia Parkway with their condensations and dramatizations of the erotics of encounter, from another angle of a great painter at once baroque, surrealist, and many other things, to make the last point.

THE FINAL POINT

In the beginning, the pointing gesture of surrealizing art insists. It forces our gaze, as the gaze is forced in mannerist and baroque movements, offering an image that *faces both ways,* crossing the boundaries of expectation both public and private. Such crossings traverse gender definitions and identity politics. They push to the heart of perception as an intimate, even erotic participation out and in, overarching and underlining all of the rest. These encounters are at once singular and multiple. Surrealism itself looks many ways, backward as well as forward: That is its point.

Notes

Preface

1. The first version of *Le Viol,* in 1934 (now in the Menil Collection in Houston), had an entire room to itself in the *Minotaure* exhibition in Brussels (Palais des Beaux-Arts) of the same year; this image was used on the cover of Breton's lecture *Qu'est-ce que le surréalisme? (What is Surrealism?)* of the same year, with René Henriquez in Brussels. Another version is used for the catalogue cover for the exhibition simply called *Surrealism* organized by Magritte in the winter of 1945–46 at the Galerie la Boétie, again in Brussels.

2. See, in particular, Xavière Gauthier, *Surréalisme et sexualité* (Paris: *Idées*/Gallimard, 1971).

3. This show, curated by Catherine de Zegher, director of the Kanaal Art Foundation in Belgium, was held at the Institute of Contemporary Arts in Boston from January 31 to May 12, 1996; the director-producer of the accompanying film was Branka Bogdanor. My thanks to Martha Otis for her suggestion that I include this in my own looking.

Look: Large and Baroque

1. Robert Desnos, *Les Nouvelles Hébrides et autres textes, 1922–1930,* ed. Marie-Claire Dumas (Paris: Gallimard, 1978), 198.

2. Among the most useful studies of surrealism and art are Rosalind Krauss and Jane Livingston, *L'Amour fou: Photography and Surrealism* (New York: Abbeville, 1985); Rosalind Krauss,

The Originality of the Avant-Garde and Other Modernist Myths, (Cambridge: MIT Press, 1985); and idem, *The Visual Unconscious* (Cambridge: M.I.T. Press, 1993); Hal Foster, *Compulsive Beauty* (Cambridge: MIT Press, 1993); Jean-Michel Rabaté, "'Ou ne sera pas': Breton et la beauté convulsive" (on the ethical significance of Breton's aesthetics) and Dawn Ades, "Visions de la matière: Breton, Cubisme et Surréalisme," both in "Lire le regard: André Breton et la peinture," *Pleine marge,* no. 13 Paris: (June 1991). Ades elucidates the ways in which Breton places Picasso's cubist works at the center of his essays on painting, identifying, as she says, "Picasso's project and the project of surrealism."

3. For an analysis of one of the most disturbing, René Magritte, and a psychoanalytic background of his images (and others), see Ellen Handler Spitz, *Museums of the Mind* (New Haven: Yale University Press, 1994).

4. See the chapters on surrealism in my *Eye in the Text: Essays on Perception, Mannerist to Modern* (Princeton: Princeton University Press, 1972), and in my *Art of Interference* (Princeton: Princeton University Press, 1988) for the background to my present rereading of my own traces. Also see my "Lecture contrariée des rapports illustrés," *Mélusine,* no. 4, "Le Livre surréaliste" (June 1981); "Regard et représentation: problématique du corps féminin tel qu'en lui-même . . . ," in *Du Surréalisme et du plaisir,* ed. Marie-Claire Dumas and Jacqueline Chénieux-Gendron (Paris: José Corti, 1987).

5. André Breton, *Communicating Vessels* trans. Mary Ann Caws and Geoffrey Harris (Lincoln: University of Nebraska Press, 1991).

6. From Heinrich Wölfflin, *Principles of Art History: The Problem of Style in Later Art,* trans. M. D. Hottinger (1932; reprint, New York: 1950), 20, 27, 82, 87–88, as quoted in Michael Ann Holly, "Wölfflin and the Imagining of the Baroque," in *Visual Culture,* ed. Norman Bryson, Michael Ann Holly, and Keith Moxey (Hanover: University Press of New England, 1994), 347. Her study of how the objects studied by the art historiographer influences the perspective taken on history itself is fascinating and forms an essential part of the contemporary theorizing about the construction of art history and the history of vision. See, on this topic also, Martin Jay, *Downcast Eyes: The Denigration of Vision in Twentieth-Century Thought* (Berkeley: University of California Press, 1993).

7. Christine Buci-Glucksmann, "Une esthétique de l'altérité," in *La Raison baroque* (Paris: Editions Galilée, 1984), 163–89. For her study of Salomé, see 190–224; for her reference to Lévinas, see 172.

8. *Anthologie de la poésie baroque française,* ed. Jean Rousset (Paris: Armand Colin, 1961; reprint: Paris: José Corti, 1988), 21.

9. See Lucien Dallenbach, *Le récit spéculaire: essai sur la mise-en-abyme.* (Paris: Seuil, 1977); *The Mirror in the Text* (Chicago: Chicago University Press, 1989).

10. *The Baroque Poem: A Comprehensive Survey* (New York: Dutton, 1974), For a resume of Baroque characteristics, see pp. 97–98.

11. Jay, *Downcast Eyes,* 36 and 46–47. For the authoritarian control, Jay cites José Antonio Maravall's *Culture of the Baroque: Analysis of a Historical Structure,* trans. Terry Cochran (Minneapolis: 1986), 47.

12. *Minotaure* (Paris: Skira, 1933), no. 1, pp. 48–52. Gérard Genette, in discussing Jean de Sponde's love poetry, points out that de Sponde and Breton make similar use of hyperbole and surprise, revealing an "equal capacity of dilatation and contraction" of poetic language. Genette's study of baroque poetry shows mainly, however, its negative side. Instead of the fluidity seen in baroque architecture and art, the poets of the period, he says, incline toward the purely rhetorical *pointe* or *concetto,* relying on rhetoric instead of substance and on a horizontal network of images with no depth or color—so that, for example, cheeks and roses abandon their color for a minerallike hardness. The baroque poets concern themselves with appearances instead of reality, with words rather than characteristics of things, with approximate likenesses instead of deep similarities. For example, to express the field of wheat mowed down, one poet writes "the gold is felled by the blade," even though "gold" and the understood "wheat" are not similar—so the intensity of the real thing is lost (*Figures* [Paris: Seuil, 1966], 252, 29–38, respectively). I take a positive view.

13. In my *Eye in the Text: Essays on Perception, Mannerist to Modern* (Princeton: Princeton University Press, 1981), I discuss and illustrate these swervings: see the chapter on "Arabesques and Serpentines," pp. 70–86.

14. Marie-Claire Dumas has addressed the problem of Breton's famous deafness, defending an interior mode of hearing.

Mode: Seeing Through

1. Ludwig Wittgenstein, *Zettel*, ed. G.E.M. Anscombe and G. H. von Wright, trans. G.E.M. Anscombe (Berkeley: University of California Press, 1967), 77e.

2. In Dawn Ades's "Visions de la matière: Breton, Cubisme et Surréalisme," in "Lire le regard: André Breton et la peinture," *Pleine marge,* no. 13, (June 1991): 23–39, she emphasizes how, for Breton, Picasso passes from a state of contradiction to one of evasion: "a real *insulation* thanks to which this mind, finding itself ideally abstracted from everything, develops an affection for his own life where what is to be desired and what have been attained are no longer mutually exclusive.") It is perhaps Breton's fascination for the topic of insulation that led to his involvement with the idea of Joseph Cornell's insulating boxes as containers for the imagination. Ades calls upon Baudelaire's prose poem "La Morale du joujou" ("The Moral of the Toy") in relation to Picasso's references to a child's world, irrational and poetic, but finds Cornell's allusions to toys "nostalgic and charming" but too literal to participate in Picasso's violence (36). I suppose it depends upon how you define violence: several of Cornell's transgressive gestures, the bespattered bird box being the most obvious, seem violent to me.

3. For a specific study of the relation between baroque and surrealist authors, see in the chapter on the Spanish poet Luis Góngora and Robert Desnos in my *Eye in the Text: Essays on Perception, Mannerist to Modern* (Princeton: Princeton University Press, 1972).

Problem: The Personal Surrealist

1. André Breton, *Nadja,* rev. ed. (Paris: Gallimard, 1962), 18–19.

2. André Breton, *Les Pas perdus* (Paris: Simon Kra, 1923), 12.

Figure: Breton's Mélusine

1. René Crevel, *Le Clavecin de Diderot* (Paris: Les Editions surréalistes, 1932; repr. in Paris: Jean-Jacques Pauvert, 1965), 69.

2. Adam Phillips, *On Flirtation: Essays in the Uncommitted Life* (Cambridge: Harvard University Press, 1994), 16. My thanks to my colleague Gerhard Joseph for discussing Phillips with me.

3. My reference is, of course, to Winnicott's notion of the "good-enough" mother, justified by Adam Phillips's reliance on a Winnicottian model.

4. André Breton, *Perspective cavalière,* ed. Marguerite Bonnet (Paris: Gallimard, 1970), 222. All subsequent references to this work appear in the text indicated as (5).

5. Robert Jay Lifton, by his enthusiasm on the subject and by inviting me several years in a row into his graduate classes to speak of it, brought back into my consciousness my long-ago fascination with André Breton's conception of Mélusine the shape-shifter. Unlike most of us, she is both mermaid and woman. But making a choice most of us would like to make, she refuses to give up any of her potential. So I see her as the heroine of feminist possibility in general.

6. André Breton, *L'Amour fou,* translated by Mary Ann Caws as *Mad Love* (Lincoln: University of Nebraska Press, 1987), 45.

7. See Barbara Johnson's study of Baudelaire in *The Critical Difference* (Baltimore: Johns Hopkins University Press, 1980), 24 and passim, from which I greatly profited in my "Decentering the Invitation, To Take the Trip," in *Le Centre absent (passage, métamorphose): En Hommage à Micheline Tison-Braun* in *L'Esprit créateur* (Baton Rouge) 34, no. 3 (Fall 1994):

8. Louis Aragon, *Le Voyage de Hollande et autres poèmes* (Paris: Seghers, 1964), 51.

9. René Crevel, "Nouvelles Vues sur Dali et l'obscurantisme," in *L'Esprit contre la raison* (Paris: Tchou, 1969), 86.

10. Octavio Paz, "Pasado in claro," in *A Draft of Shadows,* trans. Eliot Weinberger (New York: New Directions, 1972). All subsequent references to this text will be marked DS.

11. Thus my title "The Place of Poetry, the Poetry of Place," for the discussion of French poetry after the death of Breton in Denis Hollier, *New History of French Literature* (Cambridge: Harvard University Press, 1989).

12. *Benjamin Péret,* ed. Jean-Louis Bédouin, collection Poètes d'aujourd'hui (Paris: Seghers, 1961), 107–8.

13. He is here, in "Embers at the foot of Keridwen," speaking of King Arthur's shield and the art of the Gauls, and Celtic poetry, even as he speaks of that other Arthur, Rimbaud, for whom, as we remember, the I was always already another: "Je est un autre." (*Perspective cavalière,* 136).

14. André Breton, *Arcane 17* (Paris: Editions du Sagittaire, 1947).

15. *Mélusine* is in fact the name of the original journal published by the Centre de Recherches sur le Surréalisme. No. 1 (1979), edited by Henri Béhar, was devoted to "Emission-Réception." It carried a picture of the mermaid and her fountain on the cover.

16. Breton, op. cit., 90–91.

RHYTHM: CHAR AND HIS OTHERS

1. Quoted in Jacques Dupin et al., *Exposition René Char au Musée d'art moderne de la ville de Paris* (Paris: Fondation Maeght, 1971), by Pierre Granville, "De Deux Colonnes érigées," n.p.

2. In André Breton, "The Automatic Message," in *The Surrealists Look at Art,* ed. Pontus Hulten. (Santa Monica: The Lapis Press, 1991), 143.

3. See Rosalind Krauss's study in *The Originality of the Avant-Garde and Other Modernist Myths* (Cambridge: MIT Press, 1984), for an analysis of the surrealist photographic image in its "slippage," (*décalage*) in relation to Derridean thought and to the idea of postponement (*différence*).

4. Which I have studied in my *Reading Frames in Modern Fiction* (Princeton: Princeton University Press, 1988), and more recently in "Seeing and Saving, or What Can a Woman Do, for the Late Henry James," *Raritan* (Summer 1994).

5. See my *Reading Frames in Modern Fiction* for a discussion, lengthy and obsessed, about the delay serving as a temporal frame corresponding to the spatial frame surrounding the catching on to consciousness of the Jamesian characters—"Jamesian," because they are already at a remove in representation.

6. In *Le Surréalisme au service de la révolution,* no. 12, December 15, 1929, 57–64. (quotation p. 58).

7. Pontus Hulten, ed. *The Surrealists Look at Art.*

8. Paul Eluard, "Les Jeux de la poupée" (1938). The title also reads, by a slight change of pronunciation, "Les Yeux de la poupée" ("The Eyes of the Doll"). A beautiful text, says Hulten of these notably self-centered verses (*The Surrealists Look at Art,* 22).

9. Information from Hulten, ed., *The Surrealists Look at Art,* 44.

10. "Sous la verrière," from "En Vue de Georges Braque," in *Le Nu perdu* (Paris: Gallimard, 1971), 61.

11. Seamus Heaney, *The Government of the Tongue: Selected Prose, 1978–1987* (New York: Noonday Press, 1988).

12. *Selected Poems of René Char,* ed. Mary Ann Caws and Tina Jolas (New York: New Directions, 1992), 56–57.

13. *Selected Poems of René Char,* 106–7.

14. *Selected Poems of René Char,* 78–79.

15. In "En vue de Georges Braque," in René Char, *Recherche de la base et du sommet* (Paris: Gallimard, 1971).

16. René Char, *Manuscrits enluminés par des peintres du XXe siècle* (Paris: Bibliothèque Nationale, 1990), 39.

17. Quoted in Pierre Granville, *Exposition René Char,* "Musée de la Ville de Paris (Paris: Maeght, 1971), n.p.

18. Pierre Granville, "De Deux Colonnes ériges," in op. cit.

19. It is perhaps worth noting that Char had made the snowman feminine: "Vénus solitaire en exil . . . s'éprendra de Hermès, l'audacieux venu jusqu'a elle." Granville, op cit.

20. "Bois de Staël," in Char, *Recherche de la base et du sommet,* 84.

21. Char, *Manuscrits enluminés par des peintres du XXe siècle,* 39.

22. In Char, "Alliés substantiels," *Recherche de la base et du sommet.*

23. Char, *Recherche de la base et du sommet,* 170.

24. Char, *Le Nu perdu,* 36.

BODY: SEEING THE SURREALIST WOMAN

This chapter is a modified version of my essay "Seeing the Surrealist Woman: We Are a Problem," which appeared in Mary Ann Caws, Rudolf Keunzil, and Gwenn Raaberg, eds., *Surrealism and Women* (Cambridge: MIT Press, 1991).

1. Jean-Pierre Cauvin and Mary Ann Caws, trans. and eds. *Poems of André Breton* (Austin: University of Texas Press, 1982), 35.

2. I am taking a potshot at my own "Ladies Shot and Painted," in Susan Suleiman, ed., *The Female Body in Western Culture* (Cambridge: Harvard University Press, 1986), reprinted in longer form in Mary Ann Caws, *The Art of Interference: Stressed Readings in Visual and Verbal Texts* (Cambridge, England: Polity, 1989; Princeton: Princeton University Press, 1990). See also Susan Gubar, "Representing Pornography: Feminism, Criticism, and Depictions of Female Violation," in *Critical Inquiry* 13 (Summer 1987), 712–41.

3. André Breton, *Mad Love,* Trans. Mary Ann Caws (Lincoln: University of Nebraska Press, 1988), 92.

4. André Breton, *Communicating Vessels,* Trans. Mary Ann Caws and Geoffrey Harris (Lincoln: University of Nebraska Press, 1990).

5. *Les Vases communicants* (Paris: Gallimard, 1955), 98.

6. Xavière Gauthier, *Surréalisme et sexualité* (Paris: Gallimard, 1971), 25.

7. I am of course referring to Breton's great and famous poem, "L'Union libre," in *Poems,* 48–49.

PERSON: TANNING'S SELF-PORTRAITURE

1. Dorothea Tanning, *Birthday* (Santa Monica: Lapis Press, 1986), 163. Other references: Dorothea Tanning, *Abyss* (New York: Standard Editions, 1977); *Dorothea Tanning,* exhib. cat. (Malmo Konsthall, 1993), texts by John Russell ("The Several Selves of Dorothea Tanning," 10–31); Dorothea Tanning ("Souvenirs," 32–47); Alain Jouffroy ("Interview with Dorothea Tanning," 48–73); Jean-Christophe Bailly ("The Vigil of Dorothea Tanning," 74–107); Lasse Soderberg ("Small Animal Games," 108–13). See also Jean-Claude Bailly, *Dorothea Tanning* (New York: Braziller, 1996).

2. John Russell, "Dorothea Tanning," *New York Times,* September 30, 1993.

3. Four of the drawings are reproduced in my *Surrealist Voice of Robert Desnos* (Amherst: University of Massachusetts Press, 1977), and again in my *Robert Motherwell: What Art Holds* (New York: Columbia University Press, 1995). See also my *The Surrealist Painters and Poets* (Cambridge: MIT Press, 1997), the companion volume to this one. These Desnos drawings illustrate what Matta passed on to Robert Motherwell, and then to the other American abstract expressionists, as the technique of the scribble.

4. André Breton, *Communicating Vessels,* trans. Mary Ann Caws and Geoffrey Harris (Lincoln: University of Nebraska Press, 1992.

5. Much has been written about this painting, perhaps too much, because it tends to block from view some of the other creations, early and later, of equal importance. The most interesting text concerning *Birthday* is Tanning's own book, *Birthday.*

6. Tanning, *Abyss,* 3–4.

7. Ibid., xxx.

8. Tanning, *Birthday,* 63.

9. Ibid., 163.

10. Ibid., 171–2.

DOUBLING: CLAUDE CAHUN'S SPLIT SELF

1. Claude Cahun, "L'Insensé," *Le Plateau,* no. 1 (1929).

2. The self-portraits described here, and many others, are found in François Leperlier, *Claude Cahun: L'écart et la métamorphose* (Paris: Jean-Michel Place, 1992).

3. The androgynous or "Claude" part of the name appeared when, in 1914, she published "Vues et visions" in *Mercure de France,* no. 406, May 16, 1914) under the pseudonym Claude Courlis. The book was later published by Editions Crès, 1919. In 1917 she took the name Claude Cahun from her grandmother Mathilde Cahun, the sister of Léon David Cahun, an orientalist from an old Jewish Alsatian family (see Leperlier, *Claude Cahun,* 21).

4. Claude Cahun in *Aveux non avenus* (Paris: Editions du Carrefour, 1930), 72: "Je me suis aimée pour la première fois."

5. Claude Cahun, "Carnaval en chambre," *La Ligne de coeur,* 4th notebook (Nantes: March 1926); reappears in *Aveux non avenus,* 15–16.

6. Cahun, *Aveux non avenus,* 35.

7. Linda Nochlin, *The Body in Pieces: The Fragment as a Metaphor of Modernity* (New York: Thames and Hudson, 1994), 56.

8. On the mask, see Honor Lasalle and Abigail Solomon-Godeau's "Surrealist Confession: Claude Cahun's Photomontages," *Afterimage* (March 1992): 10–13. My thanks to Richard Stamelman for calling this to my attention. See also the catalogue for the exhibition of female artists entitled "Inside the Visible," in which Claude Cahun plays a major role.

9. For a discussion of this particularly animalistic striped imposition, see my chapters on Man Ray here and in *The Art of Interference* (Princeton: Princeton University Press, 1989).

10. See Leperlier, *Claude Cahun,* 92.

11. I speak feelingly here. I loved Jacqueline Lamba and her art. She gave me André Breton's first love letter to her. She gave me her friendship over a number of years, and my translation of *L'amour fou (Mad Love* [Lincoln: University of Nebraska Press, 1987]) is dedicated to her.

12. *Aveux non avenus* and *Les Paris sont ouverts* (Paris: José Corti, 1934). This work follows on the discussion of the "Front rouge" affair of 1932. Louis Aragon had written a provocative poem against the order of things as he saw them in France and was convicted of "inciting the military to disobedience, and of provocation to anarchy." Breton responded with *Misère de la poésie: L'affaire Aragon devant l'opinion publique (English)*. Aragon, in anger at this defense of his work as only counting in the domain of art (and thus not to be prosecuted), wrote against Breton's stand in the Communist newspaper *L'Humanité*. Cahun, attracted to Breton and always on his side, resigned, with Moore, from the revolutionary artist group Association des Écrivains et Artistes Révolutionnaires in 1933.

13. *Mercure de France*, February 1, 1925.

14. All quotations come from Claude Cahun's essay for Charles Ratton's exhibition of her objects, "Prenez garde aux objets domestiques," from *Cahiers d'art*, Vol. I–II May 22–29, 1936, 43, 46, and passim. The objects are described in Leperlier, *Claude Cahun*.

15. Lise Deharme, *Le Coeur de Pic* (Paris: José Corti, 1937).

16. Cahun, "Prenez garde aux objets domestiques," 43.

17. As quoted in Leperlier, *Claude Cahun*, 19.

18. Ibid., loc. cit.

19. *Mercure de France*, January 1, 1927.

FASHION: MAN RAY'S MANIPULATIONS

My warmest thanks to the Getty Center for Art History and the Humanities for encouragement and assistance during the development of this photographic essay; in particular, to Gordon Baldwin of the Photographic Study Center for his discussion of fashion photography, and to Jacklyn Burns of the Getty Museum's Rights and Reproduction Center.

1. André Breton, *Le Surréalisme et la peinture*, Paris: Gallimard, 1928; new edition revised 1928–1965, 33–34.

2. In André Breton, *Les Pas perdus* (Paris: Gallimard, 1924).

3. Mary Ann Caws, "Ladies Shot and Painted: Female Embodiment in Surrealist Art," in my *The Art of Interference* (Princeton: Princeton University Press, 1989), 111–34. This essay is also available in Susan Suleiman, ed. *The Female Body in Western Art* (Cambridge: Harvard University Press, 1985, 262–87), and in Norma Broude and Mary D. Garrard, eds., *The Expanding Discourse: Feminism and Art History* (New York: HarperCollins, 1992, 381–95). I do not yet deal in this essay with the observer's collaboration in the erotics of representation, which is my topic here.

4. Often the object exists without the person and with a glittering presence. Such depersonalized glitter emanates from a metal bracelet with no wrist inside and a superb metal necklace with glittering points that surrounds no neck. Another rayograph shows the necklace in white, with the same points: "Jewel for Elsa Triolet," it reads, and the date is 1928. It is the jewel we see and not Elsa. What matters is craft. Elsewhere, sequins float in some liquid, attached to no material, simply twinkling like little dots, needing nothing but themselves. This is high-fashion solipsism—the ornament glistening alone. These images disturb: they are perhaps the best testimony to Man Ray the surrealist.

5. Speaking of excess—and of necklaces—see also Man Ray's *Necklace* of 1965, a collage with a wire spiral around the base of the throat/neck/penis, yet another cross-dressing, all the more palpable in its irony as the *breadth* of the necklace stretched across the space of the photography of the vertical thrust (*c'est le cas de le dire,* you might say, in untranslatable French). This thrusting neck with no visage attached exceeds it on both sides . . .

6. This sofa, like two velvet lips on which to sit, originally adorned the house of the surrealist collector Edward James.

7. In my "Ladies Painted and Shot: Female Embodiment in Surrealist Art," in which I analyze the problematics of the female pose in surrealism specifically, in Man Ray's and Magritte's renderings in particular, this disquieting work is one of the key reference points, in both its cropped and original versions. This is no simple spinning wheel and no ordinary spinning of a yarn.

8. Dated as 1927, the image seems in fact likely to come from an earlier moment, since their relationship ended in 1926.

9. A rainier outdoor Kiki was filmed by Man Ray for Desnos's *Etoile de mer,* where—through a filter—we see her face under a cloche hat, as she walks with a companion along a stream.

10. For the background of this shot, see Billy Kluver and Julie Martin, *Kiki's Paris: Artists and Lovers 1900–1930* (New York: Abrams, 1989), 124. The image of her body striped with shadows "was combined with images of ordinary objects like salt and pepper grains, pins, and thumbtacks placed directly on the unexposed film in May Ray's 'rayofilm,' *The Return to Reason.*"

11. Man Ray was fully conscious of his artifacts/artifice. About one rayograph from the 1921–28 series, containing a lamp, one of a pair of dice, and the top of a cello, the whole bathed in radiance, he remarked to Nusch Eluard: "In this little corner there are all sorts of games, and objects to pass the time when you are alone—even the Queen of Spades is hidden there, and comes out of hiding only when her double comes with a slick transparent umbrella, like a peeled peach" (signed "Man"). The beautiful features of Nusch as the queen of spades form one part of the quadrilateral.

12. In the name of Rrose Sélavy, the surrealist poet Robert Desnos also wrote poems—she really got around.

13. Some of Man Ray's best critics show him as creator, as hunter of the image. I am thinking of a text by Timothy Baum, "Cachet Man Ray," in *Man Ray's Paris Portraits 1921–39* (New York: Middendorf Gallery, 1989): "Hide Man Ray" (*cachez Man Ray*). Also an album of his photographs for *Vanity Fair* (1922) called, significantly, *Les Champs délicieux*—like *Les Champs Magnétiques,* that first surrealist text by Philippe Soupault and André Breton.

DECOR: DESNOS IN MOURNING

1. Robert Desnos, *La Liberté ou l'amour, suivi de Deuil pour deuil* (Paris: Gallimard, 1962), 123. All subsequent references to this work appear in the text and are indicated as LA followed by the page number.

2. Robert Desnos, *Corps et biens* (Paris: Gallimard, 1968), 143. All subsequent references to this work appear in the text and are indicated as CB followed by the page number. In my *Eye in the Text: Essays on Perception, Mannerist to Modern* (Princeton: Princeton University Press, 1981), I discuss the relation of Desnos's poems on solitude to the sonnets or *Solitudes* of the

great Spanish poet Luis de Góngora, whom Desnos so greatly admired. These are also forms of the *vanitas* to which I am comparing these ruins.

3. See, for example, Henri Béhar, "Poéique de la déconstruction," *Le siècle éclaté* (*Théorie, tableau, texte,* no. 2, Paris: Lettres modernes, Minard, 1976), 117–40.

4. In *The Penguin Book of French Verse,* ed. Brian Woledge, Geoffrey Brereton, and Anthony Hartley (Harmondsworth: Penguin, 1961, 221–22) [my translation].

PAINTING: ARTAUD AND MONSIEUR DÉSIR

1. Pedro Calderón de la Barca, *La vida es sueño,* 1635; *Life is a Dream,* tr. Roy Campbell, in *Norton Anthology of World Masterpieces,* New York: Norton, 1956, p. 2157.

2. This essential information is found in J. Patrice Marandel's introduction to *François de Nomé: Mysteries of a Seventeenth-Century Neapolitan Painter* (Houston: The Menil Collection, 1991).

3. Of the kind that Gérard Genette points out in his work on the baroque in *Figures* (Paris: Seuil, 1966); see chapter 1.

4. Joachim Du Bellay, *Les Antiquités de Rome,* with *Les Regrets* (Paris: *Poésie/*Gallimard, 1967), 51. My translation.

5. Ibid., pp. 57–58. My translation.

6. See note 2.

7. Octavio Paz, *Early Poems,* trans. Muriel Rukeyser and others (Bloomington: Indiana University Press, 1973), 36. I have never figured out why *marzo* becomes "April" in Rukeyser's translation, except for the rhythm. I would have retained that March surf.

8. See Thomas McFarland, *Romanticism and the Forms of Ruin* (Princeton: Princeton University Press, 1981), 4.

9. McFarland, *Romanticism,* 7, 12.

10. Antonin Artaud, *Oeuvres,* 3 (Paris: Gallimard, 1961), 253.

11. In one of the conversations we had during the years 1989–91: see my *Robert Motherwell: What Art Holds* (New York: Columbia University Press, 1996). It is certainly one of the most talked-of-paintings in the world; anyone who waited, as I did, in one of the long lines in Washington for the Titian exhibit will not be surprised by that.

12. In Mark Polizzotti's *Revolution of the Mind: The Life of André Breton* (New York: Farrar Straus Giroux, 1994), 440, 446.

13. (Paris: Editions Albin Michel, 1960).

14. *Antonin Artaud: Selected Writings,* ed. Susan Sontag (New York: Farrar Straus Giroux, 1976), 362.

15. Among provocative tones, I have never heard anything to equal that of Antonin Artaud reading his "To Finish with the Judgment of God" on the French radio in 1952: it was the voice of an elderly grandmother, it was the voice of a maniac, and it was the voice—since it was the voice of Artaud—of a genius. It is now available on a compact disk.

16. Benjamin Péret, *Anthologie des mythes, légendes et contes populaires d'Amérique* (Paris: Albin Michel, 1960).

17. André Breton, *Mad Love,* trans. Mary Ann Caws (Lincoln: University of Nebraska Press, 1987), 10.

CONSTRUCTING: JOSEPH CORNELL'S METAPHYSICS OF MEMORY

1. Joseph Cornell, diary entry for January 20, 1966, in my edition of *Joseph Cornell's 'Theatre of the Mind'* (New York: Thames and Hudson, 1994), 331.

2. André Breton, *Le Surréalisme et la peinture* (Paris: Gallimard, 1965), 81. Future references to this volume will be indicated in the text as SP.

3. As Jacqueline Lamba recounted it to me.

4. Robert Motherwell recounts a wonderful Cornell story about Mallarmé, one of his own admirations. One of Motherwell's paintings used to be called *Mallarmé's Dream,* but when

Cornell insisted on calling it *Mallarmé's Swan,* Motherwell retitled it. Cornell's own collages and boxes with swans are, in a sense, homages also to Mallarmé.

5. André Breton, *Nadja* (1928; revised 1963) in *Oeuvres Complètes,* vol. 1 (Paris: Gallimard, La Pléiade, 1988), 651.

6. See my *Metapoetics of the Passage: Architextures in Surrealism and After* (Hanover: University of New England Press, 1986).

7. Cornell called these "shadow boxes." See the representations of the shadow theater at the end of the nineteenth century and the presentation by Phillip Dennis Cate and Mary Shaw in the catalogue *The Spirit of Montmartre: Cabarets, Humor, and the Avant-Garde, 1875–1905* (New Brunswick, N.J.: Zimmerli Art Museum, 1996).

8. Alain Jouffroy, "Les Hôtels de Joseph Cornell," in *André Breton et le surréalisme international, Opus international,* no. 123–24 (April-May 1991): 90–93.

9. Louis Aragon, "The Shadow of the Inventor," *La Révolution surréaliste,* no. 1, December 1, 1924, 22–24.

10. Loc. cit., 24.

11. Cornell, diary entry, January 30, 1966, 338.

12. Cornell, diary entry, February 21, 1966, 338.

13. Cornell, diary entry, March 3, 1966, 339. Cornell was a practicing Christian Scientist and read Mary Baker Eddy's writings and the Bible conscientiously, as we read often in his diary: see my introduction and comments to this publication, op. cit.

GAME: EXQUISITE EXCESSIVE CORPSE

1. André Breton, *Manifestes du surréalisme* (Paris: Jean-Jacques Pauvert, 1962), 221.

2. Salvador Dali, from Lucy Lippard, ed. *Surrealists on Art* (Englewood Cliffs, N.Y.: Prentice-Hall, 1970), 88.

3. Simone Collinet, describing the exquisite corpse game.

4. André Breton, *Communicating Vessels,* trans. Mary Ann Caws and Geoffrey T. Harris (Lincoln: University of Nebraska Press, 1990), 42 and 52.

5. As quoted in André Breton, *Le Cadavre exquis, son exaltation* (Milan: chez Arturo Schwartz, 1975).

6. André Breton, *Conversations: The Autobiography of Surrealism,* trans. Mark Polizzotti (New York: Paragon Press, 1993), 64–65.

7. As quoted in Jacqueline Chénieux-Gendron, *Surrealism* (New York: Columbia University Press, 1990), 40.

8. André Breton, *Mad Love,* trans. Mary Ann Caws (Lincoln: University of Nebraska Press, 1987), 114.

9. Examples of verbal *cadavre exquis,* in *La Revolution surréaliste* no. 9–10 (1 October 1927).

10. André Breton, *Nadja* (Paris: Gallimard, 1928), 155.

11. Breton, *Mad Love,* 19.

FACE: STILL ENVISAGING ANDRÉ BRETON

1. André Breton, *L'Amour fou* (Paris: Gallimard, 1937), translated by Mary Ann Caws as *Mad Love* (Lincoln: University of Nebraska Press, 1987), 109.

2. See my "Ladies Shot and Painted: Female Embodiment in Surrealist Art," in Norma Broude and Mary D. Garrard, *The Expanding Discourse: Feminism and Art History* (New York: Harper Collins Icon Editions, 1992), 381–96.

3. André Breton, *L'Union libre*: (Paris, Gallimard, 1931), in *Poems of André Breton: A Bilingual Anthology,* trans. and ed. Jean-Pierre Cauvin and Mary Ann Caws (Austin: University of Texas Press, 1982), 48–51.

4. See his poem about curtains and the theater, "Rideau rideau" quoted earlier. No less than Breton, Magritte is given to the dramatic curtaining of his scenes: of his stages and his skies, as well as his showers (*Le Galet*)—see *Le Palais des rideaux* (*The Palace of Curtains* 1928), *La Cour d'amour* (*The Court of Love*), and *La Joconde* (*Mona Lisa*), both of 1960. Surrealism's look is meant to be dramatic.

5. Breton, *Poems,* 70–72.

POINTING: WITTGENSTEIN AND DUCHAMP

1. Ludwig Wittgenstein, *Zettel,* ed. G.E.M. Anscombe and G. H. von Wright, trans. G.E.M. Anscombe (Berkeley: University of California Press, 1967), 123e.

2. John Hollander, *The Gazer's Spirit: Poems Speaking to Silent Works of Art* (Chicago: University of Chicago Press, 1995), 151.

3. Loc. cit., 152.

4. Ludwig Wittgenstein, *Notebooks 1914–1916* (Chicago: University of Chicago Press, 1961), 30e.

5. Ludwig Wittgenstein, *The Blue and Brown Books: Preliminary Studies for the 'Philosophical Investigations'* (Oxford: Blackwell, 1960), 70 and 84. This is the initial form of his *Philosophical Investigations,* which he had dictated to his class in Cambridge in 1933–34.

6. Wittgenstein, *Zettel,* 123e.

7. "There is . . . no objection to adopting a symbolism in which a certain person always or temporarily holds an exceptional place," says Wittgenstein, although this kind of solipsism, however pragmatically useful, can't be philosophically *justified,* which he knows. "When I made my solipsist statement I pointed, but I robbed the pointing of its sense by inseparably connecting that which points and that to which it points. I constructed a clock with all its wheels, etc., and in the end fastened the dial to the pointer and made it go round with it" (*Blue and Brown,* 71).

8. For a discussion of pointing, see Claude Gandelman, *Reading Pictures, Viewing Texts* (Bloomington: Indiana University Press, 1991), especially chaps. 1, "Touching with the Eye," and 2, "The Gesture of Demonstration."

9. See my "L'Oeil qui désigne, doigt qui pleure," in *Figures du baroque,* ed. Jean-Marie Benoist (Paris: PUF, 1983), 127–49.

10. We can, from a distance, *participate* in the thing on which we focus, by pointing at it and still leave it shown and untouched, for others to focus on in their turn: this is how Hans Gadamer defines participation, as a situation in which we are part of the whole, taking nothing away to keep it from anyone else ("The Hermeneutics of Suspicion," in *Hermeneutics,* ed. Gary Shapiro and Alan Sica [Amherst: University of Massachusetts Press, 1984]). I am thinking here also of the surrealist André Breton's discussion of what he called "the sublime point," where all contraries meet: life and death, the dream and the real, night and day. . . . We can only show it, he writes to his tiny daughter in *Mad Love,* we cannot dwell in it (*L'Amour fou* [Lincoln: University of Nebraska Press, 1987]).

11. In a most useful volume called *Relevance,* Dan Sperber and Deidre Wilson show what makes some information worth processing and how we might choose among elements. They offer the example of two people on a park bench, a couple. The boy leans back, altering the girl's view. Among the things she sees freshly—an ice-cream vendor and so forth—she sees a terrible bore coming along, and "this is the particular phenomenon she should pay attention to . . . if she is aiming at cognitive efficiency" (Cambridge: Harvard University Press, 1986), 46, 48.

12. Pointing can act as a kind of transfer, a translation of one observer's look to that of a second. Take the analogy of the pointing machine, to make a larger copy from a model. A series of points designated on the original is transferred to the corresponding points on the copy. This is the way it works for the audience: the artist or subject transfers the original look to the secondary one, by pointing out an object of interest. *Ostension,* being the sort of "behaviour which makes manifest an intention to make something manifest," generally bears a tacit guarantee of relevance.

13. See Claude Gandelman, op. cit., passim.

14. Gandelman, 21.

15. Rudolf Arnheim, *The Power of the Center* (Berkeley: University of California Press, 1982), 69.

16. See John Shoptaw's *On the Outside Looking Out* (Cambridge: Harvard University Press, 1994), on Ashbery's poetry, which has this self-portrait on the cover, as indeed did Ashbery's long poem called "Self-Portrait in a Convex Mirror."

17. In Rainer Maria Rilke, *The Book of Pictures* (Berlin: Bechtle Verlag, 1902). For a comparison of the last line and the sharp pointing instrument of the annunciating angel, see my *Eye in the Text* (Princeton: Princeton University Press, 1981), 104–124.

18. My *Eye in the Text* (Princeton, NJ: Princeton University Press, 1981), essay on Annunciation.

19. Or the stagey pointing gesture can have to do with *selection,* illustrative of Bishop Berkeley's firm conviction about the merging of the optical and the haptical, when the sense of touch is actually transferred to the vision, perfectly exemplified by the celebrated School of Fontainebleau pictures, where we see Diane de Poitiers pointing and selecting among the objects on her dressing table, representing the sometimes random relation between choice and desire.

20. My thanks to Colin Eisler for the hot-water reference. I have discussed this painting at length in my *Eye in the Text* (Princeton: Princeton University Press, 1972).

21. See Christian Prigent's discussion of this feverish canvas in his "Roue, roue voilée, roue en huit," Benoist, *Figures du Baroque,* 165–69.

22. Now it is unsettling not to know whether indeed you are invited into the spectacle or not. The main reason for our current fascination with Parmigianino's *Self-Portrait in a Convex Mirror,* where the enormous mirrored hand invites us in or shuts us out, seems to me to be about this ambivalence writ large. So the system of gesture and its staging can include the observer, as an invitation or challenge, or have the audience built in, as in Georges Seurat's peculiarly brilliant presentation of the dance, *Chahut.* Here, with the instrumental bow parallel to the outstretched legs themselves pointing to the stage lights—like a pun on footlights—and where, in the original version, the conductor's baton pointed to the uplifted skirts over the famous lack of undergarments, after all or under all, pointing and staging converge: oh what a spectacle this is.

23. See Harold B. Segel, *The Baroque Poem: A Comparative Survey* (New York: Dutton, 1972), 288, 294.

24. Wittgenstein, *Blue and Brown,* 174.

25. See René Char's poem "Madeleine à la veilleuse" ("Magdalen with the Vigil Lamp"), in which she fingers the skull and wears a homespun blouse, as in the Los Angeles version.

26. As with the text of Saint Ignatius's exercises through which we are to imagine our own bodies accomplishing the gestures of holy figures who represent us as we represent them to ourselves, the flame's finger here draws us into the picture as the pointing finger on the dada manifestoes calls us to pay attention and enter the spirit of the statement.

27. In a text reprinted in Henri Dorra, *Symbolist Art Theories* (Berkeley: University of California Press, 1994), 26.

28. See note 5.

29. Preface to Wittgenstein, *Blue and Brown,* v.

30. See my *Reading Frames in Modern Fiction* (Princeton: Princeton University Press, 1985).

31. I study this subject at some length in my *Reading Frames in Modern Fiction.*

MEETING: THE EROTICS OF ENCOUNTER

1. Pierre Reverdy, "L'Image," *Nord Sud,* XIII, March 1918, 3–5.

2. See, for an interesting discussion of Breton's blank spaces, Jean-Michel Rabaté's "Les Blancs d'André Breton (ou: Le Surréalisme de la Place Blanche," in *André Breton, la poésie, La Revue des Sciences humaines,* no. 237, 1995, 29–47.

3. As Monique Fong tells it, when she went to call on him one day, enthusiastic at meeting him, "Mademoiselle," he said, "could you come back later? You understand, we are having artichokes."

4. As Jacqueline Lamba told me.

5. Given that I have, as a mild narcoleptic, a tendency to fall asleep, driving or not, in any car, I believe Breton would not have liked me to be along, any more than Nadja.

6. See Norman Bryson on the differences among look, glance, and gaze.

7. André Breton, *Le Surréalisme et la peinture* (Paris: Gallimard, 1928, rpr. 1965), 59.

8. *Le Surréalisme au service de la révolution,* no. 11 (March 1928): 11.

9. *Le Surréalisme au service de la révolution,* no. 1 (July 1930).

10. *Le Minotaure,* no. 12–13 (date): 53; reprinted in Pierre Mabille, *Conscience picturale, conscience lumineuse* (Paris: José Corti, 1989).

11. Loc. cit., 54.

A HAUNTING LOOK

1. *Le Minotaure,* no. 8 (Month 1936): 22.

2. *Le Minotaure,* no. 11 (Month year): 43.

3. Here Breton refers to W. Bernhard, *The Philosophy of Spinoza and Brunner* (New York: Spinoza Institute, 1934), and also to "Constantin Brunner, a philosopher outside the walls," in *Cahiers du Sud,* 1964.

4. André Breton, "Exhibition X . . . Y," *Point du jour,* in *Oeuvres complètes* (city: pub, year), 72.

5. See the chapter on Cornell and Motherwell.

6. Let's take, for example, this object-poem of Breton, wherein he sees in the initials of his name AB when he is staring at them, the date 1713.

7. Breton quotes Charles Estienne *Le Surréalisme et la peinture* in *Manifeste* "22," published as a preface to the Second Salon of October (1954), 338. There are several theories about the presence of the death's head in this still life—dated 1907 and also 108—marking it as both a

vanitas (resembling one of Zurbarán, for example) and a possible elegy for a particular death. The latter hypothesis includes the death of Alfred Jarry in 1906 (although Picasso never met Jarry), and of Cézanne, also in 1906, backed up by the existence of two retrospectives of Cézanne in 1907 in Paris, one at Bernheim Jeune arousing a great deal of interest. See the catalogue *Picasso and Things,* ed. Marie-Laure Bernadec, Jean Sutherland Boggs, and Brigitte Léal (Cleveland: Cleveland Museum of Art, 1992), 54.

INDEX

Note: Pages in *italics* indicate illustrations.